EARS TO HEAR

Discovering What Jesus Says to the Seven Churches of Revelation about the Kind of Church He Wants

"He who has an ear to hear, let him hear what the Spirit says to the churches"

With study questions for groups

Forward by **Fred A. Hartley III** Author of *Prayer on Fire and God on Fire*

BILL HYER

Ears to Hear
Discovering what Jesus says to the seven churches of Revelation about the kind of church He wants
by Bill Hyer

Printed in the United States of America.

ISBN 9781498465434

www.xulonpress.com

TABLE OF CONTENTS

DEDICATION

It is most appropriate that this book
about the church,
the Bride of Christ,
should be dedicated to my bride,
Michelle,
who has loved me,
lived with me,
and been used of our Lord to transform me.
She is my best friend,
my best counselor,
and my best prayer partner.
She is the mother of our sons,
Billy and Andrew,
the cheerleader of their wives,
Rachel and Allie,
and the joy-giver of our grandchildren,
Elena, Olivia, Henry, Leah and August.
She's the best!

ACKNOWLEDGEMENTS

W hile this book is intended to be of scholarly quality, it is not intended to be a work of scholarship and, therefore, there is no effort to acknowledge by footnote ideas I may have received from other sources. However, I do want to give appropriate credit to those whose writings and lives have especially contributed to this book and my life.

Among the books that have been major sources of thought are *Commentary on the Revelation of John*, George Eldon Ladd, 1972, Eerdmans, Grand Rapids; *The Book of Revelation,* Robert H. Mounce, 1977, Eerdmans, Grand Rapids; *Revelation: Four Views: A Parallel Commentary*, Steve Gregg; *Revelation,* Leon Morris, 1987, Inter-Varsity Press, Nottingham, England; *What Christ Thinks of the Church*, John Stott; *The Revelation of John*, William Barclay, 1976, Saint Andrew Press, Edinburgh; and *The Temple and the Church's Mission,* G. K. Beale, 2004, InterVarsity Press, Downers Grove. If in any way I have written what is similar or the same as these, or any other writings, there has been no effort to plagiarize. I give credit where it is due. We are all heirs of those who have gone before us, mined the riches of Scripture they discovered and have given them to us.

I am grateful to Dr. Gordon Fee, my advisor when I was a student and Bible major at Wheaton College. He gave me a knowledge of and love for Biblical exegesis. I will never forget his fatherly look when I quipped one day in class, "Dr. Fee, can we have a little less 'exe' and a little more 'Jesus.'" For some reason, he didn't find it as humorous as I did. He graciously taught me that it is in the accurate "exe" that we will see the real "Jesus."

Among the many people who have influenced my perspective on Scripture, I want to thank Dr. R. C. Sproul. Though I don't know him personally, nevertheless, in many ways his teaching helped me to understand what Peter wrote about Paul—"some things hard to understand" (2 Peter 3:15-16).

I am especially thankful to Fred A. Hartley III, my friend, ministry and prayer partner since our days in seminary at Gordon-Conwell when we devoted our lunch hours to prayer for revival, great awakening and world missions. God has been answering those prayers through the world-wide ministry of the *College of Prayer, International*, of which he is founder and President and I am the Academic Dean. He is one of those who said I should write a book and gave helpful suggestions for it. Thanks for the amazing ride, Fred.

Special thanks to my wife, Michelle, Barb Nave, Portia McGehee, and Linda Farmer for their insightful comments and diligence in editing this work—it's hard to see your own tipos—I mean typos!

FORWARD

The Book of the Revelation is my favorite book in the Bible for one simple reason–I love Jesus and I love encountering His manifest presence. The singular expressed purpose of the Book of the Revelation is, after all, to reveal Christ, and to lead us to encounter His manifest presence. Reading Bill Hyer's new book *Ears to Hear* has taken my love to even greater heights.

If you have found the Book of the Revelation confusing or even frustrating, full of mystery, symbols and hidden imagery, you will find this book eye-opening and full of practical insight.

If on the other hand, like me, you have loved the Book of the Revelation, this book will increase your love even more.

Hundreds of books have been written trying to explain the Book of the Revelation. I have 30 of these commentaries in my personal library. None of them are more life-giving, Christ-encountering, worship-inspiring, life-transforming than *Ears to Hear.*

One thing for certain–Bill Hyer needs to write more books.

Fred A. Hartley III

INTRODUCTION

The book of Revelation is the one book of the Bible that says we will be blessed when we read, hear and heed what it says (Revelation 1:3). In it we read the very words of Jesus about many fascinating, fearful and future things, yet the first thing we read about is what He says to the seven churches (Revelation 1:11). Because of this, what He says to these churches in Revelation chapters 2 and 3 is of first importance. It is of first importance because what He says reveals His passion and purpose for the kind of church He wants.

Jesus loves His church. He died for His church, rose from the dead and ascended into heaven where He is seated and enthroned right now at the right hand of God the Father Almighty. Just as He has been doing from that moment almost 2,000 years ago until now, He is praying for us because He wants to guide and empower each of us individually and all of us together as His church to become what He wants us to be.

In the pages that follow, you will listen to the very words of the Lord Jesus Christ and learn 10 qualities and characteristics of the kind of church He wants. The book of Revelation is a book of symbols and numbers are symbolic of meaning. The number 10 is rich in meaning symbolizing completion–a complete cycle, a complete order, as well as harmony–the harmony of heaven and earth. In the first chapter of Genesis, we are told that God created the heavens and the earth and 10 times we read the words *"God said."* There are 10 Commandments which God audibly spoke from Mt. Sinai that summarize the will of God. And 10 times in the Gospel of John the Lord Jesus makes *"I Am"* declarations about Himself that reveal Who He is.

As you listen to what Christ says to each church, you will find there are certain things in some churches–not all, but some–that He commends. These things show us qualities He wants for His church and that is why He commends these churches in these areas. However, as we listen carefully at what Jesus says to each church and compare it to what He says to the other churches, we discover that His words to each individual church reveal one outstanding quality He desires for His church. The seven different churches show us seven different qualities and characteristics of the kind of church Jesus wants. Further, as we listen to what He says to all of the churches, we discover three more. That makes 10 qualities and characteristics of the kind of church Jesus wants.

Chapter one introduces Christ appearing to the Apostle John and gives an overview of what He will say to the churches. In the next 10 chapters you will find the 10 outstanding qualities and characteristics of the kind of church Jesus wants. One can find a progression of these outstanding principles that are essential to the church Christ is building (Matthew 16:18). Each can stand on it's own, but all together they are the building blocks of the church Christ is building to be the place where the glory of His living presence dwells and manifests.

In these pages, you will often read of "the manifest presence" of God, of Christ, and of the Holy Spirit. It is vital to understand what this means. Frequently, people will simply speak of "the presence of God." However, the word "manifest" is used to distinguish it from the "omnipresence of God." The "omnipresence of God" is the reality of His presence everywhere in the universe, because God is everywhere in the universe, but we don't have any awareness of experiencing it. In distinction to the "omnipresence of God" is the "manifest presence of God." This is the dimension of God's presence He freely chooses to make known so that we actually encounter and personally experience His presence in some way or another, to one degree or another, whether we realize it is God or not. It was His manifest presence that came down on Mt. Sinai, that filled the tabernacle built by Moses and temple built by Solomon, that anointed prophets, priests and kings, that filled, anointed and empowered the Lord Jesus Christ, that filled the church at Pentecost, that fills believers and churches, and that will ultimately fill the earth as the waters cover the sea. When we look at the whole of Scripture, we can see that the most common way God manifests His presence to people is to speak to them. When He does, His desire is that people will have ears to hear what He says. This book is not only intended to teach you about Christ, its purpose is to lead you to encounter the reality of His manifest presence by hearing what He says to the seven churches of Revelation.

Christ is the living word of God and this book is filled with quotations and references to Scripture. In an effort to emphasize what is an exact quotation of Scripture, it is quoted in *"italics with quotation marks."* While there are a few words that are in italics to *emphasize* a point, words of Scripture are in *"italics with quotation marks"*– for Scripture is the written word of God and you will be reading the very words of Jesus.

After every chapter study questions are provided. They are primarily intended for groups but, of course, can be used by individuals. There are 12 topics of questions for each chapter and groups can use all of them or pick and choose which ones they want to focus on. These questions are designed to lead a person to deeper insight into the Scriptures, fuller relationship with the Lord Jesus Christ, greater understanding of the kind of church He wants, and how to better live our lives in the empowering presence of the Holy Spirit.

As you travel through chapters two and three of Revelation, you will meet the seven churches that Jesus addresses. You will find there are some that are amazing and others that are awful. There are some churches that are very pleasing to the Lord, others that have some good things but not the best thing. And there are a couple that are–well, you will find out. But no matter where a church is spiritually and what is going on in the lives of those in that church, you will find one amazing truth–whether a church is following Him or failing Him, Jesus loves His church and desires every church to be the kind of church He wants it to be.

I want to be a part of the kind of church Jesus wants and I am sure you do too. So like the young man, Samuel, who said, *"Speak, Lord, for your servant is listening,"* (1 Samuel 3:10), like Mary who sat at the feet of Jesus *"listening to His word"* (Luke 10:39), and like the Apostle John who heard the very words of Jesus and wrote them down for the seven churches and us to read, let's listen to what Jesus says. May He give us ears to hear.

CHAPTER 1

THE KIND OF CHURCH JESUS WANTS

Revelation 1:9-16

I, John, your brother and fellow partaker in the tribulation and kingdom and perseverance which are in Jesus, was on the island called Patmos because of the word of God and the testimony of Jesus. ¹⁰ I was in the Spirit on the Lord's day, and I heard behind me a loud voice like the sound of a trumpet, ¹¹ saying, "Write in a book what you see, and send it to the seven churches: to Ephesus and to Smyrna and to Pergamum and to Thyatira and to Sardis and to Philadelphia and to Laodicea." ¹² Then I turned to see the voice that was speaking with me. And having turned I saw seven golden lampstands; ¹³ and in the middle of the lampstands I saw one like a son of man, clothed in a robe reaching to the feet, and girded across His chest with a golden sash. ¹⁴ His head and His hair were white like white wool, like snow; and His eyes were like a flame of fire. ¹⁵ His feet were like burnished bronze, when it has been made to glow in a furnace, and His voice was like the sound of many waters. ¹⁶ In His right hand He held seven stars, and out of His mouth came a sharp two-edged sword; and His face was like the sun shining in its strength.

So Many Different Kinds

What kind of a church does Jesus want? That's probably a question a lot of people have never answered, let alone asked. Most people have beliefs and feelings about the kind of church *they* want–just ask them! If you were to go to the paved and populated streets of New York City or a dusty and deserted road of a village in Africa and ask a person walking by, "What do you think the church should be like?" they would probably be able to give you a pretty good answer. But if you were to ask them, "What kind of church does Jesus want?"–well, that would probably be a different story. What kind of church does Jesus want?

There are so many different kinds of churches–more than all the varieties and combinations of sushi at a sushi bar. Just Google "churches" and you will find pages of different kinds of churches. From A to Z–from Assembly of God to Zealous for God–there are literally thousands of different kinds of churches to choose from, and new ones are being born every week! People have all kinds of churches they can choose from, but what kind of church does Jesus want?

After His love for His Father, the church is the most important thing there is to Jesus. Jesus loves His church. The church is His bride. The church is His body. Jesus died for His church, and then rose from the dead and ascended to heaven to be enthroned at the right hand of God the Father so that He could be Lord of His church. It is from heaven that He poured forth the Holy Spirit upon and into His church. And just as He has been doing for the last 2,000 years until this very moment, He has been praying for His church so it will be the kind of church He wants. So what kind of church does Jesus want?

What Did Jesus Say About It?

In a certain way, the entire Bible tells us about the kind of church Jesus wants. We could start at the very beginning with the opening words of the book of Genesis and go all the way to the end of the book of Revelation seeking to discover the kind of church He wants. Scholars and great Bible teachers all through church history have done that. However, just as the best way to know what someone wants is to hear it from their very own lips, so the best way to know what Jesus wants is to hear it from His lips.

One of the best places in the word of God to see the kind of church Jesus wants is from His own words recorded in the second and third chapters of the book of Revelation. If you have what is called a "Red Letter Bible," which means the words of Jesus are printed in red ink, you will see that every word in these two chapters is red. Every single word written in these two chapters comes straight from the lips of Jesus! These are the very words Jesus spoke to seven different churches, and it is by looking at what He said to these seven churches that we will get a remarkable picture of the kind of church Jesus wants.

Jesus Told John

While these are the very words of Jesus, they were written down and then sent to the seven churches by the Apostle John, one of the twelve disciples who most often spoke of himself as *"the disciple whom Jesus loved"* (John 13:23; 19:26; 20:2; 21:7, 20). In fact, the Apostle John wrote the entire book of Revelation.

In the first chapter, John tells us he was exiled to Patmos, an island in the Aegean Sea off the west coast of what is today called Turkey. He was there because he had been rejected and persecuted for his faithful testimony to the word of God (Revelation 1:9). He says he was "*in the Spirit on the Lord's day*" (Revelation 1:10). Being "*in the Spirit*," John was encountering the manifest presence of God, fellowshipping with and receiving from the Holy Spirit what God was giving him. "*The Lord's day*" is Sunday, the first day of the week, and it was named this because it was on the first day of the week that Jesus rose from the dead.

It was at this time that the living, resurrected and glorified Lord Jesus Christ Himself appears to John and speaks to him the words that are recorded in the book of Revelation. Everything in this book flows forth from this revelation of the Lord Jesus Christ and what He reveals to John. The first words John hears are the command to write what Jesus will say to the seven churches: "*Write in a book what you see, and send it to the seven churches: to Ephesus and to Smyrna and to Pergamum and to Thyatira and to Sardis and to Philadelphia and to Laodicea*" (Revelation 1:11). While what the Lord will go on to reveal in the greater part of the book is of immense importance, what He says to these seven churches is of first importance. He has something to say to each one of them, and it is from what He says to these churches that we can discover the kind of church Jesus wants.

How to Be Blessed

After hearing the command to write, John says, "*Then I turned to see the voice that was speaking with me. And having turned I saw...*" (Revelation 1:12). It's easy to think of John "turning around to see" as a mere physical act. However, in the book of Revelation actions are symbolic, as are words, numbers, colors and many other things. They express and portray particular truths and realities. "Turning around" is the "body language" the Bible uses for repentance. In fact, the Hebrew word translated "repent" literally means "to turn around." By turning around, John's action can be understood as showing what is so often needed in order to truly hear and obey the Lord Jesus Christ and that is repentance and an intentional focus on Christ. John has heard the voice behind him and in this he is fulfilling the prophecy of Isaiah, *"Your ears will hear a word behind you, 'This is the way, walk in it'"* (Isaiah 30:21). He turns around with the express purpose to see–to single-mindedly concentrate on the One Who is speaking to him. It is when he has turned around that he sees the Lord Jesus Christ.

This is what we must do if we are to be actual followers of Christ and the kind of church Jesus wants. The book of Revelation begins with this blessing: *"Blessed is he who reads and those who hear the words of the prophecy, and heed the things which are written in it; for the time is near"* (Revelation 1:3). Reading is not enough. We are to *"hear"* and *"heed."* We must turn our lives to focus on Christ, to see Him as He is and then do what He says. Then we will be blessed.

Christ in the Midst of Seven Lampstands

John says, *"And having turned I saw seven golden lampstands; 13 and in the middle of the lampstands I saw one like a son of man"* (Revelation 1:12-13). Seeing the Lord Jesus, he goes on to describe what Christ looks like in His resurrected and ascended glory. So great is His awesome appearance that John says, *"When I saw Him, I fell at His feet like a dead man"* (Revelation 1:17). Like the priests at the dedication of Solomon's temple when *"the house of the LORD was filled with a cloud 14 so that the priests could not stand to minister because of the cloud, for the glory of the LORD filled the house of God"* (2 Chronicles 5:13-14), so

John cannot stand in the glory of the manifest presence of Christ. The glory of God that once filled and dwelt in that temple built by human hands now and forever dwells in the living and glorified Lord Jesus Christ. John is so overwhelmed by the weight of His glory, majesty and power that he falls at His feet in worship like a man who has been slain.

There are a number of facets of the glory of the appearance of Christ that John describes yet he begins with that which captures his attention first: " *I saw seven golden lampstands;* [13] *and in the middle of the lampstands I saw one like a son of man."* The first thing his eyes focus on are the *"lampstands."* In the concluding words of this chapter, Christ gives the interpretation of the symbolism of the lampstands, saying, *"the seven lampstands are the seven churches"* (Revelation 1:20). It is most significant that when John describes the glorified Lord Jesus Christ, he begins and ends with His manifest presence in the midst of the churches. That is what the ultimate purpose of Christ is for His church, what His church is all about, and what His church is to be–it is to be the place where the glory of His manifest presence is revealed, encountered and experienced.

The lampstand is the symbol of a church. It is not a candle stand, for a candle and candleholder are completely different from a lamp and a lampstand. A lamp holds oil and the fire that burns the oil. The church is the lamp on the lampstand. It is the holder and carrier of the oil and the fire, the oil symbolizing the Holy Spirit and the fire the manifest presence of the Living Lord Jesus Christ. The church is the place where the manifest presence of the Living Lord Jesus Christ is to dwell and be revealed. Christ did not appear in the middle of pulpits, which would mean the church is supremely the place where the word of God is taught and preached, though it is to be preached and taught in the church. It was not in the midst of tables, which would symbolize that the church is first and foremost a place of fellowship, though that is what the church is to have. It was not in the midst of washbowls, which would mean the church is primarily a place of service. It is in the midst of lampstands, which reveals that what makes the church to be the church, what is first and foremost in the church, and what the church is to supremely be is the place where the manifest presence and glory of the Living Lord Jesus Christ is revealed, encountered and experienced.

John says Christ is in the middle of the *"seven golden lampstands."* Seven is the number of completion or perfection. This reveals that what perfects and makes the church complete is the glory of the manifest presence of Christ filling every church and His whole church. God's ultimate purpose for all creation is that the glory of His manifest presence would fill the earth as the waters cover the sea (Numbers 14:21; Isaiah 11:9; Habakkuk 2:14; Ephesians 1:22-23; Revelation 21:11, 23, 24). In accomplishing this desire, His purpose has been for His manifest presence to dwell in the midst of His people (Exodus 25:8; 29:45; Deuteronomy 12:11; Revelation 21:3). Over the course of history, God's glory filled and dwelt in the tabernacle (Exodus 40:34), then in the temple (2 Chronicles 5:13-14), then in Christ (John 1:14), and now in His church (Ephesians 3:16-21). This is symbolized in the seven golden lampstands with Christ standing in the midst of His churches. Each and every church is to be filled with the glory of His manifest presence, for this is His ultimate purpose as He speaks to each one of the seven churches. Like the seven different and distinct colors of the rainbow, when each color shines fully, and all the colors shine together, they will shine with the white light, so when each distinct and different church shines, and they all shine together, the fullness of the glory of Christ will shine forth and be manifested. His purpose will be perfected when each and every church, and His whole church is completely filled with the oil of the Holy Spirit, transformed into His likeness, and burns with the glory of His manifest presence.

A Flame of Fire and A Two-edged Sword

After revealing the foremost purpose of the church, John describes many fascinating and symbolic things about Christ's appearance. However, as we consider the kind of church Jesus wants, there are two attributes that stand out: *"His eyes were like a flame of fire"*(v.14) and *"out of his mouth came a sharp two-edged sword"* (v.16). Fire has always been one of the most powerful ways the presence of God is manifested. In a number of places, the word of God declares, *"our God is a consuming fire"* (Exodus 24:17; Deuteronomy 4:24; 9:3; Hebrews 12:29). It was in fire that God manifested His presence to Moses in the burning bush (Exodus 3:2). It was in fire that God manifested His presence on Mt. Sinai (Exodus 19:18). It was in fire that God manifested His presence when the Holy Spirit was poured forth on the praying believers in the Upper Room on the day of Pentecost (Acts 2:3). And the two-edged sword represents the word of God. Hebrew 4:12 says, *"The word of God is living and active and sharper than any two-edged sword, and piercing as far as the division of soul and spirit, of both joints and marrow, and able to judge the thoughts and intentions of the heart."*

What is important to understand about these two attributes of the Lord Jesus is that the fire of God's presence is not only light but also it can burn, and the sharp words of His mouth can pierce deep into the heart to reveal things that are hidden there. As we look at what these chapters in Revelation reveal about *the actual* Jesus Who is the living and ascended Lord of His Church, *the real* Jesus Who is revealed in the inerrant and infallible written word of God, *the authentic* Jesus Who speaks His word to His church, we will most likely discover that He is not like what many people think and believe about Him.

Is He Safe?

Over the course of church history, the predominant concept and belief in the church about Who and What Jesus is has gone through changes, and it can be seen in the art work and images of the Lord displayed in churches. Very early, and for most of church history, the predominant belief in the church was of Christ the King–the All-powerful Emperor and Judge Who is seated on His throne, to whom every soul must give an account, executing justice and rendering to everyone as they deserve. During this time in history, the culture was one in which people believed that God ordained authority and power and understood that this could be exercised by those in authority. Because of this, they revered and honored authority, especially the power and authority of the emperor or king, and this attitude was how people related to Christ. Today, we have the empathetic and gentler Jesus, most often expressed in the picture of Jesus as the Good Shepherd holding a little lamb and leading sheep. He understands people's weaknesses and is gracious toward us when we sin and fall short, and people prefer to relate to Him this way now.

What is vital for us to believe and understand is that both of these concepts are true of the Lord Jesus Christ. He is righteous and gracious. He is the all-powerful King Who is the Good Shepherd. He is the Lion and the Lamb. So we would completely misunderstand Who He really is if we were to believe either one or the other of these attributes represents the whole truth about Christ. As we will see from the words He speaks to the seven churches, He is the sovereign Lord, King and Judge who executes His righteous judgment as well as the gracious Good Shepherd Who understands and cares for His sheep because He loves us.

This reality of Who Jesus is was wonderfully portrayed in literature by C. S. Lewis in his book *The Lion, the Witch and the Wardrobe* [1]. When Lucy, one of the children, is about to meet Aslan, who represents the Lord Jesus Christ, she is told he is a lion. Realizing he is a lion, she asks, "Is he safe?" Immediately the response is, "Safe? Who said anything about safe? 'Course he isn't safe. But he's good. He's the King, I tell you."

Lewis captured the truth about the real Jesus, and it is demonstrated in the things of the world that the Lord has made. For example, we can ask, "Is gravity safe?" The answer is no, not really. But it is good and it brings blessing in our lives when we obey it. However, if we violate it, we will suffer the consequences. We can ask, "Is electricity safe?" No, not really. Yet, it is good and it brings blessing to our lives unless we violate its laws. Then we will suffer the consequences. So, is Jesus safe? Not really. But He is good.

Cleaning House

One of the foremost places Jesus demonstrated this reality of Himself was when He cleansed the temple in Jerusalem. The temple was the house of God. It was the place where His glorious manifest presence dwelt and the people of God, as well as worshippers of God from every nation in the world, were to come to draw near to God in prayer and sacrifice. However, the leadership of Israel turned the selling of the animals used for sacrifice into a money-making business and made God's house into what

Jesus called a *"place of business,"* literally in the Greek an "emporium" (John 2:16). This made Jesus angry, and He made a whip, and then went through the temple grounds, overturning the tables of the moneychangers and drove out those selling the animals (John 2:15), saying, *"It is written, 'My house will be a house of prayer for all nations,' but you are making it a robbers' den"* (Matthew 21:13). This, in effect, is what Jesus does with His words to the seven churches in Revelation–He seeks to cleanse each church so it will be a place where His presence will dwell and be manifested. This is because His manifest presence is the greatest good we can ever experience.

Many people only want a "safe Jesus," yet as we see what the Scriptures reveal about Him, He is not really what some would call "safe." His eyes are *"like a flame of fire"* and out of His mouth comes *"a sharp two-edged sword."* He is not safe, if you believe safe means never being held accountable for sin in your life, or never having to go through difficult times in order to grow and mature, or never being asked to sacrifice to advance the Kingdom of God. But one of the most important truths of life we can know and believe–the truth that will give us peace so that we will not fear in difficult times–is that the safest place to be is in the will of God. Jesus is righteous and good. Being good, He wants good for us. Being righteous, He wants exactly what He told us to pray for in the Lord's Prayer, that His kingdom would come and His will be done in our lives and in His church as it is in heaven, and sometimes that's not easy or safe.

The Truth in Love

Probably the best way to summarize what He does in these words is that He speaks the truth in love. Speaking the truth in love is a vital principle for the health of a church because it is essential for healthy personal relationships. For a church to grow the way Jesus wants His church to grow, the members must speak the truth in love. This is what the word of God tells us in Ephesians 4:15, *"but speaking the truth in love, we are to grow up in all aspects into Him who is the head, even Christ."*

Speaking the truth in love is often a difficult thing to do, and we must walk in the grace and power of the Holy Spirit to do it. Our tendency as fallen, feeble and fearful human beings is usually expressed by opting out for one of the two primary psychological defense mechanisms: fight or flight. We can go on the offensive and fight by speaking truth. This often happens when we or somebody we care about is hurt and we feel an injustice of some kind has been committed. Typically, we will let it build up and then blurt it out at some highly emotional moment–we might speak the truth, but it really isn't in love. More often, we choose to flee and emotionally avoid "the elephant in the room." Characteristically, we do this while telling ourselves we are loving the person by not opening up to them, and so we don't speak the truth. What we see Jesus doing with the seven churches is speak the truth in love, just as He says at the end of His words to the last church, *"Those whom I love, I reprove and discipline; therefore be zealous and repent"* (Revelation 3:19).

Is that Christ-like?

In speaking the truth in love, we find Jesus speaking both positive and negative things. To most of the churches, He will say positive things about what they are doing, things that please Him, specifically the way they are being the kind of church He wants. And He speaks very forthrightly and clearly about the things they are doing that do not please Him, the areas in the life of the church where they are not being the kind of church He wants. Today in the Western world and American culture, it has become popular to think we must only speak positive things to people and nothing negative. Along with this is the belief that if we say anything negative we are not being "Christ-like." However, what people so often popularly think of as being "Christ-like" is nothing like the real Jesus revealed in the word of God, for Jesus speaks the truth in love. That means He will say positive things to encourage us as well as negative things to convict us. In His words to the seven churches, there are not only positive things that please Him but also negative things where they need to repent. He does this because He loves His church and wants His good will done in every church so they will become the kind of church He wants.

Angels On Assignment

As we look at what Christ says to the seven churches, we can see a basic framework or outline composed of six parts. This is evident as we read what He says to the first church, the church at Ephesus.

First, He starts with the charge to write to the angel of each church that is being addressed. Revelation 2:1 begins, *"To the angel of the church in Ephesus write..."*

This is a fascinating statement that raises a significant question about the meaning of *"angel."* Is Jesus speaking to a spiritual being, an actual angel, or a human being?

Some believe Jesus is speaking to a human being, and a primary reason for this is that they find it strange, even weird that an angel would be assigned to a church and that Jesus would address such a being. Most who believe Jesus is addressing a human propose He is speaking to the person functioning in the role or office of the pastor of the church.

There are, however, a number of reasons why this would not be so. The most significant is the internal evidence of the book of Revelation. The Lord uses the word "*angel*," not "*pastor*," and every time the word "*angel*" is used in the book of Revelation it identifies a spiritual being, not a human being. Further, in chapter one, the Lord is described as holding "*seven stars*" in His hand (Revelation 1:16), and He interprets their meaning saying, "*the seven stars are the seven angels of the seven churches*" (Revelation 1:20). Later on in Revelation, a "*star*" is used as a symbol of an angel (Revelation 12:4). Jesus says these "*stars*" are specific "*angels*" that are "*of*" each one of "*the seven churches.*" This means they belong to the church in some way. This is the immediate context preceding what the Lord goes on to say in chapters two and three when He addresses "*the angel*" of each of the seven churches.

Another reason this would not be a human being is that if Christ intended His words to be addressed to the pastor He could have used that title for the actual designation of "pastor" is used elsewhere in the New Testament (Ephesians 4:11). And that is the point, to believe Jesus is addressing a pastor is an interpretation of the meaning of the word "*angel*" and not a literal understanding of its meaning. Not only that, but if Christ were addressing a pastor, it would be the only time in the Scripture this word is used of such an ecclesiastical office. More than this, it would mean that a major transition had taken place within the period of the writing of the New Testament in regard to the government of a church and was now being confirmed by the Lord. This would be a transition from that of the rule by elders (Acts 14:23; 20:17; 1 Timothy 3:1ff.; Titus 1:5ff.) to that of a single individual having authority. While this did eventually take place in church history, this passage would be the only place in the New Testament that could be interpreted to support this transition.

If Jesus were addressing a human being, it would be more likely to understand the Greek word *"angelos"* to express its literal meaning which is "messenger." The Lord Jesus did use the word *"angelos"* of John the Baptist. Quoting the prophecy of Malachi 3:1, He said, *"This is the one about whom it is written, 'Behold, I send My messenger ahead of You, who will prepare Your way before You.'"* In this passage, Jesus said John was *"a prophet,"* in fact, *"the messenger"* sent before Him to prepare His way (Matthew 11:9-10). If Jesus were addressing a human being, it is more likely He would be speaking to the person who would be given the responsibility to deliver the Lord's message to the church. This person would be functioning in the role of prophet and not a pastor.

The passage Christ quotes concerning John the Baptist is Malachi 3:1 which is based on Exodus 23:20 and states, *"Behold, I am going to send an angel before you to guard you along the way and to bring you into the place which I have prepared."* Exodus is speaking of a spiritual being, an actual angel who was given an assignment from God concerning the people of God to guard and lead them. Scripture reveals angels are given many different assignments from God, one being that of a "messenger" to deliver the word of the Lord. This is what took place many times in the Old and New Testaments, as we know, for example, from the Christmas story accounts of different angels speaking God's word to people such as Zachariah, Mary, Joseph, and the shepherds (Matthew 1:20; Luke 1:11ff; 1:26ff; 2:9ff.). This is what took place with the book of Revelation. It begins in the very first verse of the book stating, *"The Revelation of Jesus Christ, which God gave Him to show to His bond-servants, the things which must soon take place; and He sent and communicated it by His angel to His bond-servant John"* (Revelation 1:1). This *"angel"* is not a human being, but a spiritual being assigned by the

Lord who "*communicated*" His message to John. This verse is the foundational context of Jesus addressing "*the angel of the church in...*" Just as the Lord Jesus gave an angel the assignment to communicate to John the contents of the book of Revelation, so the Lord Jesus is addressing an angel assigned to each church who is to communicate that message to the church.

This reveals the amazing truth that the Lord Jesus has assigned an angel to each church. Most everyone knows the Bible tells us we have guardian angels, but how many know that churches have angels? Hebrews 1:14 says of angels, "*Are they not all ministering spirits, sent out to render service for the sake of those who will inherit salvation?*" Just as angels are sent to serve individuals, so angels are assigned to churches, and Jesus addresses each angel of the seven churches with the message He has for it. How this took place, we do not know. Yet we must take seriously that just as John said the message of the book of Revelation was "*communicated*" to him by the Lord's "*angel*" and we do not know how that took place yet we know it did, so also just because we do not know how the angels communicated Christ's words to the churches does not mean that this could not or did not happen.

The real world is one in which the spirit realm interfaces, influences and impacts the earthly realm. And as we see from what Jesus says to the seven churches as well as the whole book of Revelation, it is also a world not only inhabited by angels but also of the devil and demons. In fact, Jesus explicitly speaks about the reality of the devil and his influence in the lives of people in four of the seven churches. We live in a spiritual world, and Christ's holy angels are a strategic aspect of the unseen spiritual world and warfare that every church and every Christian experiences, whether they know it or not.

What He Says About Himself

During His earthly ministry, the Lord Jesus made amazing claims about Himself. He said He came to fulfill the Law and the Prophets (Matthew 5:17), He could forgive sins (Matthew 9:2), He could give eternal life to all who truly believe in Him (John 6:47), He is the only way to God (John 14:6), and whoever has seen Him has seen God the Father (John 14:9). Among the most profound claims are His seven "I AM" statements throughout the Gospel of John (John 6:48; 8:12, 58; 10:9, 11; 11:25; 14:6; 15:1). However, the greatest collection of claims Christ makes about Himself in all of Scripture is in what He says to the seven churches. These are found in the second part of the outline where the Lord Jesus identifies Himself with specific titles or attributes. Many of His attributes refer to the description of His glorious appearance given by John in chapter one, some of His claims are what He told John, and others are distinct claims based on other verses of Scripture. They are revelations of Who He is, what He has, and what He does, and each claim applies to each church in its own particular situation.

In Revelation 2:1, Christ says He is *"the One who holds the seven stars in His right hand, the One who walks among the seven golden lampstands."* As we have already seen, in chapter one Christ revealed that the seven stars are symbolic of the seven angels of the churches and the seven lampstands are symbolic of the seven churches (Revelation 1:20). Each of the titles and attributes of Jesus display His character and authority and are relevant in making known the kind of church He wants.

Jesus Knows All About It

The third thing Christ says to each church is His dec-laration *"I know..."* Every letter has His words, *"I know."* He then gives specific details about each church and that reveals His intimate knowledge of each church. This includes such things as His familiarity with every member of each church and their names, the quality of the spiri-tual life of the church, and the spiritual environment and atmosphere of the city in which they are living.

For some Christians, such knowledge of our lives by Christ can be comforting while for others it can be threat-ening. For some, there is great assurance to understand that Jesus knows everything that is going on in our lives and especially, as these letters show, the trials and suf-fering we are going through and enduring. To others who are not walking in the light, this can be fearful for as Jesus says to the church in Pergamum, *"I am He Who searches the minds and hearts, and will give to each of you according to your deeds"* (Revelation 2:23).

Praise and Problems

The fourth part of the outline of each letter is the main body and consists of Christ's words of commendation or criticism that are appropriate for each church. He praises the things that please Him and points out the places they have problems. It is in this section that we find the one thing He is most concerned about in each church. He says something different to all seven churches and it is from what He says that we discover the first seven qualities and characteristics of the kind of church He wants. His words to the church in Ephesus are:

> *I know your deeds and your toil and perseverance, and that you cannot tolerate evil men, and you put to the test those who call themselves apostles, and they are not, and you found them to be false; ³ and you have perseverance and have endured for My name's sake, and have not grown weary. ⁴ But I have this against you, that you have left your first love* (Revelation 2:2-4).

It is in what Christ says in these words that we will discover the first quality of the kind of church He wants.

It may be surprising to some that Jesus has something *"against"* a church. However, when Jesus says this, He is declaring what the prophets said to the people of Israel when they were living in sin. For example, Hosea 4:1, says, *"Listen to the word of the Lord, O sons of Israel, for the Lord has a case against the inhabitants of the land, because there is no faithfulness or kindness or knowledge of God in the land"* (see also Hosea 12:2; Micah 6:2).

On the other hand, some may think this is how Jesus thinks about them all the time. The truth is that when we are in Christ, He loves us, forgives all our sins, and there is no condemnation or rejection by Him of us personally. But that does not mean He simply overlooks every sin and act of rebellion, nor that churches are not disciplined and pay the consequences for their unrighteous, sinful and rebellious deeds.

Think of it in terms of human endeavors, for example, of great football coaches. People want the team they cheer for to have great football coaches that produce winning teams. A great football coach will seek to make the players on the team better by telling them what they are doing right as well as what they are doing wrong and how they can improve. A coach who simply overlooks the failures of his team and does not have team discipline will soon be a losing coach.

Jesus is a winner, the greatest winner in all of history. He wants His church to be a winner, the greatest team in history. And as we see from what He tells the seven churches, He will praise them when they are doing well as well as point out where they are falling short, and then tell them how they can become the kind of church He wants. That's why He goes on to say to the Ephesian church,

> *Therefore remember from where you have fallen, and repent and do the deeds you did at first; or else I am coming to you and will remove your lampstand out of its place– unless you repent. ⁶ Yet this you do have, that you hate the deeds of the Nicolaitans, which I also hate* (Revelation 2:5-6).

These are strong words, words that tell the church where they are failing and need to repent as well as words of praise where they are the kind of church He wants.

Promised Rewards

Christ's words of promise to those who overcome are a fifth part of each letter. The promise to the one who overcomes is one of only two things Jesus says to all the churches. These are promises of eternal reward to those who are faithful followers of Christ. They are gifts and blessings the overcomer will receive in the New Heaven and Earth described in the final two chapters of the book, Revelation 21 and 22. We see this in what Christ says to the church in Ephesus in Revelation 2:7, "*To him who overcomes, I will grant to eat of the tree of life which is in the Paradise of God.*"

Every letter has these words of challenge to overcome along with the promise of eternal reward to those who do. As Christ Himself was encouraged and motivated through His time of suffering on the cross by fixing His eyes on *"the hope set before Him"* (Hebrew 12:2), so He also encourages and challenges each church and every believer with the promise of their eternal reward. No matter what challenges a church faces, the Lord wants each and all to overcome so that they can receive all the good, great and glorious blessings He wants to give them.

Are You Listening?

The summit of each letter is the sixth part where Jesus leaves it to each church as to how they will respond. It is His word of encouragement, even command, to hear what the Spirit is saying to the churches. He says, *"He who has an ear, let him hear what the Spirit says to the churches"* (Revelation 2:7). This is the only other thing Christ says to each church, and it is His last, culminating and final word to all the churches.

Once again we see the real world that Jesus lives in. It is the world where the spirit realm interfaces, influences and impacts the earthly realm and our personal lives. These words reveal how Christ wants His church to listen to, respond and obey the influence and leading of the Holy Spirit. This is a foundational characteristic of the kind of church Jesus wants to build because it is being like Him in His humanity. Taking to Himself human nature to live fully as a human being, yet without sin, He was completely dependent upon the Holy Spirit to accomplish the work the Father had given to Him (Luke 4:18). He was filled with power of the Holy Spirit and led by the Holy Spirit, and He wants His church filled with and led by the

Holy Spirit. The key to this is listening to what the Holy Spirit says.

The real world Jesus lives in is one in which He speaks through the Holy Spirit to every church and to each person in the church. Sadly, as history demonstrates, many churches do not have ears to hear and suffer the consequences. The kind of church Jesus wants has ears to hear and listens to the Holy Spirit. Having ears to hear is critical to the church living in and ministering by the empowering presence of the Holy Spirit. In fact, it can be said that this is the most critical characteristic of the kind of church Jesus wants for this is the one thing He tells each and every church to do (Revelation 2:7, 11, 17, 29; 3:6, 13, 22). While he gives promises to all the churches if they overcome, listening to what the Spirit says is the one thing Christ commands all the churches to do.

Let's Dig In

Revelation chapters 2 and 3 are a quarry of the wealth of Christ's very own words just waiting to be uncovered. As we mine the riches of what He says to each of the seven churches, we will bring forth *"the gold, silver and precious stones"* of the qualities and characteristics of the kind of church He wants to build (Matthew 16:16; 1 Corinthians 3:12). We will find it's a church that's like Him because it is filled with love for Him. We will see it's one in which His people live in the real world He lives in because they understand how the spirit realm influences and impacts their lives, whether it is the spiritual forces of darkness and the devil or the spiritual powers of light and God. We will become aware of how it's a church in which His own overcome their enemies and, most importantly, listens to what the Holy Spirit is saying. Ultimately, we will find that because it encounters and experiences His manifest presence it lives in and reveals the glory of the Living Lord Jesus Christ. That's the kind of church Jesus wants. That's the kind of church I want to be a part of, and I know it's the same for you. So let's dig in together and discover the riches He has for us, and may He give us ears to hear what He says.

Study Questions
Chapter 1

1. Briefly share one personal highlight from the chapter.

2. How much thought have you given to the kind of church Jesus wants? How much do you think Jesus really cares about it?

3. Do you think the mindset of most people in your church is that they are looking for the kind of church they want or the kind of church Jesus wants? Why?

4. What do you think it means to be "*in the Spirit*"? Is this something you experience in your personal relationship and walk with the Lord?

5. Why is repentance so important for hearing God's voice?

6. What does the author say is the ultimate purpose of the church as it is symbolized in the lampstand? Is this a new thought for you? How should this make a difference in your life and your church?

7. Is there any thing that you have believed about Christ and what is "Christ-like" that is different from how He is revealed in the book of Revelation? How do you personally relate to C. S. Lewis' depiction of the Lord Jesus as Aslan the Lion, especially that he is not safe but he is good?

8. Is it difficult for you to speak the truth in love to someone? If so, do you tend to choose fight or light? Why? What kinds of problems develop in relationships when we don't speak the truth in love to one another?

9. What are the six parts of the basic framework or outline of what Christ says to each church? Is there any one of these that is most interesting to you? Why?

(1)

(2)

(3)

(4)

(5)

(6)

10. What do you think about the reality of angels and of guardian angels being assigned to churches and to you?

11. How do you relate to the Lord Jesus speaking words of commendation as well as criticism? What is your response to Him having something "*against*" a church?

12. What does it mean to you to have an ear to hear what the Spirit says to the churches?

CHAPTER 2

<u>EPHESUS: HAS A FIRST LOVE FOR CHRIST</u>

Revelation 2:1-7

To the angel of the church in Ephesus write: The One who holds the seven stars in His right hand, the One who walks among the seven golden lampstands, says this: ² "I know your deeds and your toil and perseverance, and that you cannot tolerate evil men, and you put to the test those who call themselves apostles, and they are not, and you found them to be false; ³ and you have perseverance and have endured for My name's sake, and have not grown weary. ⁴ But I have this against you, that you have left your first love. ⁵ Therefore remember from where you have fallen, and repent and do the deeds you did at first; or else I am coming to you and will remove your lampstand out of its place—unless you repent. ⁶ 'Yet this you do have, that you hate the deeds of the Nicolaitans, which I also hate. ⁷ He who has an ear, let him hear what the Spirit says to the churches. To him who overcomes, I will grant to eat of the tree of life which is in the Paradise of God."

If You Find It, Don't Join It

The perfect church... have you ever thought about the perfect church? What would the perfect church be like, and what would it be like to be a member of the perfect church?

Years ago, I heard a story about a husband and wife who had become new believers in the Lord Jesus Christ and were searching for a church to join. After some time had passed, the man who led them to saving faith in Christ asked them about their search and why they had not yet joined a church. They explained that it was taking them a long time to find a church they wanted to join because they could never find a church like what they wanted. The man responded saying that while sometimes it may take time to find a church to join, it seemed the reason they had not joined a church is because what they wanted was the perfect church. They answered, indeed, that was what they were looking for! The man, who was a mature Christian, wisely replied, "Well that's a wonderful goal. But if you ever find the perfect church, please don't join it, for the moment you do, it will no longer be perfect."

The point of what that wise man was saying is that there is not a perfect church this side of heaven because there are not perfect Christians in this world. Even if this couple found a church they thought was perfect and joined it, it would no longer be perfect because they're not perfect. Not only this, they would, sooner or later, discover that no one else in the church is perfect. No matter what church we are a part of it will not be perfect because there are no perfect churches in this world.

What is the Perfect Church Like?

Nevertheless, if there actually were a perfect church in this world, what would it be like? If the truth were told, most people would probably describe the perfect church as being a church they are comfortable in. It would be a church that is what they want, a church like them, a church that is, in effect, made in their image and likeness. But the perfect church is not like any of us, nor what we may want or be comfortable in. This is because Christ is not making His church into the image and likeness of any of us. The church is being made into the likeness of Him, and this means the perfect church is like Him! This is God's purpose for us. Romans 8:28-29 tells us

> *that God causes all things to work together for good to those who love God, to those who are called according to His purpose. 29 For those whom He foreknew, He also predestined to become conformed to the image of His Son, so that He would be the firstborn among many brethren.*

God is working in every detail of our lives as Christians, and all of us together as His church, to become like Christ.

The kind of church Jesus wants is one that's like Him. And because of this, as we listen to His words spoken to the church at Ephesus, Christ will reveal His heart and show us the kind of church He wants. It's a church that loves Him above and beyond everything else–it's a church that has a first love for Him.

Why Start with Ephesus?

The second and third chapters of the book of Revelation record the very words Jesus spoke to seven churches that were in the area of the world that today we call Asia Minor or Turkey. It is most appropriate that Christ begins with the church at Ephesus for at least two reasons.

The church at Ephesus was the leading church of all the churches in that region of the world. The city of Ephesus was the principal city of that area, just as, for example, New York City is the leading city of the state of New York, London in Great Britain, and Paris in France. We are told in the New Testament that the church was established through the ministry of the Apostle Paul. It was the first church established by him in that part of the world, and from this church the other churches in the region were established (Acts 19:1-10). It is because Ephesus was the first and leading city of the region that it was the most influential church among the seven that Jesus speaks to. So it is fitting for Him to address them first.

The second reason why it is appropriate for Jesus to lead off with the church in Ephesus is because what He says to them is the leading quality and characteristic of the kind of church He wants. Love is the leader because what we love first and foremost will define and determine our lives and lifestyle.

Keep Up the Good Work

Before the Lord speaks to the Ephesians about His principal concern for them, He commends the church for the areas of its life in which they are the kind of church He wants, and there are three things they are doing that please Him.

First, He commends them for being a church that works hard. He says, *"I know your deeds and your toil"* (2:2). The Greek word translated *"toil"* has the connotation of "intense labor in the midst of difficulty and trouble, even labor to the point of exhaustion." This means they were hard workers.

Scripture makes it clear that while no one is saved on the basis of his or her works, people who are saved do good works. They will be working for the Lord to build His church and advance His kingdom. The great Bible teachers of the Reformation in the 16th century put it this way: While we are saved by faith alone, it is not a faith that is alone–it is a faith that works.

Jesus spoke about the vital importance of works in His Sermon on the Mount, saying,

> *You are the light of the world. A city set on a hill cannot be hidden;* ¹⁵ *nor does anyone light a lamp and put it under a basket, but on the lampstand, and it gives light to all who are in the house.* ¹⁶ *Let your light shine before men in such a way that they may see your good works, and glorify your Father who is in heaven* (Matthew 5:14-16).

Practicing what He preached, Jesus worked hard. He did the works the Father gave Him to accomplish. This is the very thing He prayed about in the Upper Room at the end of His life, saying, *"I glorified You on the earth, having accomplished the work which You have given Me to do"* (John 17:4).

For us to be like Jesus, we will be doing the work God has given us to do. One of the reasons the Ephesian church was hard working is because, from its very beginning, Paul taught them that a real Christian is a real worker. This is the very thing he wrote about in his letter to them, saying,

> *For by grace you have been saved through faith; and that not of yourselves, it is the gift of God;* [9] *not as a result of works, so that no one may boast.* [10] *For we are His workmanship, created in Christ Jesus for good works, which God prepared beforehand so that we would walk in them* (Ephesians 2:8-10).

While we have not been saved *by* our works, we are saved *for* works–the good works that God has "*prepared*" for us to accomplish. That's what Jesus commends this church for.

It's a Marathon

The second area in the life of the church that Jesus praises is that they are a church that has persevered in hard times. He emphasizes this quality of the church for He speaks of it two times, first, in verse 2, saying, "*I know your deeds and your toil and perseverance,*" and then again in verse 3, "*and you have perseverance and have endured for My name's sake, and have not grown weary.*"

One of the facts of life in this world for a true follower of the Lord Jesus is that, at times, life will become very challenging. Frequently, after a person becomes a Christian, their life does not get easier, instead it becomes harder. This is often difficult for people to understand who live in the comfortable, convenient and complacent Western and American culture. People have been told, "Have it your way," and "You deserve a break today." However, if you were to become a believer in a Muslim-ruled country, coming to saving faith in the Lord Jesus as the Son of God and being baptized in His Name could mean your life is on the line. Just like Jesus, a true believer in Christ perseveres through trials and difficulties. Jesus said, *"In the world you shall have tribulation, but take courage, I have overcome the world"* (John 16:33).

The Christian life is not a sprint–it's a marathon. I know from talking with people who have run a marathon that it is extremely demanding. For most running a marathon race, somewhere along the way they hit what is called a "wall." It is a "wall" not only because their energy has been depleted but also because their bodies are so stressed it is painful to keep on going. For some, it's too much, and they give up and drop out. Nevertheless, many keep going and persevere through the pain to finish the race.

That's what Jesus did. He persevered through the pain of personal rejection, false accusations, unjust condemnation, the trauma of crucifixion, and the agony of death on the cross. He calls us to follow Him, saying, *"If anyone wishes to come after Me, he must deny himself, and take up his cross daily and follow Me"* (Luke 9:23). The kind of church Jesus wants is a church like Him because it doesn't drop out of the race when things get tough, when life becomes painful, when we hit a "wall." It perseveres through whatever pain and problems we encounter.

Do They Pass the Test?

The third thing Christ commends the Ephesians for is that they maintain doctrinal purity. This is a church that is not only teaching and preaching the truths of the word of God, it's holding people accountable who don't. Jesus identifies two ways in particular in how they are doing this. In verse 2 He says, *"...you cannot tolerate evil men, and you put to the test those who call themselves apostles, and they are not, and you found them to be false."* Then in verse 6, He says, "*Yet this you do have, that you hate the deeds of the Nicolaitans, which I also hate.*" "Cannot tolerate" and "hate"–these are the two greatest "sins" of the present, prevailing popular culture that is called "politically correct." How many people are influenced by the spirit of the world instead of the Holy Spirit of God and believe that Jesus would never hate anything because He is so tolerate of how people live their lives? As we see from His very own words, He hates evil and does not tolerate evil deeds. Just as Jesus says later to the church in Thyatira, "*I am He who searches the minds and hearts; and I will give to each one of you according to your deeds*" (Revelation 2:23), so He wants His church to righteously evaluate and discern the fruit of people's lives. In other words, we are to "*test*" the doctrine and deeds of people in the church to maintain the health of the church.

Church history tells us that the Apostle John, who recorded these words of Jesus, lived in Ephesus, and it is most significant that He wrote in his first letter these words:

> *Beloved, do not believe every spirit, but test the spirits to see whether they are from God, because many false prophets have gone out into the world. ² By this you know the Spirit of God: every spirit that confesses that Jesus Christ has come in the flesh is from God; ³ and every spirit that does not confess Jesus is not from God; this is the spirit of the antichrist, of which you have heard that it is coming, and now it is already in the world* (1 John 4:1-3).

The church in Ephesus took seriously this word, for Jesus says to them that they "*put to the test those who call themselves apostles, and they are not, and you found them to be false"* (Revelation 2:2). Whoever these false apostles and Nicolaitans were, what they taught, and what they did is not what is important, for the Scripture doesn't tell us. What is important is that the Ephesian church did not tolerate their false teaching or immoral deeds and maintained doctrinal purity and righteous living according to the truth of the word of God. Like a person who conscientiously watches what they eat and drink so they can maintain good physical health, this church watched the spiritual diet of the church to maintain good spiritual health.

These three areas that Jesus commends show us three qualities of the kind of church He wants. He wants a church that works hard, that perseveres through difficult times, and that is doctrinally and morally pure because it preserves and proclaims the purity of the word of God.

Duty But Not Devotion

Even though the Ephesian church had these excellent qualities, they didn't have that which is the leading quality and characteristic of the kind of church Jesus wants. Consequently, He speaks the truth in love to them, saying, *"But I have this against you, that you have left your first love"* (Revelation 2:4). Tragically, Jesus exposes the Ephesian church as being a church of duty and not devotion. They are a church full of "Marthas" who are busy with all their *"preparations"* but not "Marys" who want to sit in the presence of Jesus to love and adore Him. Jesus said to Martha that her sister Mary was doing the *"one thing that is necessary, for Mary has chosen the good part, which shall not be taken away from her"* (See Luke 10:38-42). The Ephesian church had been like Mary at one time, but they left their first love for Christ and became Marthas.

51

Their relationship with Jesus had become like that of a marriage where two people who once loved each other and couldn't wait to get married and spend their lives together had drifted apart in their hearts and no longer longed to be in each other's presence. They are married, they go through the motions of marriage, they fulfill their duty, but they have lost their delight in one another. They no longer enjoy one another–they have left their first love. This is a sad reality that occurs in many marriages and it has been the theme of popular songs throughout the ages. Maybe you have heard of the song from the 60's by the Righteous Brothers, "You've Lost That Lovin' Feelin,'" or the one by Blues singer, B.B. King, "The Thrill is Gone"? Whether you heard these songs or not, you get the idea. The person they are singing about has lost their first love, and that is what Jesus says happened to the church in Ephesus.

Watch Your Step

The Greek word translated "*left*" is a very strong word and means "to forsake or to send away." This is the very thing that happened to the people of Israel. Through Jeremiah, God said,

> *Go and proclaim in the ears of Jerusalem, saying, "Thus says the LORD, 'I remember concerning you the devotion of your youth, the love of your betrothals, your following after Me in the wilderness...' For My people have committed two evils: They have forsaken Me, the fountain of living waters, to hew for themselves cisterns, broken cisterns that can hold no water"* (Jeremiah 2:2, 13).

When the hearts of God's people are no longer filled with first love and devotion for Him, they will be filled with something else–things that will not satisfy or last.

The Lord does not view this as something that merely happened as an oversight, like an unattended campfire that dies out because someone forgot to put sticks on it or stir it up. Jesus regards their loss of love as a deliberate choice. They have walked away from Him. Whether it was conscious or unconscious, an oversight or a misstep, one significant choice or a series of minor choices, other things arose in their lives to distract them, causing them to depart, and it had a major consequence. The priority in their hearts was no longer their love and devotion to Him–they had left their first love.

The Worst Thing that Could Happen

This was a disastrous choice in their relationship with Christ. We see this from what He says in verse 5, *"Therefore, remember from where you have fallen." "Fallen"* is the word theologians and Christians use to identify the result of the very first sin of the human race, the sin of Adam, when he chose to not believe the word of God and disobey His command–he fell into sin. *"Fallen"* is the word the Lord used to describe what happened to Satan when he rebelled against Him, saying, *"How you have fallen from heaven, O star of the morning, son of the dawn!"* (Isaiah 14:12). *"Fallen"* is the word that depicts the worst thing that can happen to anyone in their relationship with God.

It is vital to understand what God says is the root cause and motive of His people falling away–it is that they no longer love Him. This is demonstrated by their deeds. They no longer love Him so they do not obey Him. Reaffirming what God repeatedly said to His people throughout the history of the Old Testament, Jesus stated, *"If you love me, you will keep my commandments*" (John 14:15). Love is not mere sentiment, or a positive emotional feeling. While it certainly can involve this, the reality of love for God is revealed in our obeying His commandments, and the greatest commandment is to love God.

The Most Important Thing

Love of God is the most important thing there is in life because God is the most important Being there is in life. Jesus responded to the question, "*What commandment is the foremost of all*," by stating,

> *The foremost is, "Hear, O Israel! The Lord our God is one Lord; ³⁰ and you shall love the Lord your God with all your heart, and with all your soul, and with all your mind, and with all your strength*" (Mark 12:29-30).

God is to be first and "*foremost*" in our lives and we do this by loving Him first and "*foremost*" above all other things. We are to love Him with all our heart, all our soul, all our mind, and all our strength, which is to love Him with a first love. This means that to love God with a first love, we can't have a divided heart (Psalm 86:11). Worse, we can't be half-hearted. Even worse, we can't be a hypocrite, having an appearance of religion on the outside but little real relationship and love of God on the inside. The kind of church Jesus wants is not a church that is merely motivated by duty. It is moved by devotion. He loves us and wants a church on fire with love for Him.

If we had lived in the first century and looked at the church in Ephesus from the outside, we probably would have said it is an outstanding church that loves God because of the things Jesus commended them for. Jesus

Himself says they are a church that works hard, and hard work can come from love. He said it is a church that is persevering in difficult times, and perseverance can come from love. And He said it is a church that maintains doctrinal purity, and the desire to maintain doctrinal purity can come from love of God. In spite of these things, as God spoke to the prophet Samuel, *"Do look at appearance, for man looks on the outward appearance, and the LORD look at the heart"* (I Samuel 16:7). The Lord Jesus saw the hearts of the people of the church of Ephesus and what He saw was that they had forsaken their first love for Him. While outwardly they were the leading church, inwardly they had lost their first love. They had left the leading quality of relationship with God. They had fallen away.

First love for God is the priority of the qualities and characteristics of the kind of church Jesus wants. This is because first love for God means God is the priority above all the other things in our hearts and in the life of our church. God expressly stated this to His people in the first of the Ten Commandments: *"You shall have no other gods before Me"* (Exodus 20:3). We cannot overlook the words *"before Me."* God takes it Personally when anything else comes before Him, ahead of Him, or in front of Him. He is God, and He is to be God in our hearts and lives. He is the Supreme Being for Whom we are to have the supreme love. We are to have a first love for Him, loving Him with all our hearts, all our minds, and all our strength.

Don't Forget

The gravity of the Ephesians lack of love to God is seen by the ominous threat and warning of judgment that Jesus gives to the church. He says in verse 5,

Therefore remember from where you have fallen, and repent and do the deeds you did at first; or else I am coming to you and will remove your lampstand out of its place–unless you repent.

In Scripture, the word *"remember"* is not merely recalling something or some event. It is a word of covenant relationship and means "to bring to mind in order to act accordingly." After the flood that destroyed everything on the earth that had breath, Scripture says, *"But God remembered Noah and all the beasts and all the cattle that were with him in the ark; and God caused a wind to pass over the earth, and the water subsided"* (Genesis 8:1). It is not that God had a memory loss about the only righteous man on the planet and then thought of him again. Everything in His plan and purpose for the human race was riding in the ark with Noah. God remembering Noah meant He called to mind His covenant promise to act according to His commitment. We read in Exodus 2:24 when it was the appointed time for God to save His people from slavery in Egypt and bring them into the land He had promised to give the descendants of Abraham, *"So God heard their groaning; and God remembered His covenant with Abraham, Isaac, and Jacob."* It is not as though God had amnesia about His covenant with His people and then it dawned on Him what He said He would do. Remembering meant He would act according to His covenant commitment. When we celebrate the Lord's Supper, Jesus told us, *"Do this in remembrance of Me"* (1 Corinthians 11:24-25). We are to remember Jesus and what He did for us and then act as His true disciples and followers. God constantly told His people to remember and not forget because to forget would be to deny the heart of the covenant relationship with God, and that would have disastrous consequences (See Deuteronomy 4:10; 5:15; 8:2, 18; 9:7; 15:15; 24:9).

The Light Will Go Out

The disastrous consequence of a church leaving their first love for Christ is that the Lord says He will remove their lampstand. A lampstand is that which holds a lamp. A lamp is that which holds oil, and oil is that which burns with fire. A church is to be a spiritual lampstand that holds the oil of the Holy Spirit and burns with the fire of the manifest presence of Christ. For Christ to remove the lampstand means He would cause the light of His manifest presence to be withdrawn and taken away. The light will go out. The church will no longer encounter and experience the reality of Christ's living, manifest presence, with His works and answers to prayer. They may continue as a church that outwardly meets and goes through religious rituals and motions, but the Holy Spirit will not be moving in it. The light and power of Christ's manifest presence will be gone and they will become a church that is spiritually dead.

This may seem harsh to some, perhaps many. And it may seem to not be at all what they would think Jesus would do. Nevertheless, we must understand how Jesus thinks and feels and hear what He says. If a church–no matter how good it looks outwardly to humans–does not love God first and foremost, it is not doing what is of first and foremost importance to God. It is actually denying the very thing it was created by God to be and do, which is to be a church that loves Him above everything else, a church with a first love passion, a church that reveals the reality of His manifest presence. And if a church leaves what is first and foremost to God, it is like salt that has lost its flavor and is worthless. Jesus said, "*It is no longer good for anything, except to be thrown out and trampled under foot by men"* (Matthew 5:13).

Think of it this way: if a police officer who wears the uniform of a policeman becomes crooked, he is denying the very thing he represents and he should be removed from being a police officer. If a doctor acts in a way that harms and kills his patients, he is denying the very thing he is to be and should be removed from the practice of medicine. If a judge is corrupted by bribes and renders the guilty innocent and the innocent guilty, he is denying the very thing he is to do and should be removed from office. Accordingly, Jesus says if a church stops loving God first and foremost He Himself will remove His manifest presence from that church, and in the end it will cease to exist. And isn't that what happened throughout church history, and even to this church? How many great churches have there been that were once very influential and powerfully used of the Lord, churches like the one in Ephesus, but no longer exist? Jesus meant what He said.

The Fruit Reveals the Root

Loving Christ with a first love is the leading quality of the kind of church Jesus wants. And if a church has lost its first love, what is it to do? They are to do what anyone and everyone who falls into sin is to do, they are to repent. Jesus says, *"Repent and do the deeds you did at first"* (Revelation 2:5).

What is absolutely critical about what Jesus says is that repentance is demonstrated in actions–not mere words, but works–you *"do the deeds you did."* All of church history shows us that people can profess repentance but never really repent. They can be convicted of their sin against God and others, can feel sorrow and grief for what they have done, can confess their sin and even say they repent. Yet if they do not demonstrate it by their deeds and actions, they actually didn't repent. The most sobering example of this is Judas, who was chosen by Jesus to be an apostle, but betrayed him for thirty pieces of silver. Afterward, he felt remorse, gave back the money, and confessed, saying, "*I have sinned by betraying inno-cent blood*," and then went and hanged himself (Matthew 27:3-5). John the Baptist preached, "*Bear fruit in keeping with repentance*" (Matthew 3:8). Jesus said, "*You will know them by their fruits*" (Matthew 7:20). The fruit reveals the root of real repentance.

Jesus says love–first love–is demonstrated in deeds. This is a fact of life in the real world. What happens when a man and a women fall in love? They don't merely go through motions while dutifully mumbling the words, "I love you." They have words that declare their desire and devotion of love, but most of all deeds that demonstrate the reality of their love. There can be any number of things that they do to demonstrate their love and devotion for each other, but the one thing above all others that demon-strates their love and devotion is that they want to be in each other's presence. More than any other thing, they want to be with each other. When we have a first love for Christ, a love like Mary had for Him, we will want to be in His presence more than anything else and we will do it.

A Man with a First Love for God

This is the very thing we see demonstrated in the life of David, the man who God Himself said was "*a man after My own heart*" (Acts 13:22). We see David's heart of love, devotion and desire to be in God's presence revealed in his Psalms. And think about it–why are so many of the psalms written by David–73 of the 150? These are not just poems of a romantic expressing his feelings, or the journal of a person's thoughts in times of distress. They are the word of God, the Holy Scriptures inspired by the Spirit of God for the purpose of revealing the heart of a man after God's own heart.

While many Christians may only read the psalms to find comfort and assurance in times of trouble, the greatest thing about David's psalms is they express his fervent, even ferocious first love for God and show us how we are to love the LORD with a first love. We read in Psalm 27:4,

> *One thing I have asked from the LORD, that*
> *I shall seek: that I may dwell in the house of*
> *the LORD all the days of my life, to behold*
> *the beauty of the LORD and to meditate in*
> *His temple.*

What do you desire most in your life? The one thing David desired more than anything else was to dwell in the house of the LORD all the days of his life. He did not want a "drive through" experience of attending a worship service once a week. He wanted to continuously dwell in the house of the LORD. Why was that? It's because in the house of the LORD David personally experienced the reality of God's manifest presence in which, as he wrote, there is *"fullness of joy"* and *"pleasures forever"* (Psalm 16:11). More than anything else, he wanted to live in God's manifest presence because He loved God more than anything else.

David knew what it was like to enjoy God and what it was like not to be in His presence, and it is in such a time that we also see his passion for God's presence. In Psalm 63, while experiencing a spiritually dry time in his life, he wrote,

> *O God, You are my God; I shall seek You
> earnestly; My soul thirsts for You, my flesh
> yearns for You, in a dry and weary land
> where there is no water. ² Thus I have seen
> You in the sanctuary, to see Your power and
> Your glory. ³ Because Your lovingkindness is
> better than life, My lips will praise You. ⁴ So I
> will bless You as long as I live; I will lift up my
> hands in Your name* (Psalm 63:1-4).

Amazing! David regarded the manifest presence of God as better than life itself! He loved God and His presence and it is because of this that he was a man after God's own heart–a man with a first love for God. He understood what theologians and Bible scholars said is the ultimate purpose of our lives, which is to glorify God and to enjoy Him forever.

This is Why It's the Leader

Do you have a first love for Christ? That is what the Lord Jesus wants us to have, and it is for this reason that it is the leading quality of the kind of church He wants. He desires a church to have a fervent love and devotion for Him, a church filled with people who love Him with all their hearts, minds, and strength. Whether it is in our corporate worship as a church, or in a group of believers with whom we have gathered to worship, study the word of God, pray and minister to each other, or being alone with God reading His word, listening to Him speak to us and us speaking to Him in prayer, the kind of church Jesus wants is a church that loves Him with a first love. When we love Christ with a first love, we will demonstrate it by our deeds in our love for one another, our service and work for Him, and our witness to the lost. Most of all, we will demonstrate it by our desire to be living in His manifest presence more than anything else in life. His passion is for us to want His manifest presence more than anything else because we want Him more than anything else. That's why first love is the leader on the list of qualities of the kind of church He wants. May He give us ears to hear and hearts that are on fire!

Study Questions
Chapter 2

1. What would you consider to be a perfect church? How much does your desire to be in "the perfect church" influence your relationship to the church?

2. What does the author say the perfect church is? In what way should this influence your life?

3. Why is it appropriate for Jesus to begin with the church in Ephesus?

4. What are the three qualities that Christ commends in the church of Ephesus? Are these qualities in your life and in your church? How can you develop them in your life?
(1)
(2)
(3)

5. What was the one quality the church of Ephesus lacked that is so important to the Lord Jesus? Why is this the first and leading quality of the kind of church Jesus wants?

6. What is the root cause and motive for God's people falling away from a first love for Christ? How is this demonstrated in their lives?

7. In the light of Christ's words to the church in Ephesus, do you have any concerns about your walk with the Lord? How will you live your life when you have a first love for Christ?

8. When you consider your relationship with Christ, do you believe you are motivated more by duty or by devotion? Would you say Christ is first and foremost in your life? Why?

9. What is the biblical meaning of the word *"remember"*?

10. What is the significance of Christ's words *"I will remove your lampstand"*? Do you think Christ really would do this?

11. What is the sign of true repentance?

12. What do you learn from the life of David? What do you desire most in your life?

CHAPTER 3

SMYRNA: FAITHFUL IN THE TIME OF TESTING

Revelation 2:8-11

And to the angel of the church in Smyrna write: The first and the last, who was dead, and has come to life, says this: [9] "I know your tribulation and your poverty (but you are rich), and the blasphemy by those who say they are Jews and are not, but are a synagogue of Satan. [10] Do not fear what you are about to suffer. Behold, the devil is about to cast some of you into prison, so that you will be tested, and you will have tribulation for ten days. Be faithful until death, and I will give you the crown of life. [11] He who has an ear, let him hear what the Spirit says to the churches. He who overcomes will not be hurt by the second death."

Counted Worthy

The year was 155 A.D. A man by the name of Polycarp, who had just been arrested and taken into the public arena of the city stood before a hostile and bloodthirsty crowd of Romans and Jews. While his hands were being tied behind him, wood was being placed around him in order to execute him by burning him to death in a fire.

Polycarp was now an old man, at least 86 years old. He did not grow up in a Christian home, but as a young man he came to saving faith in the Lord Jesus Christ. He had been mentored and discipled by John who was one of the twelve disciples of Jesus and wrote the gospel of John, the letters by his name, and the book of Revelation. For some time, Christians had been suffering severe persecution in the Roman Empire. They were regarded as "atheists" because they did not worship a god that could be seen with physical eyes and as a politically dangerous religious cult whose rapid growth needed to be stopped.

In a sweep of the city, Polycarp was arrested and taken to the arena where, just before arriving, 14 other Christians had already been slaughtered by lions. Seeing that he was a gentle old man, the Roman official took pity on him and made a proposal that, if Polycarp would only offer a small pinch of incense to the statue of Caesar, he would escape torture and death. So he makes the offer to Polycarp, "Swear by the fortune of Caesar, and declare, 'Death to the atheists,' and I will set you free at once! You have but to insult Christ." Polycarp replies, "I have served Him for eighty-six years and He has never done me any wrong. How can I blaspheme my King who saved me?" The Roman now demands, "Swear by the fortune of Caesar!" Polycarp responds, "You flatter yourself if you hope to persuade me. In all truth I solemnly declare to you: I am a Christian." Losing patience, the Roman says, "I have the lions here to use as I see fit." "Give your orders," says Polycarp. "As for us Christians, when we change it is not from good to bad. It is splendid to pass from the evil of this world into God's justice." "If you do not repent," declares the Roman, "I shall have you burned at the stake, since you are so contemptuous of the lions." "You threaten me with a fire that burns for an hour and then dies down. But do you know the eternal fire of the justice that is to come? Do you know the punishment that is to devour the ungodly? Come, don't delay! Do what you want with me." With that, the Roman official pronounced judgment, and while he is praying and thanking God that he is counted worthy to die as a martyr, Polycarp is executed for his faith in the Lord Jesus Christ, being burned at the stake.

Polycarp died as a martyr in the city in which he had lived and served the Lord Jesus Christ for many years. The name of that city was Smyrna, the city of the second of the seven churches that the Lord Jesus Christ spoke to as recorded in the second and third chapters of the book of Revelation. And listening to what Jesus says to the church at Smyrna, we find the second quality and characteristic of the kind of church Jesus wants. It is to be faithful–faithful all the time, but most importantly, faithful in the time of testing.

It All Begins and Ends With Him

Jesus begins His address to the church in Smyrna declaring Who He is using titles of Himself that are relevant to the current situation of the church. He says He is, "*The first and the last, Who was dead, and has come to life*" (Revelation. 2:8). This is a restatement of His declaration to John in chapter one, "*I am the first and the last, ¹⁸ and the living One; and I was dead, and behold, I am alive forevermore, and I have the keys of death and of Hades*" (Revelation 1:17-18). In these words, the Lord declares the mystery and the glory of His Person–that He is God and man.

First of all, He is "*the first and the last.*" In these words, Christ reveals His divine nature, that He is God, God the Son. It is a reference to and quotation of Isaiah 44:6

which says, "*Thus says the LORD, the King of Israel and his Redeemer, the Lord of hosts: 'I am the first and the last, and there is no God besides Me.'*" Being "*the first*" He is God. Being "*the first*" establishes that everything else begins with Him. Being "*the first*" makes known that nothing happens in the universe apart from Him permitting and ordaining it. As John wrote of Him in the first words of his gospel, "*He was in the beginning with God. ³ All things came into being through Him, and apart from Him nothing came into being that has come into being*" (John 1:2-3).

Being "*the last*" means that everything ends with Him. Being "*the last*" makes known that He is the goal for everything that happens in the universe. Being "*the last*" establishes that the ultimate purpose of everything is His glory. As Paul wrote in His magnificent doxology in Romans 11:36, "*For from Him and through Him and to Him are all things. To Him be the glory forever. Amen.*"

Being "*the first and the last,*" the Lord Jesus is the sovereign ruler over everything that happens, and nothing can happen apart from Him permitting it to happen. In declaring this about Himself, Jesus reveals He is sovereign over everything that happens in the lives of His people, and specifically His church in Smyrna.

Death Has No Power Over Him

Jesus then speaks of what happened to Him as a human being, that He is the One "*who was dead and has come to life.*" God cannot die, but human beings do. Being the Son of God incarnate in human nature, the Lord Jesus has two natures. He is truly and completely God and truly and completely human–two natures united in one Person. What is true of one nature is true of Him as a Person. He died as a human being according to His human nature when His human spirit was separated from His physical body. At the time of His death He prayed, "*Father, into Your hands I commit my spirit*" (Luke 23:46). His spirit left His body and He "*was dead.*" His body was buried in a tomb, and then, on the third day, His spirit reunited with His body and He became the One Who "*has come to life.*"

Because Christ was raised from the dead, He "*is never to die again, death no longer is master over Him*" (Romans 6:9). His power, dominion and mastery over death is symbolized in the glorious reality that He now and forever possesses "*the keys of death and of Hades*" (Revelation 1:18).

What Could Be More Relevant?

These attributes of the Lord Jesus are most relevant for the church in Smyrna because, as He will go on to tell them, they are about to go through a time of testing. What could be more relevant to people who are going through a time of testing than to know and believe that the One they trust and believe in and have dedicated their lives to is the first and the last, the sovereign ruler over all things, and everything that will happen in their lives in their time of testing is in His hands? What could be more comforting than to know and believe that everything that will happen in their lives has the goal and ultimate purpose to bring glory to Him? And above all, what could be more strengthening than to know and believe that because He was dead and is now alive forevermore, everyone who will suffer death because of their faith in Him will leave this world to enter into true life in His presence in heaven and, then, one day be raised from the dead to become like Him forever? In the words of the Apostle Paul,

> *for if we live, we live for the Lord, or if we die,*
> *we die for the Lord; therefore whether we*
> *live or die, we are the Lord's.* [9] *For to this end*

Christ died and lived again, that He might be Lord both of the dead and of the living (Romans 14:8-9).

I Know What You're Going Through

After declaring these truths, Jesus speaks of His intimate and personal knowledge of their lives, and there are three things in particular He says. First, "*I know your tribulation*" (Revelation 2:9). The dominant characteristic of the church in Smyrna the Lord recognized is that they experienced "*tribulation.*" The Greek word translated "*tribulation*" means "pressure, stress, or affliction." Because it is singular, "*tribulation*" and not "tribulations," it indicates that tribulation and affliction was not an intermittent occurrence but an ongoing experience for the believers in Smyrna.

It was difficult being a Christian in Smyrna, just as it is for many Christians in parts of the world today where they are being persecuted and put to death. Because the church in America and the Western world has enjoyed peace and the blessings of religious freedom, it is challenging for many, if not most to fully identify with and understand the experience of believers who have suffered such persecution and tribulation. However, as many are aware, the religious freedoms that Christians have enjoyed are continuously eroding to the extent that, today, the one religious group that is the most openly spoken against and persecuted is Christians–Christians, that is, who stand up for the word of God, believe Jesus is the only way of salvation, and contend for righteous moral living that opposes ungodly behavior.

Rich is Better

Delving deeper in letting them know His under-standing of what they are experiencing, He says, "*I know your poverty, but you are rich*" (Revelation 2:9). In the Greek language, there are two words that can be trans-lated "poverty." One word means "to have enough, but nothing extra." The other means "to have nothing at all, to be virtually bankrupt and destitute." It is the second word that Jesus uses. This kind of poverty was one cause of their tribulation and suffering.

This is another place where most Christians in the United States, as well as the Western world have diffi-culty identifying with the believers in Smyrna because they have so many material blessings. Many Christians in the affluent American culture have been taught what is called "a gospel of wealth and prosperity," meaning that it is always God's will for all Christians to have material wealth and prosperity in this world. This, however, is not what we see Jesus teaching or living. He Whom the Scriptures declare "*became poor, so that you through His poverty might become rich*" (2 Corinthians 8:9) does not condemn the believers in Smyrna for their material pov-erty but instead commends them, saying, "*but you are rich*" (Revelation 2:9). This, in fact, is the very opposite of the seventh church, the lukewarm church of Laodicea, which said, "*I am rich, and have become wealthy, and have need of nothing.*" Jesus reproved them saying, "*You do not know that you are wretched and miserable and poor and blind and naked*" (Revelation 3:17).

There is a saying, "I've been rich, and I've been poor, and rich is better." This is true. So the real question is what are the real riches that are better? The believers in the church in Smyrna were not rich in the wealth of this world. They were wealthy with the real riches of heaven that

Christ gives. While they were poor in the fleeting material things of this world, they possessed the true spiritual riches of treasure that will last forever.

The Real World

What we see from this is that the church in Smyrna had one of the most important qualities of the kind of church Jesus wants–they were living in the real world, the world that Jesus lives in. The real world is not the one secular materialists of the Western culture live in, nor is the physical realm all there is so that when we die that is end of our existence. The real world is one in which the spiritual realm is eternal. It is the real world the Apostle Paul wrote of to the Corinthians saying,

> *For momentary, light affliction is producing for us an eternal weight of glory far beyond all comparison, [18] while we look not at the things which are seen, but at the things which are not seen; for the things which are seen are temporal, but the things which are not seen are eternal* (2 Corinthians 4:17-18).

Because the Christians in Smyrna lived in the real world, they looked at what is eternal and, because of this, understood the true values of life. They were living their lives as Jesus did, not for the riches of this world, but for the true riches of the glory of God that is beyond all comparison.

In His Sermon on the Mount, the Lord Jesus spoke of those who are persecuted because of Him and, because of this, they will have great reward in heaven. He said,

> *Blessed are you when people insult you and persecute you, and falsely say all kinds of evil against you because of Me. ¹² Rejoice and be glad, for your reward in heaven is great; for in the same way they persecuted the prophets who were before you* (Matthew 5:11-12).

And later He said,

> *Do not store up for yourselves treasures on earth, where moth and rust destroy, and where thieves break in and steal. But store up for yourselves treasures in heaven, where neither moth nor rust destroys and where thieves do not break in and steal, for where your treasure is, there your heart will be also* (Matthew 6:19-21).

The church in Smyrna lived in the real world, investing their lives in the true riches of eternal treasures in heaven. They did this because their hearts were right with God and they were faithful to the Lord Jesus.

Falsely Accused

Like a sudden blast of lightning out of heaven, the third thing Jesus tells them is that He knows *"the blasphemy by those who say they are Jews and are not, but are a synagogue of Satan"* (Revelation 2:9). The Greek word translated *"blasphemy"* can mean *"slander"* and that's what it means here. Slander is speaking lies about someone or falsely accusing them so as to discredit their reputation. This was another major reason the believers in Smyrna were suffering tribulation and testing—people were lying about them.

The foremost slanderer in the universe is Satan whose name "the devil" means "the slanderer." He is the one who never stops speaking lies, falsely accusing and slandering God's people because, as Jesus said, that is his nature (John 8:44; Revelation 12:10). Here again, Jesus speaks about the real world. It is one in which the invisible, spiritual realm interacts with, influences and impacts the visible, physical realm. Jesus speaks of these two realms from which the slander against the Christians of Smyrna is coming. In the invisible, spiritual realm, Satan and his demons are influencing the thinking, attitudes, actions and words of people in Smyrna. In the visible human realm, there are those who are speaking lies and false accusations against the believers in Smyrna. Just as the Holy Spirit works in and through believers to accomplish God's will, so the unholy spirit of the devil works in and through people to accomplish his will.

Not What They Say They Are

Who are the people who are slandering the followers of Christ in Smyrna? Jesus identifies them as *"those who say they are Jews and are not but are a synagogue of Satan"* (Revelation 2:9). This is a shocking declaration. Christ makes a definite distinction between the physical, ethnic lineage of these people and their actual spiritual state before God. Physically they are *"Jews."* This means they are children of Abraham according to the flesh (Romans 9:3). Ethnically, they are of the heritage of the covenant people of Abraham, Isaac and Jacob, but spiritually they are of the devil. When they gather to worship in their *"synagogue,"* though their outward worship is of the God of Abraham, Isaac and Jacob, the spirit that is working in them is Satanic. Far from being a synagogue of God, the Lord Jesus Christ says they are a *"synagogue of Satan."*

Jesus, of course, is not making an anti-Semitic slur speaking about all Jews or Jewish people as such, for He was a Jew and will always be a Jew. The Scriptures are clear that God's covenant with the people of Israel will never be revoked or replaced (Romans 9:4; 11:1-2, 28-29). This is evident from the fact that there have been many Jews through the centuries who have come to saving faith in Jesus as Messiah and Lord, people such as John who wrote these words, Paul, and all of the earliest Christians. They are all members of His body, His church, and Jesus, in effect, calls them "true Jews."

However, the *"Jews"* in Smyrna Christ is speaking about are those who have rejected Him and are of the devil. Instead of their worship service being one in which the Holy Spirit of God is working and manifesting God's glorious presence, the spirit filling, leading and ruling in their hearts is Satan (Acts 5:3; 1 Corinthians 12:2; Ephesians 2:2). This is the very thing Jesus said to many Jews of His day who did not believe in Him yet claimed they were true Jews because they were physically children of Abraham. He said, *"If you are Abraham's children, do the deeds of Abraham. You are doing the deeds of your father. You are of your father the devil, and you want to do the desires of your father"* (John 8:39, 41, 44). Instead of being of God, they are antichrist for, as John wrote in his letter, *"Who is the liar but the one who denies that Jesus is the Christ? This is the antichrist, the one who denies the Father and the Son"* (1 John 2:22).

Paul wrote about the critical difference between physical heritage and actual spiritual relationship with God that makes one a true Jew. He said,

> *He is not a Jew who is one outwardly, nor is*
> *circumcision that which is outward in the*
> *flesh.* ²⁹ *But he is a Jew who is one inwardly;*
> *and circumcision is that which is of the heart,*
> *by the Spirit, not by the letter; and his praise*
> *is not from men, but from God* (Romans
> 2:28-29).

A true Jew is one who believes Jesus is the Christ, the Son of God, and the reason he does is because the Spirit of God has worked inwardly in his heart and he has been born of the Spirit. The evidence that he has come to true saving faith in the Lord Jesus is that he has a changed heart and wants to do the desires of the Holy Spirit, and this is demonstrated by doing the deeds God wills for his life.

The same can be said of people today who profess to be Christian. There are many who were born and grew up in a Christian home, were baptized, go to church and profess to be a Christian yet live a lifestyle manifested in disobedience to Christ doing the desires of the flesh and not the Holy Spirit (see Galatians 5:16-24). As Paul wrote to Titus about such people, "*They profess to know God, but by their deeds they deny Him*" (Titus 1:16; see also 1 Corinthians 6:9-10; Galatians 5:21; Ephesians 5:3-5). They are not true Christians but, as John wrote of them, they are "*liars*" (1 John 2:4). Perhaps Jesus would say of them that they are a "synagogue or gathering of Satan." A true Christian is one who has been born of the Spirit, whose lifestyle is led and governed by the Holy Spirit, and the evidence of this is that he or she wants to do the things the Holy Spirit desires and does them (Romans 8:14; Galatians 5:16-18; 1 John 2:3-6).

Test, Temptation, and Trial

After identifying these three things that He knows about them, Jesus speaks about that which, as much as anything, will demonstrate their true faith in Him and that they are the kind of church He wants. He says,

> *Do not fear what you are about to suffer. Behold, the devil is about to cast some of you into prison, so that you will be tested, and you will have tribulation for ten days. Be faithful until death, and I will give you the crown of life* (Revelation 2:10).

The Lord speaks here about the second quality of the kind of church He wants and it is that they are faithful in the time of testing.

The Greek word that is translated "*tested*" is the same word that, depending on the context, can be translated "temptation" or "trial." These three different words–test, temptation and trial - can give us three different perspectives on the time of testing. First, there is God's perspective–it is a test. Second, there is the devil's perspective–it is temptation. And third, there is our perspective–it is a trial. A test, coming sovereignly from God, involves a temptation initiated from the devil and, by its very nature, is a trial for us because it is a trying time that proves whether or not we will be faithful and true. And we can see these three things operating in what Jesus says here to the church in Smyrna.

What's In Your Heart?

One of the most important principles we must understand about what God reveals concerning His ways with

His people is that He tests us. He tests us to see if our faith is real and genuine. The proof of genuine faith is that we will love and obey Him in the time of testing. Genesis 22:1 tells us, *"God tested Abraham."* He did this when He told Abraham to sacrifice his beloved son, Isaac, as a burnt offering. This was the time of testing for Abraham, and he passed the test being obedient and faithful to God.

This is what God said He caused to happen with the people of Israel after He had saved them from slavery in Egypt. Moses told them,

> *You shall remember all the way which the Lord your God has led you in the wilderness these forty years, that He might humble you, testing you, to know what was in your heart, whether you would keep His commandments or not* (Deuteronomy 8:2).

From God's perspective it was a test that made known what was in their hearts, whether they would love and obey Him. And the Lord Jesus tells His church in Smyrna they will be *"tested."*

When we experience a time of testing, it is very important to understand that, because it is a test from God, He is sovereign over the test, and the test will last for a limited period of time. Jesus tells the church in Smyrna that the testing will have a definite duration, saying, *"You will have tribulation for ten days."* Moses spoke of God testing His people for *"forty years."* The time of testing is up to God, and it is almost always longer than we want, and often longer than we think we can endure. Nevertheless, it will always be for the time that God providential permits for His purpose. And the great assurance given to us in Scripture is, as someone said, "If the Lord has brought you to it, He will bring you through it."

It is also critical to understand that the time of testing the Lord allows is not because a person has wandered away from Him and fallen into sin. If a person has simply strayed, given in to their sinful desires and is suffering as a consequence of it, that is the result of their choice. And often there will be no end to it until they repent and turn away from their sin. It is when we are walking in the Spirit, obeying God that He will allow a time of testing that will reveal what is in our hearts, just as happened to the Lord Jesus Christ Himself (Hebrews 4:15). And then, in His time, He will sovereignly bring it to an end when we demonstrate that we love Him by obeying Him. James wrote of this, saying,

> *Consider it all joy, my brethren, when you encounter various trials, ³ knowing that the testing of your faith produces endurance. ⁴ And let endurance have its perfect result, so that you may be perfect and complete, lacking in nothing* (James 1:2-4).

He's Good At It

The Lord Jesus reveals that the way God will test His people is to sovereignly allow the devil to cause *"tribulation"* and affliction. He says, *"the devil is about to cast some of you into prison, so that you will be tested"* (Revelation 2:10). A friend of mine used to say, "The devil is a good devil." He didn't mean the devil is morally good. He meant the devil does a good job at being the devil. He is, in fact, not just good at it, he's the best. He's the greatest there is at tempting people because he is *the* devil, *the* evil one, *the* enemy of God and all that is good.

The devil will work in whatever way he can to cause temptation through *"tribulation"* and suffering in order that we will sin and disobey God. In the case of those in Smyrna, Jesus says the devil will cause some to be arrested and put in prison, and others to be killed for their faith. It is because of this that Christ tells them to *"be faithful to death"* (Revelation 2:10).

There are countless temptations that can come from the devil, but they all involve disobeying Christ in one way or another. For some, it is difficult simply to publically confess that they are Christians, and they will excuse themselves by saying that "religion is a private matter." To the contrary, Jesus said, *"Everyone who confesses Me before men, I will also confess him before My Father who is in heaven. ³³ But whoever denies Me before men, I will also deny him before My Father who is in heaven"* (Matthew 10:32-33). The greatest temptation one can face is the choice to deny Christ when faced with suffering, imprisonment or death. A true Christian believes Jesus rose from the dead and guarantees eternal life for them. They will, like Polycarp and many other believers in Smyrna, *"be faithful to death."*

A Trial is a Trial

On the night before His betrayal, suffering and crucifixion, the Lord Jesus spoke to His disciples, saying, *"You are those who have stood by Me in My trials"* (Luke 22:28). A trial, by its very nature, involves difficulty, stress and suffering or it wouldn't be a trial. Not only this, the very nature of resisting temptation is to suffer some kind of pain by denying the sinful desires of our fallen nature. As the saying goes, "No pain, no gain."

While Jesus did not have a fallen, sinful nature, the Scripture is clear that He was *"One who has been tempted in all things as we are, yet without sin"* (Hebrews 4:15). These temptations were His times of testing and trial and they were for the purpose of proving that, as a human being, He was worthy of the office God had called Him to, which is the High Priest of His people. Hebrews 5:8-9 says, *"Although He was a Son, He learned obedience from the things which He suffered. ⁹ And having been made perfect, He became to all those who obey Him the source of eternal salvation."* The word translated *"perfect"* does not mean that Jesus had faults, let alone any sin. It means as a person grows to full maturity, Christ achieved the goal of the full potential of His character that was required for Him to become the High Priest who can *"sympathize with our weaknesses"* (Hebrews 4:15). His obedience in His trials perfected the quality of His character so that *"He became to all those who obey Him the source of eternal salvation"* (Hebrews 5:9). Following Christ means we will, like Him, experience trials so that we can grow into full maturity, into the full potential of who we are in Christ.

Those who have true faith in Christ will be faithful to Christ. We will be faithful in our times of testing just as Jesus was faithful in His times of testing. Centuries before He came, God spoke of Him in His role as High Priest saying, *"I will raise up for Myself a faithful priest who will do according to what is in My heart and in My soul"* (1 Samuel 2:35). The book of Hebrews tells us Jesus *"was faithful to Him who appointed Him"* (Hebrews 3:2). So faithful was Christ that He tells the church in Laodicea one of His attributes is that He is *"the faithful"*–the One Who is faithful and the true example of what it means to faithful (Revelation 3:14). The kind of church Jesus wants is like Him, faithful to do the will of God no matter what the cost of suffering in the time of testing.

You Can Trust Him

Being Himself the One who suffered, died, rose and is alive forever, Jesus encourages the church in Smyrna, saying, *"Do not fear what you are about to suffer"* (Revelation 2:10). Knowing we will go through some kind of suffering can cause us to fear–fear of the unknown, fear of the pain, fear of what we might do. When we really think about it and search our hearts, the basic cause of fear is ultimately a lack of faith. When Jesus was facing the ultimate trial of His life, knowing the suffering that He would endure, He was *"deeply grieved, to the point of death"* (Matthew 26:38) and *"being in agony,"* He prayed that He *"would not enter temptation"* (Luke 22:40-44). During all this time, there is no mention of His being afraid for He trusted the Father. And the Father brought Him through all His suffering and into His glory. The reason Jesus tells the church in Smyrna not to fear is because they can trust in Him. He will bring them through the time of testing and suffering and reward them for being faithful, just as He was. James wrote of this saying, *"Blessed is a man who perseveres under trial; for once he has been approved, he will receive the crown of life which the Lord has promised to those who love Him"* (James 1:12).

We Will Be Blessed

The ultimate purpose of a trial is to see if we have true, saving faith in Jesus. Peter wrote of this in his first letter speaking of believers

> *who are protected by the power of God through faith for a salvation ready to be revealed in the last time. ⁶ In this you greatly rejoice, even though now for a little while, if*

necessary, you have been distressed by various trials ⁷ so that the proof of your faith, being more precious than gold which is perishable, even though tested by fire, may be found to result in praise and glory and honor at the revelation of Jesus Christ (1 Peter 1:5-7).

That is what Jesus said would happen to the church in Smyrna. The true follower of the Lord Jesus Christ is willing to not only to suffer for Him but die for Him, as thousands have through the centuries, and as thousands are today in different parts of the world.

Few of us would sign up to go through times of painful testing or to be a member of a persecuted church in some part of the world, but it is not something that we should fear. Fear, which is rooted in unbelief, is a major reason why people do not want to follow Jesus–they are afraid of suffering, afraid of pain, afraid of dying. That is why the very first thing Jesus said to the church in Smyrna was, "*Do not fear*"–"*Do not fear what you are about to suffer.*" Jesus does not tell them they will not suffer, but He does tell them not to be afraid. Christ never promised that we would not suffer for Him. He tells us not to fear. Why? Because He is sovereign over it, because He has gone through it Himself, because He is with us in it, because of what God does in us when we go through it, and because of the reward we will receive in heaven. For this reason He said,

Blessed are you when people insult you and persecute you, and falsely say all kinds of evil against you because of Me. ¹² Rejoice and be glad, for your reward in heaven is great; for in the same way they persecuted

the prophets who were before you (Matthew 5:11-12).

It's Worth It All

The Bible tells us we are to *"fix our eyes on Jesus, the author and perfecter of faith, who for the joy set before Him endured the cross, despising the shame, and has sat down at the right hand of the throne of God"* (Hebrews 12:2). Jesus went to the cross, suffering the pain and shame. But His focus was not on the pain, it was on the gain–the gain of the joy set before Him. How many are there through the centuries who can say that it was going through a painful trial in their life that they came to saving faith in the Lord Jesus Christ, or that it resulted in setting them free from bondage, or that it brought them to a place where they knew for the first time how deep and wide the love of Jesus is? Paul wrote, *"For I consider that the sufferings of this present time are not worthy to be compared with the glory that is to be revealed to us"* (Romans 8:18). He also wrote, *"for me to live is Christ and to die is gain"* (Philippians 1:21). What is the gain of going through the pain of the time of testing? It is the glory that will be revealed to us and shared with us. To the true believers in Smyrna, Jesus said, *"I will give you the crown of life"* (Revelation 2:10).

I'm Ready to Die

More than 60 years ago, the Korean War began when the armies of North Korea attacked South Korea. The Northern Koreans were atheists and Communists. Due to faithful missionary efforts, many of the people of South Korea were Christians, the most numerous being Presbyterian. On a particular Sunday, in the territory where the Communists had taken control, a band of soldiers stormed into a Presbyterian church during the worship service. With their guns directed at everyone, they closed the doors, found a picture of Jesus on the wall, took it down, walked to the front of the church, and then told everyone in the church to come forward and spit on the picture or else they would kill them. After a moment of terrible tension, an elder of the church walked forward, spit on the picture, and stood to the side. He was followed by another elder, and next some other people. Then a young girl stood up, walked forward, took the picture and cradled it in her arms. Wiping the spit off the picture with her clothes, she turned to the soldiers and said, "Shoot me, I'm ready to die." Immediately there was a commotion of confusion among the soldiers. After deliberating among themselves, they gathered those who had denied Christ, marched them out of the church, lined them up, and with the pronouncement, "You are not worthy to live," shot them. But being amazed at the young girl's faith, they decided to allow her to live along with the rest in the church.

Whether we live or die, the kind of church Jesus wants is one where His people are faithful in their time of testing. They are faithful because they are ready to die for Him. More than that, they are faithful because they want to live for Him. Are you ready to die for Jesus? More importantly, are you living for Him?

Study Questions
Chapter 3

1. Briefly share one personal highlight from the chapter.

2. What is something in the chapter that was a surprise to you?

3. What does the declaration *"I am the first and the last"* tell you about Who Jesus is? What does this mean to you?

4. What is the significance of the second declaration Jesus makes about Himself? How does this attribute of Christ impact and influence your life?

5. What experiences of *"tribulation"* have you had that made it difficult for you as a follower of Christ?

6. How does the author describe the real world that Jesus lives in? Do you agree with this? How are you thinking, believing and living in light of this?

7. What is it that makes a person a true Jew and a true believer in the Lord Jesus Christ?

8. What is the second characteristic of the kind of church Jesus wants? Why is this so important?

9. Do you believe God tests people? What is God's purpose in allowing tests in your life?

10. In what ways do you experience temptations from the devil?

11. What is the basic cause of fear and how do we overcome it?

12. What are your thoughts and feelings about the young North Korean girl who said, "Shoot me, I'm ready to die?

CHAPTER 4

PERGAMUM: HOLDS TO THE TRUTH OF GOD'S WORD

Revelation 2:12-17

And to the angel of the church in Pergamum write: The One who has the sharp two-edged sword says this: [13] *"I know where you dwell, where Satan's throne is; and you hold fast My name, and did not deny My faith even in the days of Antipas, My witness, My faithful one, who was killed among you, where Satan dwells.* [14] *But I have a few things against you, because you have there some who hold the teaching of Balaam, who kept teaching Balak to put a stumbling block before the sons of Israel, to eat things sacrificed to idols and to commit acts of immorality.* [15] *So you also have some who in the same way hold the teaching of the Nicolaitans.* [16] *Therefore repent; or else I am coming to you quickly, and I will make war against them with the sword of My mouth.* [17] *He who has an ear, let him hear what the Spirit says to the churches. To him who overcomes, to him I will give some of the hidden manna, and I will give him a white stone, and a new name written on the stone which no one knows but he who receives it."*

It's Number One

Let's begin with a quiz, a short quiz. In fact, it's so short there's only one question! The question is this: of all the topics that are addressed in all the books of the New Testament, what is the one topic that is addressed more than any other? In other words, in all of the books of the New Testament–the gospels, the book of Acts, all the letters, and the book of Revelation–what is the one concern that is spoken about most often?

Of course, some may say it is love. Love is a matter of highest concern to God because the Great Commandment is to love God with all our hearts, and the second, which is like it, is to love our neighbor as ourselves (Mathew 22:36-39). But the answer is not the Great Commandment.

Others may say it is the Great Commission, which is that we are to share, preach and proclaim the gospel of salvation in Christ to the lost so they can be saved (Matthew 28:18-20). Certainly this is also a matter of foremost concern to God. But the answer is not the Great Commission.

What, then, out of all the topics addressed in all the books of the New Testament is the number one topic that is spoken about more than any other? It is doctrine–holding to the truth of the word of God by teaching and maintaining right doctrine. While we call the command to love "the Great Commandment," and the command to share the gospel "the Great Commission," holding to the truth of God's word may be called "the Great Concern."

We can see that this is "the Great Concern" of the New Testament from the fact that all the books of the New Testament except one touch on and deal in one way or another with the matter of doctrine. It is the great concern of God that His people know and hold to the truth of His word. The one book that does not address the concern about doctrine is the book of Philemon, the shortest of all the letters of Paul. Every other book of the New Testament, 26 of 27 books, touches on and deals in one way or another with the great concern of teaching right doctrine. And, as we listen to what Lord Jesus Christ says to the church in Pergamum, we will become very aware that this is the kind of church He wants–a church that holds to the truth of God's word.

The Authority of the Sword

As He does with all seven of the churches, the Lord Jesus begins by declaring a title and attribute about Himself that is relevant to that particular church. Turning to the church in Pergamum, the one and only one thing He declares about Himself is that He is *"the One who has the sharp two-edged sword"* (Revelation 2:12).

The sword would have been most relevant and meaningful to the Christians living in Pergamum because the city was the seat of the Roman Proconsul. The office of the Roman Proconsul would have been similar to the office of the governor of a state or province. As Atlanta is the capital of the state of Georgia in the United States, Victoria the capital of the province of British Columbia in Canada, and Sydney the capital of New South Wales in Australia, Pergamum was the capital of the Roman province of Asia, which today is the region of Asia Minor or Turkey. Because of this, it was the location of the residence of the Proconsul.

Because the Proconsul was the highest civil authority of the Roman government in that region, he was given the supreme civil authority of judgment. This meant he had power over life and death, granting life to the one he judged worthy of life, or sentencing to death anyone he judged to be worthy of death. That power was called "the authority of the sword" because it was symbolized by the sword, the sword being the instrument of execution of Roman citizens. Paul explicitly stated this in the book of Romans when he wrote that the civil authority *"does not bear the sword for nothing; for it is a minister of God, an avenger who brings wrath on the one who practices evil"* (Romans 13:4).

At the time in history when Jesus spoke these words, Romans would execute people who were not Roman citizens by crucifixion, as Jesus was, and as church tradition says Peter was. However, Roman citizens who were sentenced to death were given a swift and more merciful death being executed by the sword, which is how church history says Paul the apostle died. The sword was the symbol of authority and power over life and death, and Jesus, declaring to the church in Pergamum that He has the *"sword,"* would have meant He has the supreme authority of judgment and the power over life and death. It also meant He was speaking to them about a matter of life and death.

A Sword Like No Other

When we look carefully at what Jesus says, we see the kind of sword He possesses and uses is not a physical sword held in the hand but one that comes forth from His mouth. This is one of the distinct characteristics about the appearance of the risen Christ that John described in the first chapter of Revelation. He said, *"Out of His mouth came a sharp two-edged sword"* (Revelation 1:16). This is also what Jesus says about Himself later on to the church in Pergamum, warning them, *"Therefore repent; or else I am coming to you quickly, and I will make war against them with the sword of My mouth"* (Revelation 2:16). The sword Jesus possesses is not a physical sword that can only do physical harm and never touch the spiritual realm, specifically the soul. The sword coming from His mouth is a spiritual reality that has supreme authority of judgment and power over life and death in both the physical and spiritual realms of existence. There is nothing like it.

In speaking of His "*sword,*" Jesus emphasizes three things. First, He identifies it as being "*the sword.*" It is not "a sword" or "some kind of sword." It is "*the sword.*" This is "*the sword*" that proceeds from His mouth, in other words, the very word of God. The word of God is that word which "*proceeds out of the mouth of God*" (Deuteronomy 8:3; Matthew 4:4). The word of God coming out of the mouth of Jesus is that which has the almighty power to bring all things into existence, give life and hold all things together (Genesis 1; John 1:3; Colossians 1:17; Hebrews 1:2-3; 11:3). And the word of God coming out of the mouth of the Lord Jesus is that which has the power to kill. This is the very thing the book of Revelation says will take place at His second coming. Speaking of those who will be living in rebellion against Him, it foretells "*and the rest were killed with the sword which came from the mouth of Him who sat on the horse*" (Revelation 19:21). His sword has the power of life and death.

The second thing Christ emphasizes is that it is "*sharp.*" It is "*the sharp sword.*" Being the word of God, nothing is sharper. This means there is no protection, no shield, and no defense against it. It will pierce, penetrate and perform what Christ sends it forth to do (Isaiah 55:11). Hebrews 4:12 speaks of this reality in both the physical and spiritual realms saying,

> *For the word of God is living and active and sharper than any two-edged sword, and piercing as far as the division of soul and spirit, of both joints and marrow, and able*

to judge the thoughts and intentions of the heart.

The greatest heart surgeon is the Lord Jesus Christ Who does not use a scalpel held in his hand to expose a beating heart. His *"sharp sword"* that goes *"out of His mouth"* to reveal *"the thoughts and intentions of the heart."*

More than these characteristics, the third thing Jesus says about His *"sword"* is it *"two-edged."* The Greek word is literally "two-mouthed" and is sometimes translated "double-edged." Some swords have a blade that is sharp and cutting on only one side, such as a saber that was used by cavalry officers. Christ's sword is sharp and cuts on both sides. Whichever way it goes–back and forth, up and down, in and out–it will pierce, penetrate and cut. A *"two-edged sword"* is spoken of in different places in the Old Testament and it is specifically related to judgment. The Judge Ehud had a *"sword with two edges"* with which he killed the obese, idolatrous, Gentile king Eglon (Judges 3:16, 21). Most significant Psalm 149:5-6 speaks of the LORD's people having a *"two-edged sword to execute vengeance on the nations."*

The sword the Lord Jesus possesses is *"the sharp, two-edged sword"* that goes out from His mouth. It is not a mere symbol but the very reality of His sovereign authority and power over life and death to execute His righteous judgment upon all as they deserve. In declaring this attribute about Himself, He is telling the church in Pergamum that He has the supreme authority of judgment and the power of life and death, that their situation is a matter of spiritual life and death based on how they live their lives according to the truth of the word of God, and if they do not repent, He will use His sword to execute His judgment against them.

He Knows His Own

After declaring this attribute, Jesus tells them He understands what is happening in Pergamum not only in the physical realm but also in the spiritual realm of life. He says in verse 13,

> *I know where you dwell, where Satan's throne is; and you hold fast My name, and did not deny My faith even in the days of Antipas, My witness, My faithful one, who was killed among you, where Satan dwells.*

The Lord is intimately familiar with the details of their lives saying He knows where they *"dwell."* This is because He has a deep, personal knowledge of all who are His, and He calls His own by name (John 10:3). Jesus knows His own, and if you have real and true faith in Him, He knows you, your name, and everything about you. What a comfort and joy this is, to know there is nothing in our lives Christ does not know about as well as care about.

This is revealed when He speaks of one person in particular, a man by the name of *"Antipas."* Christ uses the possessive two times of Antipas, speaking of him as *"My witness"* and *"My faithful one."* These words reveal the love and affection the Lord has for His own, especially those who are faithful to Him. The Greek word translated *"witness"* is *"martys,"* the word from which we get out English word "martyr." In his faithful witness to the Lord Jesus, Antipas was literally a martyr being *"one who was killed among you."* He was an example of what Jesus spoke about to the previous church, the church in Smyrna, that they be *"faithful to death"* (Revelation 2:10).

What's the Climate Like?

The Lord then reveals He is very aware of the spiritual climate and atmosphere of the city of Pergamum where they live. He says He knows it is a spiritually dark and extremely dangerous place because it is the location *"where Satan's throne is"* and where he *"dwells"* (Revelation 2:13). While the Bible tells us the devil *"prowls around like a roaring lion, seeking someone to devour"* (1 Peter 5:8) and, in fact, that he roams about on the whole earth (Job 1:7), nevertheless, we see from what Jesus says here that there can be a place on the earth where he *"dwells"* and has his *"throne."* It is an actual place from which he exercises his dark and evil authority and power, and Jesus identifies that place at that time in history as being in Pergamum.

One of the ways Satan exercised his influence, power and rule in Pergamum was by persecuting and killing Christians. Jesus says to the church, *"You hold fast My name and did not deny My faith even in the days of Antipas, My witness, My faithful one, who was killed among you"* The time of testing that Jesus spoke about that was to come upon the second church, the church in Smyrna, had already come to the church in Pergamum. They were being faithful to Jesus during this persecution and He commends them for being in this way the kind of church He wants.

The Main Problem

However, after declaring the attribute about Himself that is relevant to their situation, revealing His intimate knowledge of their situation, and commending them for how they are being the kind of church He wants, He identifies the one overall area in the life of the church where they were failing. In this we see the third quality and characteristic of the kind of church Jesus wants–it holds to the truth of God's word. He says in verses 14 and 15,

> But I have a few things against you, because you have there some who hold the teaching of Balaam, who kept teaching Balak to put a stumbling block before the sons of Israel, to eat things sacrificed to idols and to commit acts of immorality. [15] So you also have some who in the same way hold the teaching of the Nicolaitans.

While Jesus identifies particulars, the one overall principle He has against them is that *"some hold the teaching of..."* This means there are those in the church who are believing and maintaining false doctrines. Two times He speaks of this, saying, in verse 14, *"you have some who hold the teaching of Balaam,"* and in verse 15, *"you also have some who in the same way hold the teaching of the Nicolaitans."* *"Hold"* means "to receive, to embrace and to live by." There are *"some"* in the church who have received, embraced and are living by certain *"teaching."* *"Teaching"* is another word for "doctrine." In other words, they are not holding to the truth of God's word but have received, embraced and are living according to false doctrine.

The Real Issue

There are not a few Christians today who are "allergic" to doctrine. They believe doctrine is bad and should be avoided for different reasons, the main being that it separates and divides Christians. The story is told about an associate of Billy Graham who was preaching in a series of meetings, and after one service a man came up to him, patted him on the back and enthusiastically said, "That was great preachin'. You didn't preach no doctrine, nor nothin'!" Such people are examples of the proverb, "The road to hell is paved with good intentions."

While the intention to not divide Christians is righteous, the reality is that everyone holds to some kind of doctrine. Everyone has received and embraced something they believe about God, the Lord Jesus Christ, the Holy Spirit, salvation, and virtually every other area that touches on the Christian life, whether they know it or not. The issue is not "doctrine or no doctrine." It is whether we have right doctrine that holds to the truth of the word of God or false doctrine. And it is absolutely clear that this was the primary concern of the Lord Jesus about His church in Pergamum–there were some who were holding to false teachings.

Not only this, one of the foremost purposes of doctrine is that it does divide, for as Hebrews says, *"the word of God"* pierces *"as far as the division of soul and spirit"* and is a *"judge the thoughts and intentions of the heart"* (Hebrews 4:12). It is doctrine–right doctrine that holds to the truth of the word of God–that divides between truth and lies, what is of God and what is of the devil, and who are true believers in the Lord Jesus Christ and those who are not. Doctrine exposes to the light not only those who are deceived but deceivers–those whom Jesus spoke of as being wolves in sheep's clothing (Matthew 7:15).

So What!

Because the kind of church Jesus wants is one that holds to the truth of God's word, there are two critical things for us to observe about what He says regarding false doctrine in this church. The first is that it is not the whole church that has turned away from the truth of God's word, it's *"some."* He says in verse 14, *"you have some who hold the teaching of...*" and in verse 15, "*you also have some who in the same way hold the teaching* of..." It is not as if the whole church had become "apostate," meaning they all had completely fallen away. It is only "*some*" in the church, or as Christ says, "*you have some.*"

Why is Jesus so concerned that there are "*some*"–not all–only some in the church who are not holding to the truth of the word of God? There are at least two reasons.

Contrary to His Nature

One reason, and perhaps the most important, is Christ's own nature. His very nature is truth. He said, "*I am the truth*" (John 14:6). Being truth itself, He loves the truth and hates what is false. That which is a lie and not the truth is that which is contrary and opposed to His very nature. Being the truth, He taught the truth–the truth of the word of God. Being the truth, He understood that the truth of the word of God is essential to right and righteous relationship with God. In His prayer for all who would believe in Him, He said to the Father, "*Sanctify them in the truth; Your word is truth* " (John 17:17). To "*sanctify*" means to "make holy." To become holy means that we become like Christ with the foremost purpose of being able to live and dwell in the manifest presence of God for only that which is holy can continue to live in the awesome, holy manifest presence of God (Leviticus 10:3; Psalm 24:4; Ephesians 1:4; Hebrews 12:14). Only that which is true is of God and can remain in His manifest presence.

Jesus made it clear that one of the consequences of false doctrine is bondage to sin and only the truth of God's word makes people free. He said, "*If you continue in My word, then you are truly disciples of Mine; [32] and you will know the truth, and the truth will make you free*" (John 8:31-32). Jesus loves the truth of His word and hates false doctrine because He loves His own and wants us to walk in freedom from sin and in right relationship with God.

Not only is His very nature truth, Jesus revealed this is the nature of the Holy Spirit. He said, *"When He, the Spirit of truth, comes, He will guide you into all the truth"* (John 16:13). In saying He is *"the Spirit of truth,"* Jesus says the Holy Spirit not only communicates what is true and will *"guide into all the truth"* but that His very nature is truth. The Holy Spirit being God, the third Person of the Trinity, is truth. Being God, He cannot lie, for as Hebrews 6:18 states, *"it is impossible for God to lie."*

This, of course, is the absolute opposite of that most unholy spirit whose nature is to lie and deceive–the devil. Jesus said, *"Whenever he speaks a lie, he speaks from his own nature, for he is a liar and the father of lies"* (John 8:44). False doctrines come from the devil and his demons, and the Holy Spirit warned against this in the word. He inspired Paul to write in 1 Timothy 4:1 saying, *"But the Spirit explicitly says that in later times some will fall away from the faith, paying attention to deceitful spirits and doctrines of demons."*

Jesus' concern for right doctrine is because He is the truth, He loves the truth, and He sent the Holy Spirit to guide us into all the truth. He wants all His disciples–not some, not many, not even most–but all to live in true freedom from sin and the beauty of holiness in our relationship with God. The only way this happens is by holding to the truth of God's word.

It Will Make You Sick

The second reason Jesus is concerned about *"some"* in the church who are teaching false doctrine is expressed in the proverb quoted in Scripture, *"a little leaven leavens the whole lump of dough"*(1 Corinthians 5:6). The context of these words in 1 Corinthians 5 is that Paul is dealing with sexual sin in the church, but the proverb applies to every area of life. A little false doctrine taught by some in the church will work its way into the whole church. Changing analogies from the kitchen to medicine, we could say, "a little virus makes the whole body sick." This is how Paul described false doctrine in 2 Timothy 2:17 saying, "*Their talk*-literally "*word*"-*will spread like gangrene*-or cancer." Jesus is concerned about "*some*" in the church who hold to false doctrine because just like leaven, false doctrine can work its way into the whole church, and just like cancer, false doctrine will make a church sick. Even worse, not only can it make it sick, it can kill it.

What Does He Think About It?

The second thing to understand about what Jesus says about the false doctrine some hold in the church in Pergamum is the nature of the false doctrine being taught. He identifies two false teachings: "*the teaching of Balaam*" (Revelation 2:14) and "*the teaching of the Nicolaitans*" (Revelation 2:15).

The second false doctrine, "*the teaching of the Nicolaitans,*" must have been popular and spreading among the churches because in speaking to the first church, the church in Ephesus, the Lord commended them, saying, "*Yet this you do have, that you hate the deeds of the Nicolaitans, which I also hate*" (Revelation 2:6). We do not know what the teaching of the Nicolaitans actually was, whether it was named after a person who originated it or it summarizes their teaching. One of the first deacons was named "Nicolas" (Acts 6:5). However, he was a man highly recognized as being "*full of the Spirit and wisdom*" (Acts 6:3), and there is no indication that he was the source of this corrupt teaching. It is possible to speculate that the name *"Nicolaitan,"* which means "victory, conquering or prevailing of the people," indicates they were promoting power and rule by the people and thus not by Christ. This would, in effect, be similar to the people of Israel wanting a human king to rule over them and not the LORD by His Spirit through gifted and called individuals (1 Samuel 8:7; Ephesians 4:7-11).

What is vital to understand about what Jesus says is how this *"teaching"* impacted the church. What the doctrine was is not the issue. What is important for us to see is its effect on the church and what Christ thought about it. The root was the false doctrine and this was producing bad fruit in their lives. It was how they lived their lives–their *"deeds"*–that Jesus specifically says He hates (Revelation 2:6). Pull up the root and you will no longer produce the bad fruit.

You Can't Do That

It is important for us to understand that Christ's concern for the church in Pergamum is that there were *"some"* in the church who claimed to be true followers of Christ and yet held doctrine and taught people that they could live in a way Christ hates. There are, of course, doctrines that are not essential to what we believe and how we live, and the Bible tells us to love and give freedom to these differences of *"opinions"* while we *"accept one another just as Christ also accepted us to the glory of God"* (Romans 14:1-15:7). But there are other doctrines–essential doctrines–that lead to *"deeds"* that Christ *"hates."*

Christ's words are sobering. They were not only relevant to this church in the first century but apply to every church in every century. Today, we live in a culture that would "demonize" the Lord Jesus Himself for His "hate speech" because He literally says He hates what they are doing and He righteously judges people to be "*evil*" (Revelation 2:2). Sadly, there are more and more people, not merely in the secular, godless culture, but in the visible church that claim "God is love" and that "Christ is tolerant" of the moral choices and behavior of anyone and everyone no matter what their "*deeds*" are, especially in the area of sexual behavior. Such doctrine is, in principle, the same as "*the Nicolaitans,*" for it is teaching people that they can claim to be followers of Christ yet live in a way He hates. Christ's very own words declare He hates the doctrine and deeds of these people.

We need to hear what Jesus says about the doctrine and the "*deeds*" of these people. This is because there are not a few in the Church today who claim to believe the Bible and yet wrongly separate what a person believes from how they live their lives–"*to their own destruction*" (2 Peter 2:1ff; 3:16). This was, in fact, what the whole book of Jude was about–people in the church "*who turn the grace of our God into licentiousness,*" which means a license to sin (Jude 4). While we can distinguish fruit from root, the fruit is directly connected to the root.

Perhaps the most common example of this is when people hold to the teaching that if you simply make an profession of faith in Jesus, meaning that you give some kind of outward assent that Jesus is your Savior–merely say a prayer at some time in your life, or have even been baptized–you are saved and will automatically go to heaven when you die. They hold that it doesn't matter how you live your life–if you prayed "the prayer" or made a profession of faith you are saved and going to heaven! This is the kind of religion Jesus hates because it separates what a person professes to believe from how they actually live their lives. It teaches that how you live your life doesn't matter, that a person can live their life dominated by disobedience to the commands of Christ, live in rebellion against His rule, walk according to the sinful desires of flesh and not the desires of the Spirit, and will nevertheless still be blessed by God and go to heaven. There is one word Scripture consistently uses of such people and such teaching–deceived. Paul warned, *"Let no one deceive you with empty words, for because of these things the wrath of God comes upon the sons of disobedience"* (Ephesians 5:6). John himself wrote,

> *Little children, make sure no one deceives you; the one who practices righteousness is righteous, just as He is righteous; [8] the one who practices sin is of the devil; for the devil has sinned from the beginning. The Son of God appeared for this purpose, to destroy the works of the devil* (1 John 3:7-8).

While no one is saved on the basis of their deeds, the life a person lives demonstrates what they actually believe in their heart.

That's the Old Testament!

This brings us to the nature of the first false teaching Jesus speaks about, that *"there are some who hold the teaching of Balaam, who kept teaching Balak to put a stumbling block before the sons of Israel, to eat things sacrificed to idols and to commit acts of immorality"* (Revelation 2:14). There are two critical things we need to grasp about what Christ says here that are relevant to a church holding to the truth of God's word.

The first is that what Jesus speaks about and applies to the church in Pergamum is taken out of the Old Testament Scriptures. The reason this is important is because now, in our time in the history, there are not a few people who interpret the Bible in a way that is summed up in the statement, "Oh that's the Old Testament, but we are now in the New Testament." What this practically means is that what is taught in the Old Testament does not, for the most part, apply to us in the church because, with the coming of Jesus, the teaching in the Old Testament is no longer relevant to us. This is not what Jesus taught.

What is true is that with the coming of Christ–His death, resurrection and ascension–certain things in the Old Testament have been fulfilled, and we are no longer under those requirements. Those have to do with outward ceremonial and civil laws that Jesus fulfilled (Matthew 5:17-18; Hebrews 7:11-12; 8:13). But the moral laws of God are eternal, as are the spiritual principles revealed in the Old Testament Scriptures (Matthew 5:19; Romans 10:8-10; 15:4; Galatians 5:14). This should be obvious, first of all, from the fact that the very words Jesus spoke are a reference to an event that took place in the Old Testament that had specific application to the church in Pergamum. It is most significant to observe that one out of 22 ½ verses of the New Testament is a quotation of the Old Testament[2]. What is also often forgotten is that the only Bible Christians in the early church possessed was the Old Testament. It is absurd to think believers in Pergamum would have responded to what Jesus said about Balaam and Balak saying, "Oh, that's the Old Testament and it doesn't apply to us now because we are in the New Testament!" If we are to hold to the truth of the word of God, we must hold to what God has revealed in the whole of Scriptures, which means understanding the spiritual laws and principles revealed in the Old Testament and how they apply to us today. This is the very thing Paul wrote to the Corinthians. After citing specific events in the history of the people of God in the Old Testament, he said, *"Now these things happened to them as an example, and they were written for our instruction, upon whom the ends of the ages have come"* (1 Corinthians 10:11).

I Had No Idea

The second observation to make from what Jesus says is that He speaks about what happened in the history of God's people with Balaam and Balak. The sad fact is that many in the church today have no idea who these two men were or how the events in regard to them would apply to the church in Pergamum as well as to us today. The reason is because so many simply do not know the word of God, let alone the Old Testament, which is the portion of Scripture Jesus refers to. Nor do they know and understand the spiritual laws and principles that are revealed by God in His word in these accounts. *"All Scripture is inspired by God and profitable"* means the Old Testament as well as the New (2 Timothy 3:16). If we don't know the Scriptures, we will not be able to hold to the truth of the word of God. We will, then, not be able to live according to it, and will suffer the consequences.

This is the very thing Jesus is speaking about and applying to the church in Pergamum. There were *"some"* who were not holding to the truth of the word of God and, because of this, they were violating the spiritual laws and moral principles that God teaches in His word. The specific example Christ quotes is the spiritual laws and moral principles in the account of Balaam and Balak. So what is Jesus referring?

Spiritual Laws Revealed

As we are primarily told in Numbers 22-25, at that time in the history of the nation of Israel God delivered His people from Egypt by His almighty power and they were approaching the land that He had promised to give them. Leading up to the event with Balaam and Balak, Israel had defeated powerful nations that had attacked them. So Balak, who was the king of the nation of Moab, realizing that the military might of Israel was spiritual and that he did not have the power to defeat them, hired a man by the name of Balaam to come and use spiritual power to defeat Israel by releasing a curse on them.

Regrettably, there are many Christians in the secularized, Western culture who, while professing to believe the Bible, do not actually live in the real world of the Bible because they do not know about, let alone believe in the reality of the power of curses as well as blessings. Yet everything in this event concerning Balaam and Balak that Jesus speaks about is based on the reality of the spiritual power of curses being released to cause evil and blessings operating to cause good.

Balak hired Balaam to curse Israel in order to defeat them. Yet every time Balaam went about the ritual actions to release a curse upon Israel, God overruled it and would not allow the power of the curse to be released upon His people. Instead, He turned the curse into a blessing (Numbers 23:11; Nehemiah 13:2). Why was this? It is because of another spiritual law that operates in the universe, another law of God's kingdom that many people do not understand today. It is that Israel was the covenant people of God, and being in covenant with God, if they lived in obedience to Him, were faithful to love Him and keep His commandments, God would be faithful to them, to protect them and defeat their enemies (Leviticus 26:6-8; Deuteronomy 28:7). One aspect of His covenant faithfulness was to protect them from the power of curses being sent against them (Numbers 22:12; 23:8; Proverbs 26:2). This is what Balaam understood, and he encountered it every time he attempted to release a curse against Israel–he could not because God would not permit it.

But Balaam knew and understood another aspect of this spiritual law or principle of God's kingdom, that God's covenant promise of protection is not automatic. It is conditional upon His people living faithful to Him by keeping His commandments (Leviticus 26:3; Deuteronomy 28:1). If they sinned against God and did not repent, they would not only remove themselves from God's promised protection, God Himself would bring His own judgment upon them (Leviticus 26:14ff.; Deuteronomy 28:15ff.). So the way Balaam got the people of Israel to forfeit the protection God promised and bring His judgment on them was to get them to sin against God. He did this by teaching Balak to entice some of the people of Israel to commit the most serious sin of all–idolatry–along with sexual immorality. He had Balak send immoral woman among the people of Israel so that they would sin against God and violate the covenant. Thousands sinned with the result that God's judgment came. The Bible says 24,000 died in one day (Numbers 25:9)!

What Does That Mean for Us?

This is what Jesus specifically applies to the church in Pergamum. He said, *"you have there some who hold the teaching of Balaam, who kept teaching Balak to put a stumbling block before the sons of Israel, to eat things sacrificed to idols and to commit acts of immorality"* (Revelation 2:14). They were teaching that God's people could sin against Him, committing the sins of idolatry and sexual immorality, which is having sex of any kind outside the bonds of marriage. In this way, they were holding to false doctrine, and Jesus said they would suffer the consequences. Applying these spiritual laws and moral principles revealed in the word of God in the Old Testament, Jesus said the judgment of God would come upon these people in the church in Pergamum and He Himself would be the One who would execute it. He tells them, *"Therefore repent; or else I am coming to you quickly, and I will make war against them with the sword of My mouth"* (Revelation 2:16)!

In these sobering words of warning from the Lord Jesus Christ we see that the kind of church He wants is one that holds to the truth of God's word. In order to do this, we must *know* the word of God–all of the Scriptures, the Old and New Testaments. Further, we must *believe* the word of God–all of it, not just the parts that are comfortable and convenient or that conform to the values and the worldview of the Western, secular culture we live in. And, most of all, we must *live according to* the word of God, demonstrating it with the fruit of our lives.

The great evangelist of the 19th century, D. L. Moody said about the Bible, "This book will keep you from sin, or sin will keep you from this book." The testimony of thousands, even millions throughout the course of church history is that their lives have been enriched, transformed and blessed when they have taken hold to the truth of God's word and let it take hold of them. When we know and live according to God's word, we will be able to discern what Christ is saying, we will walk in the light of His presence, He will be faithful to keep His promises, and we will be the kind of church He wants.

Study Questions
Chapter 4

1. Briefly share one personal insight from the chapter.

2. What topic is addressed more than any other in the New Testament? What do you think about this great concern of the Bible? How important is it to you?

3. When Jesus said He has the sharp two-edged sword, how would the church in Pergamum have understood this in light of the their culture and the Roman government? How do these words of Christ apply to you and your culture?

4. How is Christ's sword unique? What does this mean to you?

5. How personal was Christ's knowledge of the individuals in the church in Pergamum? How do you respond to this? Do really believe Christ knows your name and has love and affection for you?

6. What do you think about Christ's words concerning the spiritual climate and atmosphere of Pergamum? How would you describe the spiritual atmosphere of the place you live?

7. What is the third quality of the kind of church Jesus wants? Do you believe the Bible is the written word of God and is true?

8. Why do you think so many Christians don't care about knowing and understanding Biblical doctrine? What are the consequences of false doctrine?

9. What is your response to the author's statement that one of the foremost purposes of doctrine is that it is to divide?

10. Why is holding to the truth so important to Jesus?

11. In what ways are the Old Testament Scriptures relevant for us today? How does this make a difference in how you view the Bible, its teachings and its application in your life?

12. Do you understand the distinctions between the ceremonial, civil and moral laws of the Old Testament? How do these areas of Scripture apply to your life today?

CHAPTER 5

THYATIRA: EXERCISES CHURCH DISCIPLINE

Revelation 2:18-29

And to the angel of the church in Thyatira write: The Son of God, who has eyes like a flame of fire, and His feet are like burnished bronze, says this: [19] *"I know your deeds, and your love and faith and service and perseverance, and that your deeds of late are greater than at first.* [20] *But I have this against you, that you tolerate the woman Jezebel, who calls herself a prophetess, and she teaches and leads My bond-servants astray so that they commit acts of immorality and eat things sacrificed to idols.* [21] *I gave her time to repent, and she does not want to repent of her immorality.* [22] *Behold, I will throw her on a bed of sickness, and those who commit adultery with her into great tribulation, unless they repent of her deeds.* [23] *And I will kill her children with pestilence, and all the churches will know that I am He who searches the minds and hearts; and I will give to each one of you according to your deeds.* [24] *But I say to you, the rest who are in Thyatira, who do not hold this teaching, who have not known the deep things of Satan, as they call them—I place no other burden on you. [25] Nevertheless what you have, hold fast until I come. [26] He who overcomes, and he who keeps My deeds until the end, to him I will give authority over the nations; [27] and he shall rule them with a rod of iron, as the vessels of the potter are broken to pieces, as I also have received authority from My Father; [28] and I will give him the morning star. [29] He who has an ear, let him hear what the Spirit says to the churches."*

Hidden in Plain Sight

"The elephant in the room"–how often have heard you that, or even said it yourself? It is a figure of speech that comes from the image of an elephant. It is something large, something taking up space, something "right there" in the open that everyone sees, and yet everyone ignores.

The "elephant in the room" is a problem. It is an issue that people know about, a matter that is making life difficult. Yet no one wants to address it, confront it or talk about it, so everyone pretends as if it's not there. They evade and avoid it, run away from and rationalize it, dodge and duck it, tolerate and don't talk about it–anything they can do to act as if it's not there. But everyone knows it's there because it's as big as an elephant, an elephant in the room! So they live with the problem that's making life miserable, that's stinking up the place, that everyone is walking around because they don't want to step in it. That is what was happening in the church in Thyatira.

The church in Thyatira is the fourth of the seven churches Jesus addressed. What is ironic about what Jesus says to this church is that the city of Thyatira was regarded as the least important of the seven cities, and the church was considered the least of the seven churches, yet it was to this church that Jesus spoke the greatest number words.

While there are a number of things Jesus says to the church, there is one thing that stands out. It's the most important thing in all He says. There was a problem in the church. It was a big problem right there in plain sight, that everyone knew about, yet nobody was doing anything about–it's the "elephant in the room." Perhaps some in the church wanted something done about it, but no one was doing anything . Consequently, Jesus, speaking the truth in love, addresses this major problem in this church, and as He does, we learn about the fourth characteristic of the kind of church He wants–it is a church that exercises church discipline.

The Son of God

Once again, the Lord begins His address to this church by declaring both a title and attributes of Himself that are relevant and meaningful to the situation and culture of the church. He says three things to them.

He begins by declaring He is *"the Son of God."* It's amazing that every once in a while you will hear someone who denies the deity of the Lord Jesus make the claim that He never said He is the Son of God. It is impossible to deny that is what He does here–He affirms He is *"the Son of God."* He is not "a son of God," nor "the foremost son among many sons." He is *"the Son of God,"* meaning, He is *the one* Son, *the only* Son, *the only begotten* Son of God, Who in His eternal nature is God the Son (see John 1:18; 3:16).

What is relevant about this title to the church in Thyatira is that the local patron god of the city, whose name was Tyrimnos, was believed to be a son of god–a son of Zeus, who was the supreme god in the Greek pantheon of gods. A local patron god is believed to be a spirit that is one of the many gods that inhabit the spiritual realm of this world and have authority, power and influence over a region, district, city or any smaller area. Being the local patron god of the city, Tyrimnos was believed to be the god that protected and blessed the city of Thyatira.

Many passages of Scripture reveal that spirits are given authority, power and influence over territories, peoples and areas of life. These spirits can be holy angels of God or unholy, Satanic spirits. Deuteronomy 32:8 reveals, *"When the Most High gave to the nations their inheritance, when he divided mankind, he fixed the borders of the peoples according to the number of the sons of God"* (ESV). *"The sons of God"* is a designation of spiritual, angelic or celestial beings who were directly created by God and given authority over different peoples and territories, being assigned within their particular *"borders."* Job 1:6 gives a brief account of *"the sons of God"* coming before the throne of God with Satan being among them, saying, *"Now there was a day when the sons of God came to present themselves before the Lord, and Satan also came among them."* These are spirits that are not visible to the physical eye and have various areas of rule and authority. Colossians 1:16, states, *"For by Him all things were created, both in the heavens and on earth, visible and invisible, whether thrones or dominions or rulers or authorities—all things have been created through Him and for Him."* Just as holy angels are given assignments and authority from God for His purposes over territories, peoples, and areas of life, so also fallen angels, who followed Satan in His rebellion against God, have been given their own assignments and authority from Satan for his evil purposes in their assigned areas. There is a hierarchy of evil spirits which is described in Ephesians 6:12 as *"the rulers, ... the powers, ... the world forces of this darkness, ... the spiritual forces of wickedness in the heavenly places."* In Daniel 10:20-21, the angel sent by God to give revelation to Daniel identifies three high level spirits or angelic beings over territories and people, these being *"the prince of Persia," "the prince of Greece,"* and *"Michael,"* who is identified as *"prince"* over the people of Israel. Michael, of course, is a holy angel of God, assigned to the people of God, and the other two *"princes"* are principal or ruling Satanic spirits over the territories of Persia and Greece.

Tyrimnos, being the local patron of the city, was believed to be the god that protected and blessed the city of Thyatira. In the Greek language such a god was called a *"diamonion,"* which to them meant a "divine being, deity or god." Because of this, the people of the city would render worship and honor to it in one way or another, such as a parade or festival. The Greek word *"diamonion"* is the word translated in the New Testament as *"demon"* (Matthew 7:22; 8:31), and that is what Tyrmnos was–a demonic spirit having authority, power and influence over the city of Thyatira.

What is most relevant about this to the church in Thyatira is that when Jesus declares He is *"the Son of God,"* He is stressing He is the one true Son of the one true Living God. He is the One Who has supreme authority and power over all His people and over all demonic powers. He will protect and bless His people, no matter where they live. And because of this, they are to worship and honor Him (Psalm 2:12).

Fire!

The Lord then focuses on two of His attributes, that He *"has eyes like a flame of fire, and His feet are like burnished bronze."* Both of these attributes describe the fire of the manifest presence of God in the Lord Jesus–He is burning with fire! These could be applied in different ways to the church in Thyatira, but as we see from what Jesus says, this fire has to do with testing and judgment. *"His feet,"* being like *"burnished bronze,"* reveal the strength and stability of His character. He was tested and proven faithful and true as He walked through the fiery trials of life and death, overcame them, and became victorious and glorious. And His *"eyes,"* which are like *"a flame of fire,"* depict His all-knowing insight and understanding of all things, especially the hearts of all human beings. Psalm 11:4 says of the Lord that *"His eyes behold, His eyelids test the sons of men."* Because of these things, Christ can render perfect, pure and all-powerful judgment according to the deeds of a person. He speaks of this later in verse 23 saying, *"I am He who searches the minds and hearts; and I will give to each one of you according to your deeds."*

The Big Picture

After declaring His title and attributes, the Lord makes them aware of His knowledge of them as a church. He says in verse 19, *"I know your deeds, and your love and faith and service and perseverance."*

Jesus speaks here of His understanding of the church as a whole. It's the big picture of the church. We deduce this from what He goes on to say to this church, that it had in it both those who were pleasing to Him and those who were not, which is true of most churches. There were a number in the church who were holding to false doctrine, and this resulted in their doing deeds that would bring severe judgment against them from the Lord Jesus. Yet there were others He speaks of in verse 24 as *"the rest in Thyatira who do not hold to this teaching."* These were the ones who were faithful followers of Christ. Overall, the church was to be commended.

By looking at the qualities the Lord commends, we see areas in which they are the kind of church He wants. It was not a church whose goal was, as someone cynically said, "nickels and noses"–outward appearance in numbers of money and people. The characteristics He commends are inward qualities of character. These qualities were manifested and demonstrated in their *"deeds"* because that which makes known the true character of a person is not simply what they profess but what they produce. A tree is known by its fruit.

The good fruit in this church is their *"love and faith and service and perseverance."* These four qualities summarize the Christian life. *"Love"* is love of God and other Christians, and it is the greatest demonstration that we are disciples of Christ (John 13:34-35). *"Faith"* is not only believing in the truth of Who God is, it is being faithful to Him in all circumstances of life (James 1:3). *"Service"* is the work of ministry, the service that results from one giving their time and energy to advance the kingdom of God and build the church, especially according to one's spiritual gift (1 Corinthians 12:5; Ephesians 4:12). And *"perseverance"* is continuing to press on, not fading or falling away because of difficulties and trials (James 1:12). All these qualities are the fruit of the Holy Spirit, coming from a person being filled with and walking in the Spirit (Galatians 5:22; Ephesians 5:18). These qualities were demonstrated in the life of the Lord Jesus, and in having these qualities of character, the believers in Thyatira were like Christ.

It's Getting Better

Not only this, but the Lord commends them because they are growing in these qualities. He says, *"your deeds of late are greater than at first"* (Revelation 2:19). One of the most wonderful things about our walk and relationship with the Lord is our ever-increasing capacity to receive more, be filled with more, and manifest more of the empowering presence of the Holy Spirit so that we can bear more fruit of good *"deeds."* That is what was happening in the lives of most in this church.

It is significant that Jesus says *"of late."* This indicates that those in the church He is speaking about must have experienced some kind of reviving work that "got them off the bench and into the game" in a greater way than before. It is clear that He is commending them for their *"greater"* commitment to love and serve Him. It was by growing in these Christ-like qualities that they were the kind of church Jesus wants, one that is bearing the fruit of the Spirit and growing in greater capacity and commitment to know Him and make Him known.

Thyatira, We Have a Problem

It is after revealing His title and attributes that are relevant to their situation in Thyatira, His knowledge of their situation, and commending them for the areas of their Spirit-filled character that Christ then identifies the one overall area in the life of the church where they are falling short. In this we hear Him revealing the fourth quality of the kind of church He wants. The Lord says to them in verse 20,

> *But I have this against you, that you tolerate the woman Jezebel, who calls herself a prophetess, and she teaches and leads My bond-servants astray so that they commit acts of immorality and eat things sacrificed to idols.*

Just as He did with the third church, the church in Pergamum, the Lord makes reference to the history of the people of Israel recorded in the Old Testament that was relevant and applicable to the church in Thyatira. He identifies a woman in the church as *"Jezebel"* who *"leads My bond-servants astray so that they commit acts of immorality and eat things sacrificed to idols"* (Revelation 2:20). This woman was teaching doctrine that was similar to the false doctrine that was being taught in the church in Pergamum which Jesus spoke of as *"the teaching of Balaam, who kept teaching Balak to put a stumbling block before the sons of Israel, to eat things sacrificed to idols and to commit acts of immorality"* (Revelation 2:14).

The two great sins the Lord exposes in this church are idolatry and sexual immorality. Throughout the history of the Bible, we find these two sins are continually connected, so much so that the sin of idolatry, which is the worship of any other god than the LORD, is called "spiritual adultery, prostitution or harlotry" (Deuteronomy 31:16; Jeremiah 3:1; Ezekiel 23:3-21; Hosea 1:2). Idolatry combined with sexual immorality and perversion is what took place in the nations of the world, and these sins continually plagued the people of God.

What Else is New?

Just as this was a continuous problem in the nation of Israel, so also it has been and continues to be a major problem in the church. One of the root causes of why churches and denominations choose to no longer hold to the truth and authority of Scripture is sexual sin. Desiring to live according to their sinful desires instead of the commandments of God, people choose to no longer believe God is righteous, hates sexual sin, never changes, and will execute His judgment against those who sin this way and do not repent (1 Corinthians 10:8; 1 Thessalonians 4:1-8; Hebrews 13:4). So they create their own god, which is idolatry. Paul warned of this taking place in the church, writing,

> *For the time will come when they will not endure sound doctrine; but wanting to have their ears tickled, they will accumulate for themselves teachers in accordance to their own desires, ⁴ and will turn away their ears from the truth and will turn aside to myths* (2 Timothy 4:3-4).

This is the Problem

This is what was happening in the church in Thyatira, as it was in the church in Pergamum. But whereas the key concern of Christ with the church in Pergamum was that there were "*some*" in the church who were not holding to the truth of God's word, in the church in Thyatira the key concern is that the church "*tolerates*" one particular person–a very influential person in the church whom He identifies as "*the woman Jezebel*" (Revelation 2:20). Her influence was sinister, for He says she "*leads My bond-servants astray.*" This was the critical problem–the "elephant in the room" in Thyatira. Instead of confronting and dealing with this influential person who is teaching false doctrine that is leading God's people into sin, they were tolerating her. In this we see the fourth quality of the kind of church Jesus wants–it exercises church discipline.

The Whole Enchilada

Church discipline is the exercise of jurisdictional authority given and mandated to the church by the Lord Jesus Christ, the Head of the Church. Church discipline is fundamental to the purpose of the Great Commission, which is to "*make disciples of all nations... teaching them to observe all I commanded you*" (Matthew 28:19-20). It's not just "*teaching*"–it's "*observe.*" It's not just some–it's "*all.*" It's not what He suggested–it's what He "*commanded.*" It's what a friend calls "the whole enchilada," and some more solemnly call "*the whole counsel of God*" (Acts 20:27 ESV).

Making disciples involves teaching and training God's people in the truth of His word so that they live righteous lives, grow in Christ, and promote the purity, peace and unity of the church. A foundational verse for church discipline is 2 Timothy 3:16 which says, "*All Scripture is inspired by God and profitable for teaching, for reproof, for correction, and for training in righteousness.*" In this verse, we see the two primary ways in which godly and proper church discipline is exercised.

First and foremost is "*teaching*" the word of God so that a person is "*trained in righteousness.*" The root meaning of the word "discipline" is "teach," and that is why a person who is mentored by Jesus is His "disciple." Jesus said a true disciple of His is a person who is taught, trained and continues to live according to the truth of His word (John 8:31). When we love Jesus, we will love His word and keep His commandments (John 14:15).

The second way church discipline is exercised is "*reproof*" and "*correction.*" This is the formal exercise of authority, according to the word of God, to confront and deal with sinful behavior that is not repented of. This is the very thing we see Jesus doing with the seven churches– He is exercising church discipline. He speaks the truth in love to them, confronting them about the things in their lives He has against them so they will repent and become the kind of church He wants.

Of All the Wicked Women, She's the Worst

The church in Thyatira was not exercising the second kind of church discipline. The specific problem Jesus addresses is that they *"tolerate the woman Jezebel"* (Revelation 2:20). His words are very strong and specific–not merely "a woman" but *"the woman."* She is a person who has position, prestige and power in the church, and that is most likely one of, if not the real reason why the church avoided confronting and dealing with her.

Jesus calls her *"Jezebel."* Undoubtedly, this was not her actual personal name as was that of *"Antipas"* who died as a martyr for Christ (Revelation 2:13). It was the spiritual name Christ gave to her. Christ often gave people "nicknames" which revealed their character, such as the name "Peter," which means "rock," that He gave to Simon (Matthew 10:2). The name *"Jezebel"* reveals how evil this woman was and the extent of her influence in the church. Of all the wicked women in the history of the Old Testament who exercised evil influence in the lives of the people of God, there was none more malevolent and malicious than Jezebel.

The history of Jezebel, her influence and her ultimate death are recorded in 1 Kings 16 through 2 Kings 9. She was the wife of Ahab, who himself was one of the most wicked kings in the history of Israel (1 Kings 21:25). Ahab and Jezebel were instrumental in bringing into Israel the idolatrous worship of the god Baal, which involved sexual sin. In her time, Jezebel was perhaps the greatest enemy of the LORD and His prophets, and through her evil influence many of the true prophets of the Lord were killed (1 Kings 18:14).

Prophetess, Teacher, Leader

Jesus identifies three prominent characteristics about her. She *"calls herself a prophetess, and she teaches and leads My bond-servants."* The Scriptures tells us there were many women in the Old and New Testaments who were *"prophetesses"* (Exodus 15:20; Judges 4:4; 2 Chronicles 34:22; Luke 2:36; Acts 2:17-18; Acts 21:19; 1 Corinthians 11:5). They were, of course, women who received revelation from God for His people because they were called and gifted by the Holy Spirit. This woman was not called by God but promoted and placed herself in this role, for, as the Lord says, she *"calls herself a prophetess."*

Second, we see she was a teacher of some prominence, for Christ says, *"she teaches My bond-servants."* Clearly, she was not simply teaching a Sunday school class for children. It is unmistakable that she was having great influence with many people in the church in the role and function of a teacher. Evidently, one of the appeals to her teaching was that she claimed to have great insight and understanding, not merely of basic Christian doctrine, but of the spiritual realm so that she could make *"known the deep things of Satan"* (Revelation 2:24). Such *"things,"* of course, are fascinating to many. However, because of its very nature, it is an area that is filled with deception and falsehood, which is what this woman was actually teaching.

She was also a leader for, as the Lord says, she *"leads My bond-servants."* Undoubtedly, she was highly esteemed, being seen as an unusually spiritual and gifted person. She was even seen as "a spiritual mother" having close ties to a number in the church with such a degree of bonding that Christ calls these people *"her children"* (Revelation 2:23). Unquestionably, there was a great degree of love and loyalty by these people for her because of her leadership in their lives. Nonetheless, while she was a popular and powerful person in the church, she was a false teacher whom Christ says *"leads My bond-servants astray"* (Revelation 2:20). She was a false prophet–a wolf in sheep's clothing–and for this reason, Jesus calls her *"Jezebel"*- the name of the most notorious female false prophet in the Old Testament.

Spirits Speaking

In calling her *"Jezebel,"* the Lord is not only identifying her evil spiritual influence but also the name of the evil spirit or demon that is operating in and through her. Just as Jesus identified and named demons in His ministry on earth so they could be cast out (Mark 5:9; 9:25), even now as the risen, exalted, Lord of heaven He continues to identify and name the demon that is operating in and through this woman in the church in Thyatira. It is a spirit that can be called a "Jezebel spirit," and it was operating in her to such a degree and with such powerful influence that Jesus identifies her with it calling her *"Jezebel."* While this may seem strange to some, this is the real world of the Bible. It is the real world Jesus lives in, and it is the real world today.

The Bible shows us the real world is one in which spirits speak to and through people. For example, Christ gave assurance to His followers who are arrested and required to give testimony that *"it is not you who speak, but it is the Spirit of your Father who speaks in you"* (Matthew 10:20). This is the very thing that took place with Stephen, as Acts 6:10 says, *"But they were unable to cope with the wisdom and the Spirit with which he was speaking."* Paul writes that *"one speaking by the Spirit of God says, 'Jesus is Lord'"* (1 Corinthians 12:3). The Holy Spirit will speak to and through people to lead others to faith and obedience to Jesus as Lord whether it is through preaching, teaching, testifying in a court or in conversations.

While the Holy Spirit can speak through people, it is very important to realize that demons can also speak through people in the church to teach false doctrine and lead God's people astray. This is what Paul spoke of in 1 Timothy 4:11, writing, *"But the Spirit explicitly says that in later times some will fall away from the faith, paying attention to deceitful spirits and doctrines of demons."* The Holy Spirit, speaking through Paul, says that demons will speak to and through people and their teaching will result in people falling away from the faith, which is the purpose of these evil spirits.

It is because of this reality of spirits working in and speaking through people that the Scriptures caution in I John 4:1-3,

> *Beloved, do not believe every spirit, but test the spirits to see whether they are from God, because many false prophets have gone out into the world. ² By this you know the Spirit of God: every spirit that confesses that Jesus Christ has come in the flesh is from God; ³ and every spirit that does not confess Jesus is not from God; this is the spirit of the antichrist, of which you have heard that it is coming, and now it is already in the world.*

The word of God clearly shows us that evil, unclean spirits–or demons–can and do speak through people who have prominent and influential positions in a church. This is what was happening in Thyatira. A demon that can be named *"Jezebel"* was operating in and through this woman and in the lives of real believers, those whom Jesus called *"My bond-servants."* They were being deceived and led "*astray*" by her influence and her teaching was leading them into "*idolatry*" and "*sexual immorality.*" While they were His sheep, they were no longer following their Shepherd but had wandered away into sin.

They Won't, So Jesus Will

This woman was "the elephant in the room," and the church was not exercising church discipline to confront and deal with her. Jesus says they "*tolerate*" her. The root meaning of Greek word translated "*tolerate*" is "leave," and depending on its context it can also be translated "let alone, let be, permit, neglect, or disregard." That is the very thing this church was doing with this woman and her evil influence in this church. They were leaving her alone, letting her be, disregarding her, willfully permitting her to continue to cause the bad fruit of sinful behavior in the church. So Jesus Himself demonstrates the very thing He is telling them to do, and there are two things about how He deals with her sin that show us how to exercise church discipline.

Take Time

First, He exercised patience. He says in verse 21, "*I gave her time to repent, and she does not want to repent of her immorality.*" This is how God deals with people when they sin. He is patient and forbearing, giving us time to come to our senses and face the reality of our sin so that we will "*repent*" (Luke 15:17; 2 Timothy 2:25-26).

Repentance, which in the Hebrew language literally means "to turn around" and in Greek "to change one's mind," takes place when a person actually has a change of heart, turns away from and no longer commits their sinful deeds. That which is most critical is what is in a person's heart–they *want* to repent and obey Jesus as their Lord more than they want to continue living in their sin. When we stumble and fall into sin, the Lord will be "*compassionate and gracious, slow to anger, and abounding in lovingkindness and truth*" toward us (Exodus 34:6). He "*is patient,*" wanting us "*all to come to repentance*" (2 Peter 3:9). Graciously, He gives us time to repent. And just as He is patient with us when we sin against Him, we are to be gracious and patient with people when they sin against us and give them time to repent.

But the heartbreaking reality is that some, even many do not really want to repent and the evidence of this is made known over time. This is what the Lord said of "*the woman Jezebel,*" "*she does not want to repent*" (Revelation 2:21). After giving her sufficient time to "*bear fruit in keeping with repentance*" (Matthew 3:8), the lack of good fruit demonstrated she had not repented, and the reason she did not repent is that she did not "*want to repent.*" The lack of good fruit of her life revealed what was in actually in her heart.

Sometimes people "*tolerate*" and excuse the sinful behavior of people saying, "We don't really know what's in a person's heart." While to a certain degree this may be true, the Bible never states this, and this is not what Christ said. The Lord stated that a person's "*deeds*" make known what is in their heart. He said that what a person says can actually reveal what is in their heart "*for his mouth speaks from that which fills his heart*" (Luke 6:45). A number of times He said, "*You will know them by their fruits*" (Matthew 7:16, 20; 12:33). If people are given time to repent and don't, that's the fruit of their lives that reveals what's actually in their hearts.

Take the Right Steps

After graciously giving her time to repent, we see the second thing Jesus does to deal with this woman's sin, which is He exercises church discipline. There are steps the Lord has set forth for the process of church discipline when a person does not repent. These are recorded in Matthew 18:15-17:

> *If your brother sins, go and show him his fault in private; if he listens to you, you have won your brother. But if he does not listen to you, take one or two more with you, so that by the mouth of two or three witnesses every fact may be confirmed. ¹⁷ If he refuses to listen to them, tell it to the church; and if he refuses to listen even to the church, let him be to you as a Gentile and a tax collector.*

Every Christian and every church is to apply these steps in the process of church discipline when confronting a person who *"sins"* and does not repent. They are, first, *"in private,"* second, *"two or three,"* then third, *"the church."* One of the greatest failures among Christians is that they do not follow what the Lord Jesus has instructed us to do. Instead of first going to the person *"in private,"* they go to other people to complain, talk about and even attack that person behind their back. This is sinful behavior in itself.

Another problem is that people who have been hurt and carrying an offense from being sinned against may get *"two or three"* people to go with them but only to "be on their side" against the person. The only "side" believers are to be on is Christ's side, and His side is that of truth, love and mercy. It is the truth–*"every fact"*–that is to be *"confirmed"* in love and mercy so the person can be restored.

The Apostle Paul instructed the church in Galatia, *"if anyone is caught in any trespass, you who are spiritual, restore such a one in a spirit of gentleness; each one looking to yourself, so that you too will not be tempted"* (Galatians 6:1). The word *"spiritual"* does not necessarily mean a higher level of spirituality. It means those who are walking in the Spirit and not the flesh. They are to *"restore"* the person so that he or she is no longer walking in the flesh but in the Spirit. They are to do this by walking in the Spirit themselves as they bear the fruit of the Spirit, which is *"gentleness"* (Galatians 5:23). When this takes place, the church has *"won"* them (Matthew 15:15).

Why?

This brings us to that which is perhaps the most important thing about church discipline–the motive. What is to be our motive for going to a person so that they will deal with and repent of their sin? Why should we not *"tolerate"* sin but confront "the elephant in the room"?

There are actually a number of reasons. Leading the list is love–love for God, His church and the person who is sinning. This is the very thing the Lord says at the conclusion of all that He says to the seven churches, *"Those whom I love, I reprove and discipline"* (Revelation 3:19). We are to be like Christ and exercise discipline in love. Because we love our Lord, because we love the person who has sinned, and because we love the people who are being harmed by the sinful behavior, we are to follow the steps in the process of church discipline that Christ sets forth.

Church discipline is vital for the life and spiritual health of the church. Its purpose is to *"restore"* a person who has stumbled and to remove from the church *"the leaven"* of sin that is corrupting it. Yet of all these things, the ultimate motive to exercise church discipline is the glory and honor of the Lord Jesus Christ. It is so that His church can become like Him, living in His manifest presence and revealing His likeness.

What's the Difference?

The distinction between patience and the need for exercising church discipline is critical as we can see from what Christ has *"against"* the church in Thyatira. They were not being patient. Instead, they are wrongly tolerating and giving place, position and prestige to *"the woman Jezebel."* The church is a community, the body of Christ, and we live in relationships with one another. Because of this, a person who is unrepentant can and will have a harmful affect in a church as well as well as others in the body of Christ. The Lord does not want us to *"tolerate"* the elephant in the room.

It's Not that Easy

Confronting people about their sin is not easy, and there can be a number of reasons why this is difficult. Sometimes we may think, "Who am I to say anything" and, because of this, feel that we have no "right" to talk to them. The issue isn't who we are or aren't, or what right we have. It is what is right, for it is God's will for us to live righteously before Him.

Probably the greatest reason we have difficulty confronting a person about their sin is that we're simply afraid. We might be afraid that the person may react by saying we are "judgmental," "mean-spirited" or "intolerant," which would be a false accusation if we are acting in love like Christ. We can be afraid the person may not only reject what we say but reject us, and this would result in a break down in our relationship with that person, as well as with other people who have a loyalty to him or her. This might actually turn out to be true, but it is not our responsibility as to how a person reacts. It is our responsibility to do God's will. Or we might simply not want the person to feel bad or uncomfortable, which is often more about us feeling bad than the person feeling bad.

On the other hand, think about it this way: If your neighbor's house is on fire and causing the houses in the neighborhood to catch fire, would any of those reasons be valid or an excuse to not go and tell your neighbor their house is on fire and causing others to burn? "I will let his house burn, along with others because who am I to tell him." Or, "He will think I am judgmental, mean-spirited and intolerant, so I will just let his house keep on burning." What about, "He might not like what I tell him and it will break down my relationship with him"? And then there's, "It will make him feel bad." If we love them, we will tell them.

Revive Us Again!

One of the greatest revivals in the history of the church was the Reformation of the 16th century. At the core of what took place was that the Reformers confronted the false teaching and abuses taking place in the Roman Catholic Church. They became known as "Protestants" because they protested the sin in the church. During this time of great struggle, the Roman Catholic Church claimed it was the one true church and Protestants were heretics. Because of this, the Protestant leaders had to identify what the Bible says are "the marks of the true church." They identified three. First, right doctrine is preached and taught, which is the third characteristic of the kind of church Jesus wants–it holds to the truth of the word of God. Second, that the sacraments or ordinances of baptism and the Lord's Supper are correctly administered according to the word of God. And third, that church discipline is exercised. As we hear from what Jesus says to the church in Thyatira, this is an essential quality of the kind of church He wants–it is a church that exercises church discipline. May the Living Lord Jesus Christ, the Head of the church, gives us ears to hear what He is saying and the grace to love Him and those who are failing Him so that we will become more and more like Him.

Study Questions
Chapter 5

1. Have you ever experienced an "elephant in the room" problem? What happened?

2. What is the first declaration Jesus makes about Himself and why was it relevant for the church in Thyatira?

3. What does Deuteronomy 32:8 reveal about who *"the sons of God"* are and their purpose? What do you think about this?

4. What does the Greek word *"diamonion"* tell us about who Tyrimnos really was? Do you think this is a reality in our day?

5. What do the attributes of Jesus' eyes being like a flame of fire and His feet like burnished bronze reveal about Him? How is this relevant to you?

6. What are the five qualities in the church in Thyatira that Christ commends? Do you see these in your life and your church?
(1)
(2)
(3)
(4)
(5)

7. How would you describe the evil work of Jezebel—what influenced her and her influence in the church in Thyatira? Have you ever been in a church where something like this was taking place?

8. What two sins does Christ identify and why do they so often go together?
(1)
(2)

9. Tolerance is a major value in the Western culture. What is your response to Christ's criticism that the church in Thyatira tolerating the actions and influence of the woman He calls "*Jezebel*"?

10. What is the fourth quality of the kind of church Jesus wants? Has this been a characteristic of the church(es) you have attended? Do you want to be a part of a church that has this quality? Why or Why not?

11. What are the two ways godly and proper church discipline is exercised?
(1)
(2)

12. Following the example of Christ, how are believers to deal with sin in the church?

CHAPTER 6

SARDIS: IS REAL

Revelation 3:1-6

To the angel of the church in Sardis write: He who has the seven Spirits of God and the seven stars, says this: 'I know your deeds, that you have a name that you are alive, but you are dead. ² Wake up, and strengthen the things that remain, which are about to die; for I have not found your deeds completed in the sight of My God. ³ So remember what you have received and heard; and keep it, and repent. Therefore if you do not wake up, I will come like a thief, and you will not know at what hour I will come to you. ⁴ But you have a few names in Sardis who have not soiled their garments; and they will walk with Me in white, for they are worthy. ⁵ He who overcomes will thus be clothed in white garments; and I will not erase his name from the book of life, and I will confess his name before My Father and before His angels. ⁶ He who has an ear, let him hear what the Spirit says to the churches.

The Worst Thing that Could Ever Happen

These words directed to the church in Sardis may be the most severe ever spoken by the Lord Jesus Christ to a church. They give reason to ask one of the most solemn questions that can ever be asked: Of *all* the things that could ever happen to *all* the people who will *ever* live, what is *the worst possible thing* that could ever happen?

I am sure we can think of many dreadful things, such as the loss of a loved one, the loss of wealth, or the loss of health. Nonetheless, these are not the worst possible thing that could ever happen to a person because they are the loss of things in this world.

Worse than these is loss in the world to come–a person losing their soul. Jesus spoke of this saying, *"What will it profit a man if he gains the whole world and forfeits his soul?"* (Matthew 16:26). No one in this world can really imagine how horrible this will be. Most people "sell their soul" merely for a "piece of the action" in this world–fame, fortune, and, most of all, power. There have been a few people in history who actually aspired to gain and rule the world–emperors, dictators and military leaders such as Genghis Khan, Napoleon, and Hitler–but they failed. Yet even if it were possible to gain possession of *"the whole world,"* what good would it do if you lost your soul? Such a person will stand before the Lord Jesus Christ on the Day of Judgment and He will condemn them to an eternal existence separated from God being tormented in the fire of hell–they will have lost their soul (Matthew 5:22, 29, 20; 7:22; Romans 2:16). As bad as this will be for the most evil people who ever live, Jesus said this will happen not to a *"few"* but to *"many"* (Matthew 7:13-14). Losing all there is in this world cannot compare to losing your soul. Without doubt that will be the most tragic thing that will ever happen to any individual person. But is there anything that could possibly make this worse?

Most people believe in hell, and many tell others to go there all the time. Worse than this, how many know they are going to hell and speak of the certainty of it. How often do people say, "As sure as hell..."! Hell for them is certain–so sure and guaranteed that they testify to the truth of what they are saying by their affirming the certainty that they going are to hell, or at least some people are! And that will certainly be the most dreadful thing that will ever happen to them. Yet that's not the worst *possible* thing that could ever happen to a person.

The worst possible thing that could ever happen to a person is living your life in this world satisfied you are saved, confident you are a Christian, believing that when you die you will go to heaven, but then when you die and stand before Christ on the Day of Judgment you make the most dreadful discovery there could possibly be–you are not saved! You will come to the horrifying realization that you were not a real believer, that you were not a true follower of the Lord Jesus Christ, and you will hear the worst possible words that will ever be spoken to anyone coming from the lips of the Lord Jesus Christ, saying, *"Depart from Me you who practice lawlessness, I never knew you"* (Matthew 7:23). That is the worst possible thing that could ever happen to anybody. It is, in fact, what Jesus said will happen–believing you will go to heaven when you die but when you die you are condemned to spend eternity in hell.

How Many Will This Happen To?

What makes this so shocking is that Jesus said this will not happen to a few but to "*many.*" He declared,

> *Not everyone who says to Me, "Lord, Lord,"*
> *will enter the kingdom of heaven, but he who*
> *does the will of My Father who is in heaven*
> *will enter.* ²² *Many will say to Me on that day,*
> *"Lord, Lord, did we not prophesy in Your*
> *name, and in Your name cast out demons,*
> *and in Your name perform many miracles?"*
> ²³ *And then I will declare to them, "I never*
> *knew you; depart from Me, you who practice*
> *lawlessness, I never knew you"* (Matthew
> 7:21-23).

The Lord says there are "*many*" who believe they are going heaven, but are not. This means there are churches that have a few people, and others that are filled with people whose names are on the church roll but not on heaven's roll. They have an outward appearance of being alive but are spiritually dead. They have a head knowledge about Christ but not a heart relationship with Him. They are not real Christians.

This is what the Lord Jesus said was appallingly true of the church in the city of Sardis. And as we listen to what He says to this church, we can see the fifth quality of the kind of church Jesus wants–it is real.

The One Who Has the Seven Stars

As with all the churches, the Lord begins by highlighting His attributes that are relevant to the situation of the church, and He identifies two. He says He is the One "*Who has the seven Spirits of God and the seven stars*" (Revelation 3:1).

In the first chapter, John said that one of the prominent aspects of Christ's appearance was that "*in His right hand He held seven stars*" (Revelation 1:16). At the end of the chapter, the Lord revealed the meaning of the seven stars, saying, *"As for the mystery of the seven stars which you saw in My right hand, the seven stars are the angels of the seven churches"* (Revelation 1:20). What the Lord is emphasizing by saying *"He has the seven stars"* is that He is the overall guardian of the churches and one of the ways He does this is through the agency of guardian angels assigned to the churches. There are many things the Scriptures reveal about angels and their ministries, but here He emphasizes each church having an angel.

The relevance of this to the church in Sardis is that angels see and observe the life of every person. There is no such thing as "the right to privacy" in the real world revealed in the Scriptures. People may have secrets, but there is nothing secret before God. While angels are not visible to us, we are visible to them. This is alluded to in 1 Corinthians 11 where Paul gives the church instructions about how men and women are to outwardly express their submission to authority in the worship service in a culturally appropriate way and he says one of the reasons for this is *"because of the angels"* (1 Corinthians 11:10). This indicates angels are present in the worship service, see what is taking place and, because of this, know who is real and who is not. The reality of being in the presence of angels is dramatically stated later by Jesus to this church when He promises the true believer who overcomes, *"I will confess his name before My Father and before His angels"* (Revelation 3:5). While in the modern, secular Western world angels may seem to be a sentimental myth, the reality of angels and their presence was taken very seriously in church history. This is testified to in many ways–in paintings, in statues and by churches being named after angels such as Michael, of whom Scripture speaks as *"the great prince who stands guard over"* the people of Israel (Daniel 12:1).

The One Who Has the Seven Spirits

While the reality of angels and their presence in the church is significant, the most important thing is what Jesus states first, that He is the One *"Who has the seven Spirits of God."* This phrase does not mean there are seven distinct and different spirits that are *"of God."* It is a Hebrew way of speaking about the one Holy Spirit of God and the various ways His presence, power and gifts can be manifested.

The Biblical background for the phrase *"the seven Spirits of God"* is the prophecy of Isaiah concerning the coming Messiah, the One anointed with the fullness of the Spirit of God. Isaiah said,

> *Then a shoot will spring from the stem of Jesse, and a branch from his roots will bear fruit. ² The Spirit of the LORD will rest on Him, the spirit of wisdom and understanding, the spirit of counsel and strength, the spirit of knowledge and the fear of the Lord* (Isaiah 11:1–2).

Seven spirits are identified–*"the LORD," "wisdom," "understanding," "counsel," "strength," "knowledge,"* and *"the fear of the Lord."* These are all attributes *"of"* the One Holy Spirit. They are ways the Holy Spirit will manifest His presence and work in the life of the coming Messiah Who was and is the Lord Jesus Christ.

The number seven does not mean there are only seven ways the presence, power and gifts of the Holy Spirit can be manifested in and through Christ. Seven, being the symbolic number meaning complete, total or full, means that the Lord Jesus was anointed with the fullness of the Holy Spirit. He is the Messiah, the Christ, or as John the

Baptist spoke of Him saying that the Father gives Him *"the Spirit without measure"* (John 3:34). Thus, when Jesus says He *"has the seven Spirits of God"* He is affirming He is the Christ, the Anointed of God functioning in and fulfilling His God-given role as the ruler and king of God's people.

Not only this, in saying He *"has the seven Spirits of God,"* the Lord Jesus makes known He is the source from Whom and through Whom the Holy Spirit is given to His people. On the night before He died for our sins, He spoke a great deal about the Holy Spirit and that He would send the Holy Spirit to His disciples (John 14:26; 15:26; 16:7-15). After He died, rose from the dead and ascended to the Father's right hand in heaven, He poured forth the Holy Spirit upon those gathered in the Upper Room on the day of Pentecost. The Apostle Peter, being himself filled, transformed and empowered by the Holy Spirit, declared on that day the truth that the Holy Spirit is given by the Lord Jesus, saying, *"Therefore having been exalted to the right hand of God, and having received from the Father the promise of the Holy Spirit, He has poured forth this which you both see and hear"* (Acts 2:33). The Lord Jesus is the One Who *"has the seven Spirits of God"* and gives the Holy Spirit to His people to transform our lives. And just as *"the seven Spirits"* does not mean there are only seven ways the Spirit will work in the Lord Jesus, so also there many ways in which He will manifest His empowering presence in our lives.

The relevance of this to the church in Sardis is that the Holy Spirit is *"the Spirit of truth"* (John 14:17) and *"leads"* true disciples of Christ to the truth. In other words, the Holy Spirit *"leads"* us to that which is real–real about God, and real about their relationship with God (John 16:13; Romans 8:14). As John wrote in his first letter,

> *As for you, the anointing which you received
> from Him abides in you, and you have no need
> for anyone to teach you; but as His anointing
> teaches you about all things, and is true and
> is not a lie, and just as it has taught you, you
> abide in Him* (1 John 2:27).

The church in Sardis was not doing this. They desperately needed to actually and authentically receive the empowering presence of the Holy Spirit to become and live as real followers of the Lord Jesus Christ.

Like a Corpse in a Funeral Home

The actual spiritual state of the church is revealed by what Jesus says He knows about them. As with the four previous churches, He tells this church of His intimate knowledge of them and every member of the church. We know from what He said to the other churches that He knows the spiritual condition of their lives, the spiritual atmosphere of the city they live in, their struggles and sufferings, and that He knows each one by name. But whereas with the previous churches there were certain things He found in the church that He commends, the desperate situation of the church in Sardis is disclosed by the fact that He does not give them a single word of commendation!

Jesus quickly gets to the point saying, "*I know your deeds, that you have a name that you are alive, but you are dead*" (Revelation 3:1). Like a coroner who has examined a lifeless corpse and found there is no breath, pulse or heartbeat and pronounces it "dead," the Lord crisply and uncompromisingly gives His pronouncement, "*you are dead*" (Revelation 3:1). "*Dead*"! There is nothing worse that could be said to a church by the Living Lord Jesus Christ than that they are dead–spiritually dead.

He says, "*You have a name that you are alive, but you are dead.*" Like a body lying in a coffin in a funeral home during a "viewing" that has been made to look alive, and people walk by and comment about "how good he looks," the great deception in the hearts of these hypocrites in Sardis is that they believe that because they look good to people they are "*alive*" to God. But they are "*dead.*"

The Lord Jesus is very aware they "*have a name.*" He acknowledges their reputation and image–their "press release"–as it appears outwardly to people and, perhaps even to other churches. They are the place to be, the church where it is happening, the church of high esteem, for what could be more highly esteemed for a church than that it is said to be "*alive.*" But they aren't. They are not what they appear to be. They are not real.

Undoubtedly, this church had an impressive past that gave them this reputation, but what they had become was altogether different. Like a classic car that was once fast and powerful but ran out of gas and coasted until it came to a dead stop, this church puttered along on its past prestige, ran out of power, coasted and died. And contrary to the clichés of the world that "image is everything" and "perception is reality," the only perception that matters is the reality of the Lord Jesus Christ and His judgment. And His assessment of this church is that they are phonies.

According to the Lord Jesus, the church in Sardis was the first church in history that was literally full of "nominal" Christians. The word "nominal" means "in name" and a "nominal Christian" is a person who professes to be Christian but is not. They were, as Jude described them, "*clouds without rain,*" "*trees without fruit*" (Jude 12). This church was living out of the memory of their past achievements but not the present manifestation of the life-giving power of the Holy Spirit. Over the front door of the church could be placed the ancient words "*Ichabod*" which means "no glory" or "the glory has departed" (1 Samuel 4:21).

Rotten Roots

Jesus said, "*I know your deeds*" which is the fruit of their lives. From what He tells the church to do, we can establish the root causes of the bad fruit of this nominal church. More importantly, by recognizing the rotten roots we can then identify the corresponding qualities that are the roots of the good fruit of a church that is spiritually alive and real. Christ digs up five rotten roots, and four of them are exposed in verse 2 when He says, "*Wake up, and strengthen the things that remain, which are about to die; for I have not found your deeds completed in the sight of My God*" (Revelation 3:2).

The Trumpet Sounds

Like a bugler blowing his trumpet sounding reveille, Christ's first call is "*Wake up.*" The Greek word is "*gregoreo,*" from which we get the name "Gregory," and its primary meaning is "to watch." To keep watch, one must be awake and alert. Jesus is not merely telling these people who are spiritually asleep to "wipe the sleep from their eyes." He is telling them to become spiritually alert and keep watch.

What is so significant about this in the history of the city of Sardis is that it was situated on a mountainside with a cliff 1,500 feet high on one side and walls surrounding the rest of the city. Because of this, the city was believed to be an impregnable fortress that was impossible for its enemies to enter and conquer. However, its enemies gained access into the city and conquered it, not once but two times! The reason was because the watchmen who guarded the city fell asleep. They were not awake, they were not alert, they were not watching, and they paid the price. The church in Sardis was now a defeated and dead church because they were not spiritually awake, alert and watching.

What does it mean to be awake and watching? Scripture uses this metaphor for prayer. In Isaiah 62:6-7, God says,

> *On your walls, O Jerusalem, I have appointed watchmen; all day and all night they will never keep silent. You who remind the Lord, take no rest for yourselves; ⁷ and give Him no rest until He establishes and makes Jerusalem a praise in the earth.*

"*Jerusalem*" can be spiritually applied to the church (Galatians 4:26; Hebrews 12:22), and on the walls of the church, which are the places of protection, are watchmen who are to stand alert praying. They are "*to never keep silent,*" which means they are to "*pray without ceasing*" (1 Thessalonians 5:17).

Perhaps the most poignant place where this metaphor is used of prayer is when the Lord Jesus is in the garden of Gethsemane aware that He is about to be betrayed, arrested and then suffer and die, and He asks His disciples to "*watch and pray*" with Him (Matthew 26:41). But they did not and fell asleep.

People who are spiritually alive and awake pray. Like the disciples gathered in the Upper Room before Pentecost, they are "*continually devoting themselves to prayer*" (Acts 1:14; Romans 12:12). People and churches that are spiritually dead do not pray, that is, really pray. They will have formal, ritualistic, religious prayers, but not prayer that comes from real heart relationship with

God. Sardis was a spiritually dead church, and the first and foremost evidence of it was that it was a church without prayer. Because of this, Jesus tells them to "*Wake up.*"

Scripture and church history record that prayer is the first thing that ignites revival and brings a church back to life. When Christians are real, and when their church is real, they will be spiritually awake and alive because their lives will be rooted in real relationship with God that results from real prayer.

Unplugged From the Power

Like the blast of a canon across the bow of a ship, Christ's next salvo is "*strengthen what remains.*" The second characteristic of a church that is not real is that it is spiritually weak and it doesn't know it. Resting on the reputation of their "*name,*" they didn't realize how weak they were spiritually, and even the little strength they had was waning! This church was in real trouble because the vast majority of the people in it were not connected to the real power.

This is the kind of church that Paul warned about in the last letter of his life, 2 Timothy, saying, "*But realize this, that in the last days difficult times will come*" (2 Timothy 3:1). The New Testament speaks of "*the last days*" as beginning with Christ's death, resurrection, ascension and outpouring of the Holy Spirit to give His church power to live for Him and manifest His presence (Acts 2:17; Hebrew 2:1). Paul goes on in 2 Timothy to list things that will happen during this time in history and he culminates it all in verse 5 saying people will be "*holding to a form of godliness although they have denied its power.*" Like an electric toaster that's unplugged from the power outlet, the bread can go into the slots but will not be toasted because there is no radiating heat, so these churches will go through the motions of worship but no one's life is changed. They are not plugged into the power, and even deny it. This is what was happening in Sardis.

Real Christianity is all about power–the power of God to manifest His kingdom and transform lives. Jesus lived His life and ministered in the power of the Holy Spirit (Luke 4:14, 18). He promised His disciples, "*You will receive power when the Holy Spirit has come upon you*" (Acts 1:8). Paul wrote, "*For the kingdom of God does not consist in words but in power*" (1 Corinthians 4:20). And to Timothy he wrote, "*God has not given us a spirit of timidity, but of power*" (2 Timothy 1:7). Where does the real power of real relationship with God come from? It comes from the Holy Spirit. It is for this reason Paul told the Ephesian church he was praying for them "*that God would grant you, according to the riches of His glory, to be strengthened with power through His Spirit in the inner man*" (Ephesians 3:16).

Real spiritual life and power come from the Holy Spirit. Everything we do–our worship, our walk, our work, our witness and our warfare–is to be in the power of the Holy Spirit. But the church in Sardis was spiritually dead because people in the church had closed their hearts and were unplugged from the power of the Holy Spirit. The tragedy is that this is the kind of church that too many people experience today. Because of this, they think that is all there is to Christianity–a weak, powerless religion that makes no difference in people's lives. They go through outward religious motions but don't experience the reality of the transforming power of God in their lives. Because these churches are not real and experiencing the real power of the Holy Spirit, young people who grow up in these congregations leave the church. They have been "vaccinated" from the living Christ because they experienced a dead, diseased form of Christianity and have built an immunity that prevents them from being "infected" by the real thing. They are like the tragic generation described in Judges 2:10, *"There arose another generation after them who did not know the Lord, nor yet the work which He had done for Israel."*

A church that is real is alive because it is rooted in real relationship with Christ that results from prayer that brings the power of the Holy Spirit. When people live in the power of the Holy Spirit, they will encounter real problems but they will have real spiritual strength to live for Christ and be transformed to become like Him.

A Cruise Ship

The third characteristic of a dead church is heard in Jesus words *"for I have not found your works completed"* (Revelation 3:2). The Greek word translated *"completed"* literally means "full or fill." Like a cook serving a half-baked meal, a farmer who plowed but did not plant, or a painter who put on the primer but not the paint, Jesus says they only partially completed their tasks and assignments. Their work is inadequate and, because of this, unacceptable.

Sadly, this happens too frequently in churches. People volunteer for a job or are even ordained to an office in their church for a specific role and responsibility such as elder or deacon and then fail to "show up." They joined the team, put on the uniform but quit in the middle of the game. They are like the man who became a small group leader and quit because he was "burned out"–after two meetings!

Why does this happen? Why don't people complete the job given to them? It's because they are complacent and not really committed. They don't have hearts that are passionate about living for Christ, serving Him and advancing His kingdom.

The word of God tells us, "*we are His workmanship, created in Christ Jesus for good works, which God prepared beforehand so that we would walk in them*" (Ephesians 2:10). Because of this, we are told, "*Whatever you do, do your work heartily*–with all your heart, with passion–*as for the Lord rather than men*" (Colossians 3:23). When people have a passion for what they do, they want to accomplish the goal to fulfill the work, and to do it with excellence. They work "*heartily*" to complete the task because they want to succeed. This is true in all areas of life. The greatest example of this is the Lord Jesus Christ Who, at the end of His life and ministry, prayed to the Father, saying, "*I glorified You on the earth, having accomplished the work which You have given Me to do*" (John 17:4).

The church in Sardis was not real because it was filled with people simply going though the motions. Instead of the church being like a battleship, it was a cruise ship, with passengers on board who were just along for the ride. They were spiritually complacent, without passion for the purpose of God, without a heart for Christ and His kingdom, and so that they didn't work "*heartily*" for the glory of God. A church that is real, a church that is alive because it is rooted in real relationship with God that results in prayer that brings the power of the Holy Spirit has a holy passion to accomplish their work for Christ with excellence. They do this because, like Christ, they are living for the glory of God.

The Wrong Perspective

Insight into the fourth characteristic of a dead church is seen in the closing phrase of verse 2 where Christ exposes the basic motive in their hearts that determines how they make their decisions. They are the words *"in the sight of My God."* These words reveal the perspective from which Jesus lives His life. What is the governing principle in His heart for how He makes His decisions and chooses His actions? It is that He is utterly aware that there is absolutely nothing He does that is not seen by God, whether it is His outward actions or the inward thoughts and attitudes of His heart. He lives His life in this reality because it is reality. He lives His life from the perspective that God sees and knows everything and we will give account to God for all that we do. As the book of Hebrews says, *"There is no creature hidden from His sight, but all things are open and laid bare to the eyes of Him with whom we have to do"* (Hebrews 4:13). It is from this perspective that every real believer in the Lord Jesus Christ is to live their life–with the absolute awareness that everything we do, everything we think, everything we are is seen and known by God. Knowing and believing this, we will *"walk in the light as He Himself is in the light* (1 John 1:7), and we will be real.

But phony, fake and counterfeit Christians are not living their lives *"in the sight of God"*–to be seen by God, to be pleasing to God, for the glory of God. The primary motive and standard for decisions in their hearts is people and what people think. Their decisions are made from the perspective of being seen by people and, most of all, being approved and esteemed by people. That is the motive that controls their thoughts, emotions and attitudes, and it is the rotten root that brings forth the bad fruit of their actions and deeds.

This is the very thing Jesus exposed about the most notorious religious phonies in history, the scribes and Pharisees, who were His supreme opponents. Probably the premier place we see Jesus doing this is in the 23rd chapter of the gospel of Matthew. It compiles a catalogue of denunciations by the Lord Jesus of the scribes and

Pharisees whom He continuously called *"hypocrites."* He exposes the motive of their hearts that led to their religious hypocrisy, saying, *"They do all their deeds to be noticed by men"* (Matthew 23:5). This is the rotten root of religion that is not real–professing to love God but living for the praise of people. Because of this, Jesus denounced them for their worthless worship and hollow holiness saying, *"Woe to you, scribes and Pharisees, hypocrites! For you are like whitewashed tombs which on the outside appear beautiful, but inside they are full of dead men's bones and all uncleanness"* (Matthew 23:27).

Most Christians have no problem with Jesus saying such a thing to the scribes and Pharisees who were His greatest opponents and engineered His death. Yet how many can imagine Christ saying this to a church, to those who claim to be His followers? But that is the very thing He does with the church of Sardis. They have an outward façade of a *"name"* that appears to people to be *"alive" "but inside they are full of dead men's bones."* The root reason is because the basic motive in their hearts was that they are not living their lives in the sight of God and for His glory but in the sight of men and for their praise.

Two enormously important words of Christ reveal the root motivation in the heart of a person who lives for the glory of God. They are *"My God."* He does not merely live in the sight of God. He lives *"in the sight of My God."* These are the words of covenant commitment to God (Genesis 17:7 Ruth 1:16). These are the words the Lord Jesus spoke to Mary Magdalene immediately after He rose from the dead when He said, *"I ascend to My Father and your Father, and My God and your God"* (John 20:17). These are the words that reveal Jesus has a heart relationship with the Father, a real relationship with God, a heart passion and commitment to His Father and God. These words reveal the perspective from which we are to live our lives which is, as the Latin phrase *Coram Deo* expressed it, in the presence of God.

A church that is real is filled with people who have a real relationship with God because they have hearts that are born of the Spirit. Having a real heart relationship with God, they live their lives in the sight of God and from His perspective. Because of this, all their thoughts, attitudes and actions are motivated for the glory of God. They fulfill what Jesus said is the greatest commandment, which is to *"love the Lord your God with all your heart"* (Matthew 22:36-37).

Inward Pollution

The fifth rotten root that Jesus digs up in this spiritually dead church is that it is not pure but instead polluted by the world. Jesus speaks of this in verse 4 where, addressing the remnant in the church who are still alive, He says, *"But you have a few names in Sardis who have not soiled their garments but they will walk with me for they are worthy."* *"Garments"* is a Biblical metaphor for a person's life and lifestyle because it is what a person "puts on and wears" as they live their lives in the world. The vast majority of this church had *"soiled garments."* They are people whose lives are spiritually polluted because of their involvement and participation in the things of this world that are spiritually unholy and morally corrupt. Like the scribes and Pharisees Jesus denounced, *"inside they are full of dead men's bones and all uncleanness"* (Matthew 23:27).

There are many admonitions and warnings in Scripture to not be spiritually *"soiled"* and all the major writers of the New Testament speak to this in one way or another. Quoting the Old Testament, Paul told the Corinthians,

> *For we are the temple of the living God; just as God said, "I will dwell in them and walk among them; and I will be their God, and they shall be My people."* [17] *Therefore, "come out from their midst and be separate," says the Lord. "And do not touch what is unclean"* (2 Corinthians 6:16-17).

The writer of Hebrews said, "*Pursue peace with all men, and the sanctification without which no one will see the Lord*" (Hebrews 12:14). James warned,

> *You adulteresses, do you not know that friendship with the world is hostility toward God? Therefore whoever wishes to be a friend of the world makes himself an enemy of God.* [5] *Or do you think that the Scripture speaks to no purpose: "He jealously desires the Spirit which He has made to dwell in us"?* (James 4:4-5).

Peter, quoting the foundational ethical command in the Old Testament said,

> *As obedient children, do not be conformed to the former lusts which were yours in your ignorance,* [15] *but like the Holy One who called you, be holy yourselves also in all your behavior;* [16] *because it is written, "You shall be holy, for I am holy"* (1 Peter 1:14–16).

And John wrote,

> *Do not love the world nor the things in the world. If anyone loves the world, the love of*

> the Father is not in him. [16] *For all that is in the world, the lust of the flesh and the lust of the eyes and the boastful pride of life, is not from the Father, but is from the world. [17] The world is passing away, and also its lusts; but the one who does the will of God lives forever* (1 John 2:15-17).

The Lord Jesus is *"the One Who has the seven Spirits"* and His will for His church is to be filled with the manifest presence of the Holy Spirit. In order for this to take place, His people must live holy lives, lives that are set apart to Him and lived according to His will.

A church that is not real and spiritually dead is one filled with people who, while being outwardly pious, are inwardly polluted. They betray their profession of faith in Christ by their involvement and participation in the immoral ways of the world. Because of their unholy lives, the Holy Spirit withdraws His manifest presence. They will *"grieve"* the Holy Spirit (Ephesians 4:30) and *"quench"* or put out the fire of His manifest presence (1 Thessalonians 5:19). This was the culture of the church of Sardis.

The Autopsy

In these austere words to the church in Sardis, Christ revealed the rotten roots of a dead church. It is a church without prayer, without power, without passion, without perspective, and without purity, and because of this without His presence. The most dreadful thing about this dark tragedy is that it is a church filled with people who are hoodwinked by the worst deception there can be. They believe they are going to heaven when they die but they aren't. This is because they aren't real.

Nevertheless by taking the autopsy of this church, we can identify the qualities of a church that is alive. We can know the good roots that bring good fruit. It is, first of all, a church that is awake, alert and watching because it is devoted to prayer. It is a church that is strong because it is plugged into the power of the Holy Spirit. It is a church that accomplishes its work because it is passionate for the glory of God. It is a church that is living in the sight of and the light of God's presence because it has the right perspective on life. And it is a church that is filled with the manifest presence of the Holy Spirit because it is spiritually pure. When these qualities are alive and flourish in a church, it will be the kind of church Jesus wants because it is real.

Study Questions
Chapter 6

1. What does the author say is the worse thing that could ever happen? Do you believe this will actually happen? Do you think it could happen to you? Why or why not?

2. What is the fifth quality of the kind of church Jesus wants? What does this mean to you?

3. What two attributes of Himself does Christ highlight for the church in Sardis and what do they mean to you?
(1)
(2)

4. Have you ever done anything in secret that you didn't want anyone to know about? How much does being aware that God knows everything influence your life?

5. How is the church in Sardis different from all the previous churches Jesus has addressed?

6. How does Christ's assessment of the church in Sardis differ from that of people? How important is this difference?

7. What does it mean to be spiritually awake and watching? Is this true of your life and your church?

8. How would you describe a church that has real spiritual life and power? What is essential to have spiritual power?

9. What is your response to Christ finding the work of people in the church unacceptable?

10. Why are the two words *"My God"* so significant?

11. How much are you aware of the reality of being spiritually polluted? How does knowing this and its effect on your relationship with Christ impact your walk with Him?

12. What are the good roots that bring forth good fruit in a church that is real? Do you see these in your life and church?
(1)
(2)
(3)
(4)
(5)

CHAPTER 7

PHILDELPHIA: FULFILLS ITS ASSIGNMENT

Revelation 3:7-13

And to the angel of the church in Philadelphia write: He who is holy, who is true, who has the key of David, who opens and no one will shut, and who shuts and no one opens, says this: ⁸"I know your deeds. Behold, I have put before you an open door which no one can shut, because you have a little power, and have kept My word, and have not denied My name. ⁹Behold, I will cause those of the synagogue of Satan, who say that they are Jews and are not, but lie—I will make them come and bow down at your feet, and make them know that I have loved you. ¹⁰Because you have kept the word of My perseverance, I also will keep you from the hour of testing, that hour which is about to come upon the whole world, to test those who dwell on the earth. ¹¹I am coming quickly; hold fast what you have, so that no one will take your crown. ¹²He who overcomes, I will make him a pillar in the temple of My God, and he will not go out from it anymore; and I will write on him the name of My God, and the name of the city of My God, the new Jerusalem, which comes down out of heaven from My God, and My new name.

¹³ *He who has an ear, let him hear what the Spirit says to the churches."*

The Ceremony of the Keys

I t is the oldest, continuously running ceremony in the world. It began 700 years ago, and has been held every single night without exception from the very first day it was instituted. It is called *The Ceremony of the Keys*.

   The Ceremony of the Keys is held at the Tower of London, the historic fortress castle in the city of London, England. Construction of the Tower began in 1078 under William the Conqueror. It was the royal palace and fortress of the ruling monarchs of England, and today is the home of the priceless Crown Jewels of England. What the ceremony involves is the formal locking of the gates of the walls around the Tower of London with the keys that are the possession of the reigning monarch of England who today is Queen Elizabeth. What happens is that at exactly 8 minutes before 10 at night, a guard called the Chief Yeoman Warder, wearing the uniform of his ancient office, comes out carrying a lantern with a lit candle in one hand and in the other hand the royal keys of the gates to the Tower of London. He then meets four members of the Tower of London Guard who provide the military escort for the keys throughout the ceremony as he locks the gates. As he makes his rounds, all the guards and sentries on duty salute the keys as they pass, and he then returns to go back into the Tower. As he approaches, a sentry guard awaits him and challenges him to identify himself, saying, "Halt! Who comes there?" The Chief Warder declares, "The Keys," to which the sentry responds, "Whose keys?" He identifies the royal keys stating, "Queen Elizabeth's Keys." The sentry then permits entrance saying, "Pass Queen Elizabeth's Keys. All's well." The keys travel under the archway and into the fortress and halt at the foot of stairs where, at the top of the stairs, stand other guards. The officer in charge here gives the command to the guard and the escort to present arms saluting the keys while the Chief Yeoman Warder raises his hat in the air and proclaims, "God preserve Queen Elizabeth." The guards answer, "Amen," and immediately, at that second, the clock chimes 10:00 PM and the keys are carried into the Tower for safekeeping as the last post of the bugle sounds.

Not All Keys Are the Same

A key is an instrument that locks and unlocks a door or gate so that it can be opened and someone can enter or closed so someone will not be able to pass through. There are countless numbers of keys in the world, and they vary in significance and importance. Some keys are worthless because no one knows the door they open and close, or there no longer is a door for them to open and close. Other keys no longer open or close anything but have sentimental value because, for whatever reason, they mean something to the person who possesses them. And then there are certain keys that have the highest value because of who owns the key and what door it opens and closes. Keys not only have power to open and close doors, they can also be a symbol that represents the office and authority of the one who possesses them.

The Ceremony of the Keys demonstrates the enormous significance of the keys of the reigning monarch of England for they open and close the gates to the Tower of London. Yet while those keys are among the most valuable on earth, there is a key that is of far greater value, importance and worth than any here on earth. It is the key the Lord Jesus Christ now possesses, and He speaks of this key in His words addressed to the sixth church, the church of

Philadelphia. And, pardon the pun, it is the key to understanding the next quality and characteristic of the kind of church Jesus wants–it fulfills its assignment.

The Holy One

Once again, the risen Lord Jesus Christ begins by identifying His attributes and titles that are relevant to the life and situation of the church in Philadelphia, and He highlights three. He starts with the words *"He who is holy."* The Greek is absolute and literally says *"the holy."* This can be translated *"He who is Holy,"* but more accurately *"the Holy"* or *"the Holy One."*

Holy is one of the most important concepts there is in the Bible, as well as in other religions that have a reverence for things that are sacred. The most glorious attribute of God is that He is holy. Throughout the Scriptures, God is revealed and identified as being holy. When we are given a glimpse in Scripture of the worship of God in heaven, we are told that *"day and night they do not cease to say, 'Holy, Holy, Holy is the Lord God, the Almighty, Who was and Who is and Who is to come'"* (Revelation 4:8). We see this same reverent worship spoken of by the prophet Isaiah who wrote of his vision of God when He was taken into heaven and *"saw the LORD"* and the angelic beings calling out, *"Holy, Holy, Holy is the LORD of hosts, the earth is full of His glory"* (Isaiah 6:1-3). While God has many glorious attributes, those in heaven are not saying, "Love, Love, Love," "Compassion, Compassion, Compassion," or "Righteous, Righteous, Righteous." They never stop–in fact they cannot stop–declaring this overarching, overwhelming, and all-inclusive attribute of God that He is holy. His love is holy. His compassion is holy. His righteousness is holy, because He is holy.

The basic meaning of *"holy"* is "set apart," but it resonates with connotations and implications. God is holy, first of all, in regard to Who He is in and of Himself, and second, in regard to what He does.

The primary meaning of God being holy reveals Who He is in His essential nature. He is set apart in the totality of His Being from everything else that exists and, because of this, nothing else is like Him. He is, in the essence and substance of His being, absolutely different from everything else. He is God, and nothing else is. He is eternally self-existing, and nothing else is. He is the sovereign ruler over everything, and nothing else is. When all the creatures in heaven worship Him as *"Holy, Holy, Holy,"* they are affirming the reality that He alone is God and nothing else is. He is Who He is and nothing else is like Him.

Being holy, everything He does is holy. Sometimes people say that absolutely nothing is impossible for God to do. This is not true. God cannot sin. God cannot change. To say that God cannot sin is to affirm in negative terms what God does in the positive sense–He only does what is holy. Everything He does is holy, whether it is to act in love and grace to save a sinner or to act righteously and justly to condemn one to hell.

God is holy and cannot sin, and when a person is encounters the awesome reality of His holiness, they can become dreadfully aware of their own sinfulness. It was when Isaiah saw the absolute holiness of God that he instantly became conscious of his own sinful corruption and cried out, *"Woe is me, for I am ruined! Because I am a man of unclean lips, and I live among a people of unclean lips"* (Isaiah 6:5; see also Luke 5:8).

It is because God is holy that He is *"the Holy One."* It is undoubtedly because of his life-changing encounter with God that the favorite designation of God by the prophet Isaiah was *"the Holy One of Israel."* He used this title 23 times (Isaiah 5:19, 24; et al). Most significantly, Isaiah used the absolute *"Holy One"* two times. Directly quoting God, he wrote, *"'To whom then will you liken Me that I would be his equal?' says the Holy One"* (Isaiah 40:25). Again he directly quotes God, *"'I am the LORD, your Holy One, the Creator of Israel, your King"* (Isaiah 43:15).

Human beings, as well as other creatures, are not holy in and of themselves. They become holy when they are set apart to become God's possession in order to be in God's manifest presence and to serve His purpose. They are made holy because of their relationship to God. But God alone is holy in the essence of His being.

When Jesus declares to the church in Philadelphia that He is not merely "holy" but *"the Holy One,"* He is making the most profound claim about Himself, and this title applies to Him in three ways. Most amazing of all, He is declaring He is the God Who revealed Himself in the Scriptures of the Old Testament. No one is like God or His equal. With this title Jesus reveals His divine nature–He is God, God the Son, the second Person of the Trinity. Second, according to His human nature, He is *"the Holy One"* Who was uniquely set apart from all other human beings to become God's possession in order to be in God's manifest presence and to fulfill God's purpose for His life. This began with His incarnation when He took human nature to Himself, two natures united in one Person. Then at His baptism in water, He was anointed and empowered with the fullness of the Holy Spirit to fulfill God's purpose for His life. This, by the way, is what the demons recognized so that they called Him *"the Holy One of God"* (Mark 1:24; Luke 4;34). Further still, third, according to both His divine and human natures, He is righteous and without sin. He is *"the Holy One"* and no one is like Him.

The True One

The second attribute Christ makes known about Himself is that He is the one *"who is true."* Here again, the Greek is absolute and literally says *"the true."* It can be translated *"the True One."*

Depending on the Hebrew or Greek connotations, there is a difference of implied meaning of *"true."* The Greek sense of *"the true"* is how Western culture primarily understands the meaning of the word. It has the basic idea of the state of being and what is. What is true is that which is factual, actual, and corresponds to reality in contrast to that which is false, fake, and phony. This connotation is applied to the situation in Philadelphia where Jesus goes on to speak of the ethnic Jewish people in Philadelphia who were from *"the synagogue of Satan, who say they are Jews and are not, but lie"* (Revelation 3:9). Christ is saying these Jews are not true Jews *"but lie"* about what their actual spiritual nature is. Their worship is not, as Jesus told the Samaritan woman, the kind the Father seeks, which is *"in Spirit and truth"* (John 4:23-24).

In saying He is *"the True One"* Jesus affirms He is Who He says He is, that there is nothing false, deceptive, crooked or shadowy in Him. He is, in fact, what He said He is, *"the truth"* (John 14:6). He is the One Who reveals what is true, what is actual, and what corresponds to reality in regard to God, the world, salvation, and relationship with God and one another.

The Hebrew concept of true, in contrast to the Greek notion of a state of being, understands the word as continuous action–something continues to be true because it does not vary, distort, diverge or fail. Because of this, the actions are faithful. Jesus is *"the true One"* because He was faithful to the will and purpose of God during His earthly life and ministry, and He will always be faithful.

This attribute that He is *"the True One"* is so prominent to Who Christ is and what He does that, in the depiction of Him at His Second Coming recorded in chapter 19 of the book of Revelation, He is *"called Faithful and True"* (Revelation 19:11).

The Lord stresses the two attributes that He is *"the Holy One"* and *"the True One"* because they apply to the church in Philadelphia in two ways. First of all, He wants them to know and believe He can be trusted and relied upon in and through every situation and circumstance in life because He is God and He is faithful. He will not fail them because He cannot fail them. That is Who He is and that is what He does. Even if no one else will be with them He will for He has promised *"I will be with you always"* (Matthew 28:20). This is what Paul personally testified to when he was arrested and brought to trial. He wrote, *"At my first defense no one supported me, but all deserted me; may it not be counted against them. 17 But the Lord stood with me and strengthened me"* (2 Timothy 4:16-17).

The second thing He wants is for them to be like Him as He was in His human nature. He wants them to be holy-set apart to God, filled with the Holy Spirit, living in the manifest presence of God, and fulfilling God's purpose for their lives. He wants them to be true and faithful to God's will and the assignment He will give them.

The Key of David

These two attributes are foundational to the third attribute of the Lord, which is that He *"has the key of David, who opens and no one will shut, and who shuts and no one opens."* As with previous churches, Jesus refers to something in the Old Testament and applies it to this church now in the New Testament period of history.

The background of this statement that He is the one *"who has the key of David"* is Isaiah 22:15-25. In this passage, God speaks through the prophet Isaiah to a man named Shebna who is identified as *"the steward in charge of the royal household"* (Isaiah 22:15). This does not mean he was like an attendant on an airplane or cruise ship, or even the butler in a stately manor house. The *"royal household"* refers to the kingdom of David and the government of God over His people.

One of the greatest covenant promises God ever made was with David and his house. He said He would give David and his sons the kingdom, which means rule over His people, so that through them God's will and purposes would be done on earth. Shebna was the steward, meaning he was one of the highest-ranking officials in the government of the kingdom of Judah, perhaps even second to the king. As such he was given the highest level of authority and power under the king in the house of David. He was assigned with responsibility to faithfully execute the affairs of the kingdom according to the will and purpose of God. But, as the passage in Isaiah 22 goes on to say, he abused this powerful office. He used it for his own worldly, self-interested desires, pursuing wealth, with all of its praise from people and earthly glory. He was not faithful to fulfill the assignment God had providentially entrusted to him.

Because of this, the Lord spoke a word of judgment against Shebna through the prophet Isaiah. His word was that He would replace him with another man, a man named Eliakim, who would be faithful to God, His will and purpose. He said,

> *I will depose you from your office, and I will pull you down from your station.* [20]
> *Then it will come about in that day, that I*

will summon My servant Eliakim the son of Hilkiah, 21 and I will clothe him with your tunic and tie your sash securely about him. I will entrust him with your authority, and he will become a father to the inhabitants of Jerusalem and to the house of Judah. 22 Then I will set the key of the house of David on his shoulder, when he opens no one will shut, when he shuts no one will open (Isaiah 22:19-22).

God says that He will take away *"the key of the house of David"* from Shebna and give it to Eliakim. This key was the symbol of the high-ranking office of *"the steward in charge of the royal household,"* the one assigned with the oversight, administration and execution of the affairs of the kingdom. It would be placed *"on his shoulder,"* which means he was to assume and carry the responsibility of this office. As the High Priest in his priestly responsibility had the ephod upon which were placed the shoulder pieces with two stones engraved with the names of the sons of Israel so that he would bear their names before the LORD (Exodus 28:12), so Eliakim would bear the responsibility for the governing of the kingdom of David. The key placed on his shoulder was the symbol of his power and authority to open and close the doors of the business of the kingdom.

In His words spoken to the church at Philadelphia, the Lord Jesus says He now *"has the key of David, who opens and no one will shut, and who shuts and no one opens."* While Jesus spoke of *"the keys of the kingdom"* that would be given to Peter (Matthew 16:19), this is *"the key,"* the key that is the symbol of His authority and power to oversee, administer and execute the business of the kingdom of God. As Isaiah foretold in another place, it is the symbol that *"the government will rest on His shoulders"* (Isaiah 9:6). The Lord is not merely the steward but the king Himself, the son of David, who in fulfillment of the covenant promise of God given to David has been made ruler over the royal house and kingdom of God. Being given the authority and power of this key, He will open and close the doors in the administration of the kingdom according to the will and purpose of God so that His will is done on earth as it is in heaven. In doing this, He will give assignments to His people in specific areas of responsibility. And, as He goes on to say, this is what He will give the church in Philadelphia–an assignment they are to fulfill.

It Seems He Can Hardly Wait

The Lord quickly moves on from His attributes to His intimate knowledge of the church in Philadelphia succinctly saying, *"I know your deeds"* (Revelation 3:8). But whereas with the other churches He listed specific things He knows about them, whether it was something He commends or something that needed to be corrected, with this church He does neither. It seems He can hardly wait to tell them what follows, saying, *"Behold!"* Like a loving parent who is excited about giving their child a present they have waited for until it is time for it to be opened, there is the sense that the Lord has great anticipation and excitement about what He will tell them. Exercising the authority and power of *"the key of David,"* He says, *"Behold, I have put before you an open door which no one can shut"* (Revelation 3:8).

We don't know what this open door was but looking at what He goes on to say we gain insight into what had led to the Lord opening this door. He says,

> *You have a little power, and have kept My*
> *word, and have not denied My name.* ⁹*Behold,*
> *I will cause those of the synagogue of Satan,*
> *who say that they are Jews and are not, but*
> *lie–I will make them come and bow down at*
> *your feet, and make them know that I have*
> *loved you.* ¹⁰*Because you have kept the word*
> *of My perseverance, I also will keep you from*
> *the hour of testing, that hour which is about*
> *to come upon the whole world, to test those*
> *who dwell on the earth.*

Two things stand out. First, they have *"little power."* Second, they have been persecuted.

Little Power

It is possible in saying they have *"little power"* that Christ meant they have little influence in the city and region because they were small in number and did not have people of wealth, position or status. This is the way many think about power. It is "the power of influence" that comes from prestige, position or, more often, politics. There are mega churches that have "large power" of influence because thousands of people attend them and identify with the "brand" name of the church. Being large, they have a greater ability to make themselves known, as well as make a greater impact in their city, region and even the world. But this is not what Jesus is speaking about.

While the book of Acts records that thousands were *"being added"* to the church in Jerusalem and they were *"held in high esteem"* (Acts 5:13-14), this was not typical of churches. Many were the size of "small groups" because they met in houses (Romans 16:5; 1 Corinthians 16:19). A collection of the churches in a region was identified as *"the churches in Galatia"* (1 Corinthians 16:1; Galatians 1:2) or the *"churches in Macedonia"* (2 Corinthians 8:1), while those in a city by the name of that city, such as *"the church of God which is at Corinth"* (2 Corinthians 1:1) or *"the church of the Thessalonians"* (1 Thessalonians 1:1). That is how the Lord identifies the seven churches of Revelation, by the names of the cities in which they are located. The vast majority of churches were not mega churches, just as most churches today number less than 100. So Jesus is not speaking about the power of influence that comes from being the biggest church in town.

Nor is He referring to the church having people of wealth, status or political power. While the New Testament mentions certain people who had such influence, people like *"Manean who had been brought up with Herod the tetrarch"* (Acts 13:1), or Lydia who was a wealthy merchant selling purple fabrics (Acts 16:14), most people in the early church were poor and had little worldly prestige, power and influence. Paul wrote of this to the church in Corinth saying, *"For consider your calling, brethren, that there were not many wise according to the flesh, not many mighty, not many noble"* (1 Corinthians 1:26). Unlike the church in Sardis that had a *"name,"* most churches are not known outside their community, let alone in their city or region. They have little power of number, prestige or position. But this also is not what Jesus was speaking about.

The Greek word translated *"power"* is *"dunamis."* This is the word Jesus used to speak of the power of the Holy Spirit He promised to His followers. It is the word He used right after He rose from the dead and told His disciples, *"Behold, I am sending forth the promise of My Father upon you; but you are to stay in the city until you are clothed with power from on high"* (Luke 24:49). It is the word He used right before He ascended to heaven promising His disciples, *"You will receive power when the Holy Spirit has come upon you; and you shall be My witnesses both in Jerusalem, and in all Judea and Samaria, and even to the remotest part of the earth*" (Acts 1:8). The power Jesus promises and is concerned about is the power of the Holy Spirit.

Jesus recognizes that, at this present time, the church in Philadelphia was experiencing "*little power,*" or a lesser degree of the empowering presence of the Holy Spirit. Why is that? It is because, while churches are like a sailing ship and are to put up their sails, only God controls the wind. *When* the wind of the Holy Spirit blows, *how* He blows, and with *what* force and effect He blows is up to God. It is as Paul wrote, "*There are varieties of effects, but the same God who works all things in all persons*" (1 Corinthians 12:6). And Isaiah said, "*Who has directed the Spirit of the LORD*" (Isaiah 40:13). The Lord promises power, but how His power is manifested is up to Him. Our responsibility is to put up the sails. His responsibly is to provide the wind of the Spirit, and He will do this as He is pleased. In contrast to church in Sardis that was waning in the power of the Holy Spirit because they, in effect, had anchored in the harbor, tied the ship to the dock and taken down the sail, there is the sense that this church had their sails up full. However, they had "*little power*" because, while there was the gentle breeze of the Spirit, in the providence of God it had not been the season for the wind of the Spirit to blow in greater power. But it was coming.

Persecuted

The confirmation that this church had its sails up is seen by three things in Christ's words to this church, one being what He doesn't say, and two being what He does say. In distinction to the previous churches, the Lord doesn't say a single negative word of criticism or correction to this church. His silence speaks loudly–this is a healthy church. More than that, there are two profoundly positive things He says. He expressly commends them for their faithful obedience, and this in the midst of persecution. Two times the Lord affirms they have kept His word. He says in verse 8, *"You have kept My word, and have not denied My name,"* and in verse 10, *"Because you have kept the word of My perseverance."* It is clear this church had suffered persecution and kept His word. This is a church that loved the Lord, for as Jesus said, *"If you love Me you will keep My commandments"* (John 14:16). The third confirmation is that He says, *"I have loved you"* (Revelation 3:9). While we know Christ loves all His churches, this is the only church of the seven He explicitly says this to. These words express what He told His disciples in the Upper Room, *"He who has My commandments and keeps them is the one who loves Me; and he who loves Me will be loved by My Father, and I will love him and will disclose Myself to him"* (John 14:21). Their faith in Him and love for Him had been proven in the time of testing by their obedience to Him. They had persevered in the difficult time of persecution, resisting the temptation to compromise and deny His name. Being the kind of church Jesus wants, they were faithful in the time of testing and had kept His word.

Prepared For a New Assignment

The church in Philadelphia had little power and a lot of persecution, and in the providence of God, these two things were essential to prepare them for their new assignment. The time of *"little power"* taught them that, as Jesus told His disciples, *"apart from Me you can do nothing"* (John 15:5). They had to understand that the power to work effectively and fruitfully is not from them but from God–He causes the wind to blow. It is the "secret" of power that is not really a secret because Jesus revealed it to Paul when He said, "*My grace is sufficient for you, for power is perfected*–or reaches its full potential–*in weakness.*" And earlier in 2 Corinthians Paul wrote, "*We have this treasure in earthen vessels so that the surpassing greatness of the power will be of God and not of ourselves* " (2 Corinthians 4:7). It is by experiencing our utter weakness that we become desperate for His power. And because the power is from God, the glory goes to God (see Judges 7:2).

Then also the time of testing revealed what was in their hearts, whether or not they would keep His commandments (Deuteronomy 8:2). Just as the Lord Jesus *"learned obedience from the things which He suffered"* (Hebrews 5:8), meaning He was trained and prepared through suffering for the ministry the Father assigned to Him as High Priest, so in their time of suffering the Philadelphians learned obedience by keeping His word and it prepared them for the new assignment God had for them. They proved they would be faithful to obey Him no matter what the cost. Just as Joseph waited in prison for years, powerless to cause what God had promised to be realized, but then, in God's time, the Lord opened the door for him to enter his new assignment for which God had prepared him (Genesis 41:1ff.), so now, having been prepared, the Lord has opened the door for this church with their new assignment that they are to fulfill. And so He tells them," *I have put before you an open door which no one can shut.*"

The Open Door

What does it mean that He has opened the door? It is a metaphor for access and entrance into an opportunity for something. Since Christ has opened the door with "*the key of David,*" which is the key of oversight and administration of the kingdom of God, He is saying He has opened a door in the spiritual realm that has the potential to success-fully influence, impact and transform lives in the earthly realm. It is a door of opportunity with favorable condi-tions that make it possible for the effectual working of the Holy Spirit so that the kingdom of God can advance and be established in greater ways.

The Apostle Paul used this metaphor in regard to his work of missions and evangelism. He told the Corinthians, *"But I will remain in Ephesus until Pentecost; ⁹for a wide door for effective service has opened to me, and there are many adversaries"* (1 Corinthians 16:8-9). Again, he told the Corinthians, *"Now when I came to Troas for the gospel of Christ and when a door was opened for me in the Lord..."* (2 Corinthians 2:12). Then also, he requested the Colossians that they be *"praying at the same time for us as well, that God will open up to us a door for the word, so that we may speak forth the mystery of Christ"* (Colossians 4:3).

There are five key principles to get hold of in what Paul says in these verses about an open door. First, and most important, it is God Who opens the door. Christ has *"the key of David"* to open, as well as, shut the door of opportunity for the gospel. Second, it comes in answer to prayer. A general principle of God's ways is that while He can do anything He intends to do, He has chosen to work in answer to prayer. That is why Paul asked people to pray for this. God opens doors when we pray for doors to open. Third, it is a specific assignment. In all three verses Paul says the open door is *"for me"* or *"for us."* Doors open for specific churches and specific people in specific places for specific kinds of ministry. Fourth, there will be opposition. Paul says, *"there are many adversaries."* Where God moves, Satan opposes. Jesus spoke of *"those of the synagogue of Satan"* who persecuted the church in Philadelphia. The name *"Satan"* means "adversary," and he will oppose the work of God through one or *"many."* Fifth, we have to go through the door. Because of the open doors in Ephesus and Troas, Paul changed his plans to take advantage of the opportunity that God had made for him to preach the gospel. As Proverbs 16:9 says, *"The mind of man plans his way, but the LORD directs his steps."* When we discern a door that God has opened, no matter what we may have planned, we must go through it to take advantage of it because it is God's providential communication concerning His direction and assignment for us.

Excitement and Expectation

When Christ opens the door to a new assignment, He does so with excitement and expectation. He is excited about the assignment because He knows it is the time for the kingdom of God to advance in this world. And He is excited for us because the new assignment is His gift to us and He knows we will experience the fullness of His joy as we bear much fruit for His glory (John 15:1-11).

Along with His excitement is His expectation for us to fulfill the assignment. Our assignment will be fulfilled, first, when we work, serve and minister in the power of the Holy Spirit. When we put our sails up full, in His time He will blow the wind of the Holy Spirit to fill them and empower us to accomplish the work. Second, it will be fulfilled as we obey Him. Being led by the Holy Spirit and keeping His word, we will execute His battle plans.

We see this kingdom principle of Christ's expectation for us to fulfill our assignments in many places, and one is the Parable of the Talents. In that day, a "talent" was not an ability, it was a measurement of weight. In the parable, a master gives three slaves different talents, meaning three different amounts of money to invest. He gives one slave five talents, a second three talents, and a third one talent. The master gives these to his slaves with the expectation that they will invest the money to increase his wealth. In other words, they were assignments from their lord to advance his interests using the talents of money he gave them. The different amounts didn't matter. What did matter was that they were to be faithful to fulfill their assignments.

The parable goes on to say that the slaves were brought before their lord to give an account of what they did. Two fulfilled their assignments. To these their master said, *"'Well done, good and faithful slave. You were faithful with a few things, I will put you in charge of many things; enter into the joy of your master'"* (Matthew 25:21, 23). One, however, did not fulfill his assignment. His master called him a *"wicked, lazy slave,"* took back what he gave that slave and entrusted it to one of the slaves who was faithful to fulfill his assignments (Matthew 25:26-28).

No One Can Stop Them

The church in Philadelphia was being given a new assignment to fulfill. The Lord had opened a door, and He assured them it was a door *"no one could shut"* (Revelation 3:8). They were to go through the door, even as they encounter opposition from *"those of the synagogue of Satan."* They were to be fully assured of His attributes that He is *"the Holy One"* and *"the True One."* Because He is Who He says He is and will do what He says He will do, they can trust and rely on Him. As they listen to Him, are empowered by the Spirit and obey Him, they will be faithful to fulfill their assignment and be the kind of church Jesus wants–and no one will be able to stop them!

Study Questions
Chapter 7

1. Briefly share one personal highlight from the chapter.

2. Besides being able to open something, what other purpose does a key serve?

3. What is the quality and characteristic of the kind of church Jesus reveals to the church in Philadelphia?

4. One of the attributes of Jesus is that He is *"the holy One."* What is your understanding of the implications of this reality in regard to your relationship to God and how you live your life?

5. The second attribute Jesus reveals is that He is "*the true One.*" How does understanding this help you grow in your knowledge of Who Jesus is?

6. Because Christ has been given the Key of David, what authority does He exercise?

7. What is Christ speaking about when He says they have "*little power*" and how did it apply to the church in Philadelphia? Do you see this in your life?

8. How does suffering prepare a person for the next assignment the Lord has for them?

9. What do you learn about the church in Philadelphia by what Jesus says and doesn't say about them?

10. What are the five key principles regarding an open door?
(1)
(2)
(3)
(4)
(5)

11. Have you ever considered that Christ wants to give you an assignment to accomplish and that He is excited about it? How does this make you feel?

12. What do you need to fulfill your assignment?

CHAPTER 8

LAODICEA: IS ZEALOUS FOR GOD

Revelation 3:14-22

To the angel of the church in Laodicea write: The Amen, the faithful and true Witness, the Beginning of the creation of God, says this: ¹⁵ *"I know your deeds, that you are neither cold nor hot; I wish that you were cold or hot.* ¹⁶ *So because you are lukewarm, and neither hot nor cold, I will spit you out of My mouth.* ¹⁷ *Because you say, "I am rich, and have become wealthy, and have need of nothing," and you do not know that you are wretched and miserable and poor and blind and naked,* ¹⁸ *I advise you to buy from Me gold refined by fire so that you may become rich, and white garments so that you may clothe yourself, and that the shame of your nakedness will not be revealed; and eye salve to anoint your eyes so that you may see.* ¹⁹ *Those whom I love, I reprove and discipline; therefore be zealous and repent.* ²⁰ *Behold, I stand at the door and knock; if anyone hears My voice and opens the door, I will come in to him and will dine with him, and he with Me.* ²¹ *He who overcomes, I will grant to him to sit down with Me on My throne, as I also overcame and sat down with My Father on His throne.* ²² *He who has an ear, let him hear what the Spirit says to the churches."*

House Cleaning

I t was probably a day like any other day in Jerusalem. Jerusalem was the center of life of the Jewish nation. It was also the center of the Jewish religion because the temple was there. The temple was the distinct location on earth where the manifest presence of God dwelt in the Holy of Holies, and every day multitudes of people from many places around the world would come to worship the God of Israel at the temple. In order to facilitate the worship of those who travelled from far away places, a number of locations around the temple complex were set up for transactions so people could exchange their money and buy animals, such as oxen, sheep, and goats, as well as other things that would then be offered in their worship to God. Many different tables were stationed around the temple complex with men seated at them for this purpose. But whereas centuries before the initial intention of these places was to help assist the worship of travellers (Deuteronomy 14:24-26), the focus of the transactions had transitioned from worship to wealth, from facilitating worshippers to making money. This day was much like any other day as the worshippers streamed into the temple complex area, but it was going to turn out very different.

Suddenly the calm of the morning was disrupted by a huge commotion as a man who had just entered the temple area began turning over the chairs and tables of the moneychangers and throwing their money on the ground. People were jumping up and scattering in different directions because he had made a scourge–a whip–and while he was swinging it and chasing the moneychangers out of the temple area, he shouted, *"Take these things away! Stop making My Father's house a house of business. It is written, 'My house will be a house of prayer for all nations,' but you have made it a den of thieves"* (John 2:16; Mark 11:17). It was Jesus, and He was consumed with emotion and passion as He confronted the moneychangers about what they were doing and what they had made the house of God to be. He was cleansing the temple and proclaiming what the true purpose of God was for that place.

Like a Consuming Fire

While all four gospels tell us about this forceful, even violent act of Jesus and the reactions of the different people to what He did, only John tells us what was going through the minds of His disciples. He reported that His disciples remembered the prophecy of Psalm 69:9, *"Zeal for Your house will consume me"* (John 2:17). As Jesus fulfilled this prophecy, they not only saw what Jesus did, they realized why He did it. It was zeal–zeal for the house of God because of His zeal for God. And His zeal was so intense that it could be described as nothing less than consuming–a consuming zeal, like a burning flame of fire. He was literally burning with passion for God and the glory of God, and that burning passion moved and motivated Him to cleanse the temple.

Is Jesus Really Like That?

How many people think Jesus is really like that– charged with emotion and passion, even burning with a consuming zeal for God? Probably most people picture of Him as a placid, calm and kindly soul, who is reserved and restrained, even serene and sedate. How many think of Jesus expressing His love and reverence for God in a way that is so filled with feeling that He would literally come into the most reverent place of worship on earth, over- turn tables and chairs, make a whip and chase people out with it, all the while shouting about what had happened to the place of worship and quoting Scripture about what was to be happening there? How many people have ideas and images in their minds of what Jesus is like according to how their Sunday School teachers presented Him, the sermons they heard, even the movies they watched that portray Him in a way that is actually very different from Him acting this way? Yet that is what the word of God tells us He did. It tells us He did this because of Who He is–He is consumed with zeal for God!

Jesus is burning with passion for God, and He wants His people to have hearts on fire with zeal and passion for Him and His house. That is the kind of church He wants–a church that is zealous for God–for that is what we hear Him saying to the seventh and last of churches, the church at Laodicea.

Can I Hear An "Amen"?

As with all of the churches, Jesus begins by declaring His attributes and titles that are relevant to the church, and He identifies three. The first is that He is *"the Amen"* (Revelation 3:14).

"Amen" is an amazing word. It is a transliteration from the Hebrew language that has found its way into most of the languages of the world. It is, in fact, believed to be the one word that is known and used more than any other word in all the languages of the world!

"Amen" comes for the root *"amam"* which means "that which is true, sure, certain." Because it has the connotation of trust and confidence, it is related to and virtually the same as the Hebrew word for "believe." Something is to be believed because it is true, sure, and certain. "Amen" can be used at the beginning of a sentence, as Jesus frequently used it saying, *"Truly, truly"*–literally in the Greek,

'Amen, amen, I say to you." This means, "I am telling you the truth which you can believe and have total trust and confidence in." It can be used at the end of a prayer when one says *"Amen."* This does not mean, "That's the end of my prayer because I have nothing more to say." It means, "I affirm the truth of what I prayed." And when someone is praying and another says, "Amen," they are affirming and agreeing with what the other person is praying.

All these connotations of the word are true of Jesus. He is the One who is true. He is the One we are to believe and have total trust and confidence in. And He is the One Who is the affirmation of the truth of the word and promises of God. Paul wrote of this, saying, *"For as many as are the promises of God, in Him they are yes; therefore also through Him is our Amen to the glory of God through us"* (2 Corinthians 1:20). Notice he says *"also"*–we *"also"* say *"amen."* Jesus Himself is the great *"Amen"* to the truth of the promises of God because He is the One Who proves them to be true. Then, we also affirm the truth, certainty and trustworthiness of God through Him saying, *"Amen, it is true,"* all to the glory of God.

Can I Get a Witness?

How can Jesus do this? It is because He is *"the faithful and true Witness"* (Revelation 3:14). A witness is one who testifies. Jesus affirms, bears witness and gives evidence to the truth of God's word and His promises. Christ is not merely a witness. He is *"the witness"*–the foremost witness. His testimony is not hearsay, nor is it even that of an expert witness. He is Himself the testimony. This is the very thing Jesus stated when the Roman governor Pontius Pilate interrogated him. He said, *"For this reason I have been born, and for this I have come into the world, to testify to the truth. Everyone who is of the truth hears My voice"*

(John 18:37). The life, words and works of Jesus testify to the truth of God. Most of all, His death and resurrection from the dead make known the certainty of God's covenant promise that He will give eternal life to all who believe in Him.

"Faithful and true" have the same basic meaning with different emphases. *"Faithful"* accentuates the reality that He is and will always be loyal and devoted. He did not waver, turn away from or fail in any way in doing the Father's will and revealing the Father's nature (John 14:8). Jesus uses the present tense, which means He was, is and will always be the faithful witness to the truth of God.

"True" stresses something being factual, actual, and real. Jesus spoke of this to the people of His day saying, *"My testimony is true, for I know where I came from and where I am going"* (John 8:14.) His testimony is true not only because He comes from the Father but also because He is *"the truth"* (John 14:6). For this reason, His testimony is absolutely reliable and trustworthy. You can count on it. You can, in fact, not only "bet your life on it," you can bet your eternal destiny on it!

The Author and Authority

The third thing Jesus says about Himself is that He is *"the beginning of the creation of God"* (Revelation 3:14). The Greek word translated *"beginning"* is "arche," and it can be translated in two different ways depending on the context.

One way is *"beginning,"* as it is here. This does not mean "the first one to be created" but "the One from Whom all creation begins–the source, the originator, the One Who got it all started." In other words, all of creation began with Him initiating it. The English word "architect" is based on this meaning. The architect is the person from whom the whole building project begins. He or she is not the first thing built but the one who initiates everything that will be built. Jesus, being *"the beginning of creation,"* is not the first thing created but the architect, the One through Whom all things were created.

This is what John wrote of Him in the opening verses of His gospel saying of He, " *In the beginning was the Word"* (John 1:1). The Greek words translated *"the Word"* are literally *"ho logos"*–"the logos"–and John's identification of Jesus as" the logos" combines both the Biblical and Greek cultural connotations of the meaning of "the logos." The first chapter of Genesis reveals God created all things through His word (Genesis 1:3ff.). The power of the word of God is what initiated and caused all things to come into existence–it all began with the word of God. In the Greek culture, "the Logos" was a technical philosophical designation for the Mind that conceived and created all the architecture and logical structure of the created order. Thus, John says of Him, *"All things came into being through Him, and apart from Him nothing came into being that has come into being"* (John 1:3). He did not come into being or existence for the simple reason that He has always existed. He is the *"I AM"* (John 8:58). But all things that came into existence began by the almighty word of Him Who is the Great Architect of the Universe.

The second way "arche" can be translated is "ruler." This comes from the idea of something "being over all, the supreme, or the highest." An arch in an archway is a structure that is over the walkway. Being over something, it rules over it.

While these two ways of using the word may seem different, they are actually related. They have the same basic meanings and connotations as the words "author" and "authority." An "author" is the beginning, the source, the creator of something. An "authority" is that which has the right to rule in an area of life. The word "authority" comes from the word "author"–the author of something is the highest authority concerning that matter.

When Jesus says He is the *"beginning of the creation of God,"* He is saying He is the author of creation–that it all started with Him. Because of this, He has authority over all of the creation of God–He is the ruler. This is what He told His disciples after He rose from the dead saying, *"All authority in heaven and on earth has been given to Me"* (Matthew 28:18). Being the Great Architect of the Universe, He is the author and authority, the originator and ruler over God's creation,

It's All About Him

When we look at these three attributes Jesus reveals about Himself, it is evident that He is making known that He is "what it's all about." Everything in creation is about Him because He is the beginning, the middle and the ultimate conclusion of creation. Starting with the end in mind, He is the *"Amen."* He is the One Who is to be believed and believed in because He affirms the truth of God's word, promises and purpose to all creation. Being the *"faithful and true witness,"* He is the One Who gives actual, factual and true testimony about Who God is and what life and creation is all about. Being *"the beginning and ruler of the creation of God,"* He is the author and the authority over all creation. Jesus is the One from Whom, through Whom and for Whom everything exists–it's all about Him.

Whose Side Are You On?

These three attributes are most relevant to the church in Laodicea because the church has lost its focus, strayed from its true purpose, and wandered from its real reason for existing. While it is a church filled with people who have professed faith in Jesus, they have lost their passion. The fire has faded, the desire has diminished, and the intensity is past tense. The real zeal that comes from real faith and love for Jesus has been reduced and replaced.

We see this in what the Lord says about their deeds, and it is not so much what they are doing but how they are doing it that is unacceptable to Him. He tells them, "*I know your deeds, that you are neither cold nor hot; I wish that you were cold or hot.*"

As He did with the six previous churches, He begins with the words "*I know your deeds,*" but that's as far as it goes. Like the spiritually dead church in Sardis, there is not one word of commendation. But it is evident that this church is even worse than Sardis, for Jesus said to Sardis "*there are a few people who have not soiled their garments*" (Revelation 3:4). At least there was a remnant in that church who were living the way Jesus wanted. When He speaks to the church in Laodicea, He not only speaks no word of approval, He finds no one to praise. There is nothing in the church that makes it the kind of church He wants.

The Lord identifies the overall spiritual climate and atmosphere of the church as being "*lukewarm.*" The cultural context of this statement that was so relevant to the church in Laodicea is that the city was situated in-between two other famous cities. One was renown for its hot water that was used for medical purposes and the other was well known for its cold water used for drinking. Just as the city of Laodicea was in-between hot and cold water, so the church in Laodicea was in-between hot and cold in its spiritual life–it was "*lukewarm.*"

He then says to them, "*I wish you were cold or hot.*" These are typical words of the Lord Jesus Christ. There is no gray with Jesus, only black or white. There is no compromise, only commitment; no give and take, only take it or leave it. He calls people to decision–to be for Him or against Him, "to fish or cut bait," to be "in the boat or out of it." He is saying, in effect, *"Choose for yourselves today whom you will serve"* (Joshua 24:15) and live it to the fullest. His desire, of course, is for them to be hot for Him for as He says later in verse 19, *"be zealous and repent."* His own love, zeal and passion for them has moved Him to speak these words of reproof and discipline so they will become zealous and consumed with burning passion for God as He is. But if not, then He would prefer them to be cold! He is drawing a line in the sand and telling them to take a stand–one side or the other. As He told the religious hypocrites, the Pharisees, *"Either make the tree good and its' fruit good, or make the tree bad and it's fruit bad; for the tree is known by it's fruit"* (Matthew 12:33).

You Make Me Sick

The zeal and passion of the Lord come to a head when He delivers an ominous word of warning, *"So because you are lukewarm, and neither hot nor cold, I will spit you out of My mouth."* The Greek word that is translated *"spit"* does not actually mean "spit." It may have been translated this way because "the religious sensitivities" of certain people reading what Jesus actually said might find it distasteful. There are, in fact, a few places in the English translations where the Hebrew and Greek words are not translated literally because it might seem crude, vulgar or even repulsive to some. This is one of those places. And while the rendering of what Jesus said as *"I will spit you out of My mouth"* might seem crude enough to some, what He actually says is, "I will vomit you out." That literally expressed the depth of His feeling and revulsion about people who are spiritually lukewarm! They are not merely distasteful to Him, they literally make Him sick. Because of this, He wants to vomit them out.

Just as there are people who may find it difficult to think of Jesus as being consumed with burning zeal and passion in His love for God, it may be even more surprising to conceive of Jesus using such gross and graphic language. This, however, is the very language of the Old Testament Scriptures. In Leviticus 18:25 the LORD spoke to His people about the sinful actions of the Canaanites living in the land saying, *"For the land has become defiled, therefore I have brought its punishment upon it, so the land has spewed out its inhabitants."* The Hebrew word translated *"spewed"* is literally *"vomited."* The LORD goes on to tell His people to keep His commandments *"so that the land will not spew*–vomit–*you out, should you defile it, as it has spewed*–vomited–*out the nation which has been before you"* (Leviticus 18:28; see also Leviticus 20:22). This is what Jesus says to this church. Being lukewarm, they are not keeping the greatest commandment to love God with all our heart, soul, mind and strength (Mark 12:30). Half-hearted love is not really love. Just as an omelet made with one good egg and one rotten egg will make you sick, so the defiled "drink offering" of their lives is making Jesus sick. The result will be His just and righteous judgment upon them–He will vomit them out.

What's the Problem?

What was this church doing that made Him feel this way? He tells them, *"Because you say, 'I am rich, and have become wealthy, and have need of nothing'"* (Revelation 3:17).

Once again the cultural context is important to understand. Laodicea was the wealthiest city in the whole region. The agricultural and commercial success of the area brought the banking industry that produced great wealth and prosperity in gold to the city. There was fertile ground that provided good grazing for sheep that were bred to produce soft, glossy black wool garments that were famous and greatly desired. The city was also well known for a school of medicine that produced a famous ointment for an eye salve. They were rich, wealthy and comfortable! But their material wealth and welfare had diluted their love for God, dulled their passion for Christ, and deceived them about their actual spiritual state.

It is important to understand that worldly wealth and prosperity are not necessarily evil or wrong for God has blessed many of His faithful followers with wealth and prosperity. Prosperity is one of the promises God made to His people when they obey and keep His commandments (Deuteronomy 28:1-14). He promised His people in Deuteronomy 8:18 that He would give them "*power to make wealth.*" But in the same chapter He warns them to not let their wealth turn their hearts from Him. That is the very thing that happened to the church in Laodicea. Jesus warned of this in His Parable of the Sower speaking about the ground that becomes infested with weeds and thorns, which represent the deceitfulness of worldly wealth and the desire for other things. The weeds choked out the word making it unfruitful (Matthew 13:22). That is the very thing that happened to this church. The deceitfulness of sin with the abundance of worldly wealth deadened their hearts to God. They became self-satisfied, thought they had no needs, and became complacent about their spiritual life. They lost their zeal for the Lord–they were "*lukewarm.*"

They Didn't Have a Clue

This church is in real trouble, but they don't know it. Jesus tells them: *"you do not know that you are wretched and miserable and poor and blind and naked."* He gives a catalogue of six spiritual aliments that expose their appalling condition.

First of all, they are *"wretched."* This word is used only one other time in the New Testament. It is after the Apostle Paul has come to the conclusion that his spiritual condition is hopeless because he has been overcome by the power of sin working in him and He says, *"O wretched man that I am!"* (Romans 7:24). The Laodiceans' spiritual condition is *"wretched"* because they are surrendering to the rule of sin and not the reign of Christ.

Second, they are *"miserable."* This word is also used only two times in the New Testament. In the other passage, Paul is describing the desperate plight of Christians if Christ has not risen from the dead and it is translated *"pitied."* If they have trusted in Christ for eternal life but He did not rise from the dead, they have been completely duped and deceived, and they are of all people most to be *"pitied"* (1 Corinthians 15:19). The Laodiceans are deceived about their pathetic spiritual condition, which is pitiful and *"miserable."*

More than this, they are *"poor."* There are two Greek words translated as "poor" in the New Testament. One is based on the word meaning "to have mercy on" and means that a person is "poor" because he does not have any more than he needs. They have enough, but nothing extra and a person has mercy on them by giving them something. The other word means "poverty stricken, bankrupt, destitute." Jesus uses the second word. What a complete contrast this church is to the church in Smyrna! To them, Jesus said, *"I know your poverty but you are rich"* (Revelation

2:9). Those in the church in Laodicea are making the positive confession about themselves, "*I am rich*," but Jesus says to them, "*you are poor*." They have the worst possible poverty, the kind that has nothing. They are spiritually "good for nothing."

"*Blind*" continues the description of their desperate spiritual condition. It is a dreadful thing to be called "*blind*" by the Lord Jesus. That is what He called His greatest critics, the religious hypocrites the scribes and Pharisees (Mathew 23:16, 17, 19, 34, 26). The glare of the Laodiceans material wealth has closed their spiritual eyes.

The Lord, then, exposes their disgraceful condition— they are "*naked*." He elaborates further on what this means in the next verse when He speaks of "*the shame of your nakedness*." This terminology comes from the third chapter of Genesis, which gives the account of the early chapter of human history. Adam and Eve sinned against God, and when they recognized the awful reality of their sinful condition they realized they were "*naked*." The ironic thing about what Scripture says about Adam and Eve is that "*the eyes of both of them were opened, and they knew that they were naked*" (Genesis 3:7). With the Laodiceans, their eyes are closed and they have no idea of their "*nakedness*."

The immediate reaction of Adam and Eve to their nakedness was shame. Shame is different from guilt. Guilt has to do with what I have done–I have sinned. Shame has to do with who I am–I am a sinner. While the psychological condition of fallen humanity is one in which people can be susceptible to false guilt and false shame, especially in a real world in which there is a devil who is "*the accuser*" of God's people (Revelation 12:10), the Scriptures are emphatic that there is true guilt and true shame before God. The modern secular world has done everything it can to rationalize sin and eradicate shame. This is not what

Jesus does. He speaks the truth in love to the Laodiceans about their true *"shame."* Shame is real because sin is real. Their destitute condition was that they had no covering for their sinful condition. They were *"naked"* and exposed and it was a shameful.

One would think with this disastrous list of spiritual diseases the Laodiceans would have an idea of how the Lord actually sees them. Yet the depth of their desperate spiritual condition is made known by the sixth thing Jesus identifies, which is actually the first thing He said to them, *"you do not know..."* They are completely unaware of all of the spiritual diseases the Lord diagnoses them as having. They are so spiritually anesthetized they have no clue!

The Greatest Loss

Letting our hearts turn from passion for Christ to the pursuit of material wealth has a cost. The Lord said, *"those who honor Me I will honor, and those who despise Me will be lightly esteemed"* (1 Samuel 2:30). Far from being honored, the Laodiceans had lost their esteem from the Lord. Worse than this, their greatest loss is His manifest presence in the church.

There is nothing more valuable, nothing more precious and nothing more to be desired than the manifest presence of the Lord. The greatest leaders of God's people understood this. Moses understood this. After Israel had committed the sin of idolatry and the Lord said that while He would fulfill His promise to lead His people into the Promised land but His manifest presence would not go with them, Moses prayed, *"If Your presence does not go with us, do not lead us up from here"* (Exodus 33:15). He went on to pray about the Lord's manifest presence, saying,

> *For how then can it be known that I have*
> *found favor in Your sight, I and Your people?*
> *Is it not by Your going with us, so that we, I*
> *and Your people, may be distinguished from*
> *all the other people who are upon the face*
> *of the earth?* (Exodus 33:16).

David understood this. He wrote, "*You will make known to me the path of life; in Your presence is fullness of joy*" (Psalm 16:11). Life, true life, the life that Jesus spoke of as "*abundant*" (John 10:10) only comes from the reality of Christ's manifest presence. Living in His manifest presence, the Holy Spirit will fill our lives and we will have the "*fullness of joy*" that comes from the well of "*living water*" that Jesus gives (John 4:10; 7:37-39). But the Laodiceans are like the Israelites of old to whom God spoke through the prophet Jeremiah saying, "*My people have committed two evils; they have forsaken Me, the fountain of living waters, to hew for themselves broken cisterns that can hold no water*" (Jeremiah 2:13). Being deceived by their worldly wealth, the Laodiceans had dug worthless wells. They had "*grieved*" and "*quenched*" the Holy Spirit (Ephesians 4:30; 1 Thessalonians 5:19) and the Lord had withdrawn His manifest presence from their church.

This is made painfully clear by what Jesus says in verse 20, "*Behold, I stand at the door and knock; if anyone hears My voice and opens the door, I will come in to him and will dine with him, and he with Me.*" This verse is often used in the evangelism of the lost inviting a person to "open the door of their heart" to Christ by believing in and receiving Him. The context, however, is that Jesus is not speaking to people outside a church but to people in a church. He is the One outside! He is on the outside of the church–standing, waiting, knocking, inviting them to hear His voice and let Him come in!

It may seem strange to some to make a categorical distinction between the church and the manifest presence of Christ in the church, but that is the very thing the Lord Jesus does. Such a distinction can be seen in many ways in Scripture. There was a difference between the places of the tabernacle and the temple and the glory of God's manifest presence that filled those places (Exodus 40:34; 2 Chronicles 5:13). When the sin of Israel had come to fullness, God withdrew His manifest presence from the first and second temples (Ezekiel 10:18; Matthew 23:38; 27:51). His presence was removed but the temples still stood until they were finally destroyed in 586 B.C. and 70 A.D. More precisely, the glory of God's manifest presence was enthroned on the Ark of the Covenant and the Ark could be removed from the tabernacle at such times as when it was carried by the priests on the journey through the wilderness, crossing the Jordan, going into battle, and even being captured by the Philistines for a period of time (Numbers 10:33; 14:44; Joshua 3:1ff.; 6:1ff.; 1 Samuel chapters 4 through 6). The tabernacle remained, but the Ark, which enthroned God's manifest presence, was not in it. One of the most significant times was after David brought the Ark to Jerusalem and placed it in a tent he had pitched and appointed Levites to worship the LORD there before the Ark while the tabernacle remained at a completely different location, Gibeon, with the priests who would "*offer burnt offerings to the LORD on the altar of burnt offering continually morning and evening, even according to all that is written in the law of the LORD, which He commanded Israel*" (1 Chronicles 16:1-7, 37-42). It was in this "*tent,*" which was "*the house of the LORD,*" that David desired to be more than any other because it was there that he would worship and encounter God's manifest presence enthroned above the Ark (Psalm 15:1; 27:4-6; 61:4). David, like Moses, understood that there was nothing was more valuable than the manifest presence of God

There is a distinct difference between the place created for God's manifest presence and His manifest presence. This is what Christ made known to the church in Laodicea, for, as He Himself said, He was outside the church. These are people who have made a profession of faith in Christ but have no idea they have lost His manifest presence. They are like a wineskin with no wine (Matthew 9:17), a lamp with no flame (Revelation 1:20), a house with no one living in it (Luke 13:35). What could be worse? What could be a greater loss? His manifest presence has been withdrawn.

Yet His love and compassion for them continues. Just as He says in the previous verse, "*Those who I love, I rebuke and discipline*" (Revelation 3:19), so His love has moved Him to stand at the door of the church and knock. He is saying in effect, "Does anyone hear? Does anyone know Who is at the door? Then open up! Open your hearts to Me, and let Me come in!" The fire of His consuming passion has compelled Him to call out to them so He can come into their lukewarm hearts. He wants to light their fire again, to fill their lives with His manifest presence so they can have real fellowship and communion with Him. While He says it to the whole church, it is an individual decision each must make.

Get With The Program

What are they to do? The Lord tells them, even commands them to "*become zealous and repent*" (Revelation 3:19). To "*repent*" is to "turn around." They are going in the wrong direction, which is away from Him. They must repent and return to a first love by becoming "*hot*" in their love and devotion for Him. Then they will be "*zealous*"–just as He is–consumed with the fire of passion and holy desire for God.

What does it look like to be zealous? One of the greatest examples in our present culture is how people love their sports team–their high school team, their college team, or their professional sports team. It is amazing how people's lives, emotions and identities are intertwined and connected to their team. While the team is actually the group of individuals who happen to be on the field and dressed in the uniform during the time the game is played that day, they speak of it as "my team." They are totally *for* their team and completely *against* the others. They devote their time, energy and money to their team. They dress in the colors of their team, with the logos and pictures branding them as being with their team and separated from all others. When their team wins, they win and are elated. When their team loses, they lose and are deflated. When they win, they have joy like that of a mother and father at the birth of a new child. When they lose, it's like a death in the family–or even worse if they lose to the chief rival! They are zealous for their team because they love their team.

That's the way the Lord was and is for the Father and His glory and the way He is for us. That's the way we are to be for Him and His team, His church. And that's the way He wants the Laodiceans to be–He wants them to get with the program. His will is for this church to be fired up with holy desire, passion and zeal for Him so it can be a winning team because that's the kind of church He wants.

Pay Me Now Or Pay Me Later

Having made clear what He wants them to become, He tells them the way this is to be done. He says, "*I advise you to buy from Me...*" (Revelation 3:18). There is a saying,

"Pay me now or pay me later." We will either pay the price of loving and following Christ as His true disciples or we will pay the price of suffering the loss of not following Him. As the saying goes, "One life will soon be past, only what's done for Christ will last."

Everyone is spending their life on something. Everyone is investing in something. And everyone will receive a return on their investment. They may spend their life on wasteful living, like the prodigal son of Jesus' parable who squandered his inheritance with loose living (Luke 15:13), and their wealth will pass away before they do. They may invest their life to accumulate the wealth of this world, the wealth that will pass away when they do. Or they may invest their life in the true riches, the wealth that will never pass away. These are the real riches that can only be bought from the Lord Jesus Christ. They are the riches He counsels them to "*buy*" from Him, and He tells them to purchase three things.

Where Should You Begin?

First on the list is "*gold.*" While Laodicea was a materially wealthy city, Jesus wants them to have the true riches. What is this gold? Christ does not explicitly say, yet it is undoubtedly faith, real faith, true faith in Christ. Just as gold is regarded as the most precious metal, faith is the most precious possession we can have in our hearts in our relationship with God. Jesus is the "*Amen,*" "*the true and faithful Witness*" to the word and promises of God, and the Laodiceans are to truly believe in and follow Him.

The gold of faith is first on the list because everything in our relationship with God begins and ends with faith. This is what the Apostle Paul expressed in his opening summary of the gospel in the book of Romans, writing, "*For in it the righteousness of God is revealed from faith to faith; as it is written, 'But the righteous man shall live by faith'"* (Romans 1:17). *"Faith to faith"* means from the beginning to the end it is all about and ultimately about faith. The righteous man not only is justified or declared righteous through faith in the saving work of the Lord Jesus Christ, he lives his whole life by faith under the sovereignty of the Lord Jesus Christ.

The contact and connection we have to reality is faith. If we believe a lie, we will be disconnected from the truth and will build our lives on a fragile, faltering and failing falsehood. We connect in our relationship with the Lord by believing the truth of what He has revealed in His word. We are saved through faith in His promise. And we continue in our relationship with Him as we walk by faith and are transformed into His likeness by the power of the Holy Spirit as we come to understand and believe the truth of His word. When we have the *"gold"* of true faith in Christ, we will love Him, live for Him and be zealous for Him.

But this is not any kind of gold–it is *"gold refined by fire so that you may become rich."* The gold Jesus speaks of is the faith that has been tried and purified–it is *"gold refined by fire."* This is not a superficial, temporary, religious faith. It is the real faith that comes from real relationship with Christ and has been proven to be true through the real trials of life. Peter writes of this kind of faith, speaking of those who

> *have been distressed by various trials, [7] so that the proof of your faith, being more precious than gold which is perishable, even though tested by fire, may be found to result in praise and glory and honor at the revelation of Jesus Christ* (1 Peter 1:6-7).

True faith is where it all begins. Real faith is refined in the fire. That is the gold that makes us rich in our relationship with Christ. When we have this kind of gold, we will spend our lives for Him.

You Need a New Wardrobe

The second thing Christ says they are to buy is *"white garments so that you may clothe yourself, and that the shame of your nakedness will not be revealed."* While the city of Laodicea was famous for the soft, glossy black wool of the sheep bred in the area, Jesus tells them to buy *"white garments."* The *"white garments"* Christ provides is the clothing of His holy and pure righteousness purchased as *"the Lamb of God who takes away the sins of the world"* (John 1:29; Revelation 5:6-9).

One of the most important principles Scripture makes known is that spiritual cleanliness and purity is essential to enter into and dwell in the holy, manifest presence of God (Exodus 19:10, 14; 28:1-5, 38, 41, 43; Psalm 24:3-4). In the book of Revelation, white garments symbolize being spiritually clean so that those wearing them can remain in God's presence. Jesus spoke earlier to the church of Sardis using this imagery, *"But you have a few people in Sardis who have not soiled their garments; and they will walk with Me in white, for they are worthy"* (Revelation 3:4). The twenty-four elders who are seated on twenty-four thrones before God are *"clothed in white garments"* (Revelation 4:4). The martyrs who had been killed for following Christ whose souls are underneath the altar were given *"a white robe"* (Revelation 6:9-11). The countless multitudes of those saved by the blood of the Lamb are standing before the throne *"clothed in white robes"* (Revelation 5:9; 7:9, 13). *"White garments"* are essential to be able to be in the manifest presence of

God. So Jesus counsels the Laodiceans to pay the price to receive *"white garments"* from Him so that His holy, manifest presence can dwell in their church.

The Laodiceans love of the world and compromise with the things of the world has made them shamefully *"naked"* and spiritually unclean. They have *"soiled their garments"* and have become spiritually defiled and this is why Christ is outside the church. They are like the High Priest Joshua who stood before the Lord with *"filthy garments"* being accused by Satan because of his *"iniquity"* and the Lord is telling them to remove *"the filthy garments"* and be clothed with *"clean"* garments so they can live in presence of God (Zechariah 3:1-5). However, the dreadful condition of the Laodiceans is demonstrated by the fact that they are not being accused by Satan who has deceived them but by the Lord who desires to save them! Christ is telling them to repent and return to Him. Like Jacob who preached the first revival sermon recorded in the Bible to *"his household, and all who were with him, 'Put away the foreign gods which are among you, and purify yourselves and change your garments'"* (Genesis 35:2), the Lord Jesus is telling them they need a new wardrobe! They need a new lifestyle! As He had cleansed the physical temple in Jerusalem, He is telling them to cleanse their spiritual lives so they can live in His holy, manifest presence.

Open the Eyes of Your Heart

Seeing the Lord is what the Laodiceans vitally need because they are *"blind."* For this reason, the third thing on the Lord's shopping list is to *"buy"* *"eye salve to anoint your eyes so that you may see."* While the city of Laodicea was famous for a school of medicine that produced ointment for an eye salve, these people need the true spiritual eye salve.

The "*eyes*" the Lord is speaking about are the eyes of the heart (Matthew 13:14-15). People with a "*hard heart*" will have "*eyes*" but cannot "*see.*" They will not understand the ways of the Lord, the power of God, nor works of His kingdom (Mark 8:17-18; Romans 11:7-8; Hosea 14:9). It is those who are "*blessed*" of God who are given "*eyes*" so they can "*see*" (Matthew 13:16; 16:17).

Being spiritually "*blind*," the Laodiceans must have the eyes of their hearts opened, otherwise they will never get it–they will never understand and receive the things of God. The only eye salve that gives the eyes of our hearts the ability to "*see*" is the Holy Spirit. His foremost work and ministry is to testify to and glorify the Lord Jesus Christ (John 15:26; 16:14). The Holy Spirit opens the eyes of our hearts to know the Lord as He truly is and understand how His kingdom works and is manifested in people's lives (John 3:2-3). We must yield to the working of the Holy Spirit in our hearts to see the Lord and His glory for, in doing this, the Holy Spirit will transform us to become more and more like Christ (2 Corinthians 3:18). It was for this reason that Paul prayed for the Ephesians that God would give them a fuller work of the Holy Spirit by giving them greater revelation of God as the eyes of their hearts are "*enlightened.*" We are to pray this, for when this takes place we will grow richer and deeper in our knowledge of and relationship with God (Ephesians 1:17-18; see also Paul's prayer in Ephesians 3:14-20).

When the eyes of our hearts are opened to "*see*" we will understand how God works, discern what God is doing, and perceive the manifest presence of God. More than this, the Holy Spirit will set our hearts alive with burning passion for Christ–to know Him, to live for Him, and to spend our lives for Him. He will give us the grace to pay the price to "*buy*" the most precious "*spiritual blessings*" that can only come to us in and through the Lord Jesus Christ (Ephesians 1:3).

On Fire Like Jesus

The word of God says, *"Our God is a consuming fire"* (Hebrews 12:29). The fire is God, and zeal and passion are our response to the fire of His manifest presence. In order to do this, we are told what to do: we are to be *"fervent in spirit serving the Lord"*–which means we are to zealous and on fire for the Lord (Romans 12:11). And we are told what not to do: *"Do not quench the Spirit"*–which means we are not to extinguish the fire of the Spirit (1 Thessalonians 5:19). Christ was filled with a consuming zeal for God and the purity of His House where His manifest presence dwelt. When Christ poured forth the Holy Spirit from heaven upon His church on the day of Pentecost in answer to the prayer of those gathered in the Upper Room, His presence was manifested with *"tongues–flames–of fire"* (Acts 2:3) and they were all filled with power and went forth to fulfill Christ's purpose. When a church loves God with all their hearts, is filled with the holy, manifest presence of Christ, and is on fire with fervent zeal from the Holy Spirit, it will be the kind of church Jesus wants.

Study Questions
Chapter 8

1. Briefly share one personal highlight from the chapter.

2. How did the disciples interpret Christ's act of cleansing the temple? What are your thoughts about what Jesus did and how He did it?

3. What is the seventh quality and characteristic of the kind of church Jesus wants?

4. Did the word *"amen"* take on greater meaning for you? If so, in what way?

5. How is Jesus *"the faithful and true witness"* and how does this relate to the cleansing of the temple?

6. What insights did you gain from Christ's attribute of being *"the beginning of the creation of God"*?

7. What is the tragic truth about the church in Laodicea?

8. What does being *"lukewarm"* mean to you? What do you think about how Jesus responded to this in the church in Laodicea?

9. What are the six "rotten roots" of the church in Laodicea? Do you see any of these in your life or church?

(1)

(2)

(3)

(4)

(5)

(6)

10. Why do you think a church or person can be so spiritually sick and not realize it?

11. Does every church have the manifest presence of Christ? If not, why might they be unaware of this reality?

12. What three things does Christ prescribe for an unhealthy church? Are you seeking to "*buy*" these from the Lord for your life?

(1)

(2)

(3)

CHAPTER 9

THE SEVEN CHURCHES: OVERCOMES

Revelation 2:7
To him who overcomes

Revelation 2:11
He who overcomes

Revelation 2:17
To him who overcomes

Revelation 2:26
He who overcomes

Revelation 3:5
He who overcomes

Revelation 3:12
He who overcomes

Revelation 3:21
He who overcomes

Worship Like You've Never Seen

It's a scene that words can hardly describe. There has been nothing like it–the numbers who are praising, the sadness turned to joy, the wonder overflowing in worship. It's the finale of the greatest worship service that has ever taken place in the history of universe. It certainly isn't like so many routine, sedate and boring worship services on earth because this one is taking place in heaven, and everyone's attention is completely focused on the throne of God and the One Who is standing before the throne. There are individuals called "elders," beings identified as "living creatures," and millions and millions of angels who are all cheering, singing and shouting as loud as they can, "Worthy, worthy, worthy." Why? What's happening?

This spectacular celebration is depicted in the fourth and fifth chapters of the book of Revelation by the Apostle John who was privileged to be there. In chapter 4, John has described the first part of the service with the worship of God the Father seated on His throne in heaven. Now, in chapter 5, the worship service has transitioned to focus on the Son–all He accomplished in His death, resurrection and ascension, and the reward for His suffering. As John looks on, he sees a scroll with seven seals being held in the right hand of God the Father. This scroll is the title deed, the right to rule over the universe, and on it is written the revelation of the future that will unfold through the course of history until it all culminates in the New Heaven and Earth. The future belongs to the one who possesses the scroll. This part of the service began with a worship leader putting everything in perspective by proclaiming with a thundering voice the most penetrating question, *"Who is worthy to open the scroll and to break its seals?"* (Revelation 5:2). After searching the whole universe, no one is found, and John begins to weep with great sorrow. But then another worship leader says, "Wait! There is One who is worthy." John is told He is "*the lion of the tribe of Judah*"–the very One Who is standing before the throne. But as John looks for the lion, he sees One Who looks like a lamb–a lamb that had been slain, having shed his blood, but now is alive, resurrected from the dead, and standing before the throne. He is the One Who is worthy, and because of this all heaven erupts in worship loudly singing and saying, "*Worthy is the Lamb*" (Revelation 5:12). Why? Why is He worthy? The reason is because He gave His life as a sacrifice to pay the penalty for sins to purchase people for God from every tribe and tongue and nation (Revelation 5:9).

What words can summarize what He did–the height of His love, the depth of His suffering, the width of His mercy, and the breadth of His compassion? Yet there is one word that captures what He did, one word that turned John's sorrow into unspeakable joy, one word that gave him absolute assurance about the glorious future of all those who will be saved by the blood of the Lamb. That word is "*overcome*." The Lamb is worthy because He has overcome, and because He has overcome He is worthy to be given the scroll, to open it, and to receive the worship of all of heaven (Revelation 5:9).

The One Who is receiving the worship of all of heaven, the One Who is the Lion and the Lamb, the One Who has overcome is the Lord Jesus Christ, and His will is for His church to be like Him. This is the eighth quality of the kind of church He wants–it overcomes.

All in the Family

Families are composed of individuals. Each individual person is unique because he or she has features that distinguish them from every other person. Even if they are "identical twins," they have characteristics that make them distinct from the other twin. Everyone is one-of-a-kind–just like everyone else! However, while each person is unique, there are certain traits that identify him or her as being a member of their family. They say things, do things and generally look like the other members of their family. This is because they have DNA that classifies them as a member of their family.

This is the way it is with the family of God. Churches are unique. They have their own particular strengths and weakness, gifts and talents, callings and assignments that make them different from every other church. This is what Jesus recognized in His commendations and criticisms of the seven individual churches in Revelation. Yet there are certain things that are to be the same for every church. These are the things Christ says to all the churches, and one of these is that each church, as well as every individual who identifies with that church, is to overcome. Seven times the Lord declares the words to the churches *"to him who overcomes."* The number of times He says this emphasizes how vital it is that each church overcomes. Numbers are also symbolic, especially in the book of Revelation, and the number seven is the number of perfection and completion. In saying this seven times, the Lord Jesus indicates that a church is not complete and will not be the kind of church He wants unless it overcomes.

Victory

The Greek word translated *"overcome"* is the verb "nikao." It means "to be victorious, conquer, or prevail." The root of the word is "nik," and it is from this root that we get the English word "Nike." This, of course, is the name of the manufacturer of athletic shoes and equipment with the swoosh logo that looks like a wing. The name Nike comes from the name of a Greek god–actually a goddess–whose name was Nike. In the depiction of this goddess in the idols of the Greeks, Nike was visually portrayed as having wings. The winged goddess was believed to be the spirit that led and gave people victory and the power to conquer and prevail. This myth gave rise to the oft-repeated phrase from that past culture "the wings of victory," as well as the name and swoosh logo of the athletic company of our present world.

Holy War

The word "*overcome*" is used in the context of a power encounter and struggle. There is a conflict–a war–with a winner and a loser, one who conquers and one who is conquered, one who is the victor and the other the vanquished. In the context of the book of Revelation, its meaning is that of being victorious in a holy war.

War is waged for the ultimate purpose of rule and having one's will done, whether it's between individuals or nations, kingdoms and empires. During the 20th century, World Wars I and II and the other conflicts were not holy wars in which people were motivated by their religion and the rule of their god. Rather, they were secular and fought for the rule of their ideology, whether it was Communism, Nazism or Democracy. The reality of a holy war has come to impact the secularized, Western world in this century with the rise of militant or fundamental Islam. A major precept of Islam is to wage holy war, or jihad, against all who do not submit to the rule of Allah, the god of Islam, and his law, which is Sharia. "Jihad," which has often been translated into English as "holy war," literally means "struggle," and the goal of Islam is to struggle and war against everyone in every place until the entire world comes under the rule and dominion of the god of Islam and lives according to his law.

Most people in the West do not understand the significance of holy war or the motivations of those who give their lives for their religion and their god because of the controlling influence of materialistic secularism and the concept of "the separation of church and state." But holy war is one of the major themes of the Old Testament. The God of the Bible is not the god of Islam[3], and the Scriptures continually tell of the holy war between the LORD and all other gods. The LORD waged holy war against the gods of Egypt to set His people free and for them to come under His rule to live according to His law (Exodus 12:12; 15:3; 20:1ff.; 2 Samuel 7:23). He waged holy war against the people and the gods in the Promised Land to give His people their inheritance (Exodus 23:27-32; Deuteronomy 7:23-25). And He continued to wage holy war against the gods and people who were the enemies of His people (Judges 3:10). Not only this, the promise of God in the Psalms to the coming King who is the Son of David was and is, *"Sit at My right hand until I make your enemies a footstool for your feet"* (Psalm 110:1). This, by the way, is the most quoted verse from the Old Testament in the New Testament.

One of the major themes woven into the book of Revelation is holy war. Jesus waged holy war to overcome (Revelation 5:9) and Revelation describes how He will return to wage holy war on His enemies (Revelation 19:11-21). Chapter 11 speaks of two witnesses saying, *"When they have finished their testimony, the beast that comes up out of the abyss will make war with them, and overcome them and kill them"* (Revelation 11:7). Chapter 13 depicts one described as *"the beast"* and saying, *"It was also given to him to make war with the saints and to overcome them"* (Revelation 13:7). Then, Revelation chapter 17 tells of the kings of the earth who have joined *"the beast"* to oppose the Lord Jesus Christ, saying, *"These will wage war against the Lamb, and the Lamb will overcome them, because He is Lord of lords and King of kings"* (Revelation 17:14). In these verses, overcoming means prevailing in war–a holy war. Perhaps most surprising of all is that the Lord Jesus says He wages war against people in churches who are sinning against Him! To those sinning in the church in Pergamum He said, *"Therefore repent; or else I am coming to you quickly, and I will make war against them with the sword of My mouth"* (Revelation 2:16).

A World At War

During His ministry on earth, Christ used the word *"overcome"* to describe the power encounter involved in setting people free from the influence and control of demons. As we know from the synoptic gospels, much of Jesus' ministry was spent in driving demons out of people and His enemies accused Him of doing this by the power of Satan. In response, He spoke a parable to His accusers about a strong man, who would have been Satan, being overcome by a stronger man, who would be Jesus, saying, *"But when someone stronger than he attacks him and overpowers him, he takes away from him all his armor on which he had relied and distributes his plunder"* (Luke 11:22). The Greek word translated *"overpowers"* is "nikao," the same word translated *"overcome,"* and Christ used it in the context of warfare. Christ delivering people from demons was a battle in the supreme holy war of the universe–the spiritual war between God and Satan over the souls of people.

As is clearly seen from what the Lord says to the seven churches in Revelation, we are living in a world at war. The real world is one ravaged by spiritual warfare involving many different battles of one kind or another on many different battlefronts. Jesus calls His church, and each individual in a church to overcome–to be victorious in the holy war wherever we encounter it.

Powerful, Not Passive

The very essence of overcoming means one struggles, one fights, one engages the enemy to win. The opposite of waging war is passivity. Passivity is the path to defeat. In fact, when one is passive in the spiritual war they are already defeated! Christ wants to empower us to overcome. Sin and Satan want to overcome us by making us passive. This is what happened with Saul and the army of Israel when they encountered the taunts and power of the giant Goliath who continuously defied the ranks of Israel–they stood on the battle line paralyzed with fear (1 Samuel 17:1-11, 24). But David, who had already defeated the lion and the bear, understood that *"the battle is the LORD's"* and becoming strong in faith and the power of God attacked and defeated the enemy (1 Samuel 17:31-49; Hebrews 11:32-33).

The Lord Jesus calls us to wage holy war so that like Him, the son of David, we will overcome all our enemies. As He said in the parable, He is the *"stronger"* man who attacked and overcame the enemy. He promises us power and He gives it to us through the empowering presence of the Holy Spirit. Paul wrote to Timothy, *"God has not given us a spirit of timidity, but of power and love and discipline"* (2 Timothy 1:7). The Greek word translated *"timidity"* means "fearful, cowardice." The Holy Spirit empowers us to be powerful, not passive, so that we can overcome. As we survey what Jesus says to the seven churches, we can identify five major enemies that are to be overcome: the world, the flesh, the devil, false prophets and death.

They Overcome The World

First on the list of enemies to be overcome is the world. It's first on the list, not for the reason that it's more powerful or more important, but because it's first on the traditional list of enemies often cited as "the world, the flesh and the devil."

The world that is our enemy is not the visible creation, nor people through out creation. It is the way of life, the culture of morals and values, and the mindset of beliefs, desires and goals that seek to control our attitudes and actions so we will think and live our lives in a way that is hostile to God and contrary to His will. It is expressed in so many ways, felt in what we call "peer pressure" or "herd mentality," and pursued in the praise and esteem of people. Its influence comes from outside, and is, like smog in a city, the ungodly spiritual atmosphere we live in and breath that pollutes our lives. It is the siren song that seduces us from the love of God to the love of its enticing attractions, vain imaginations, and devilish delights. It is a pressure that constantly seeks to compress us into its mold instead of conform us to the likeness of Christ.

The New Testament is unequivocal in its evaluation of the world–it is an enemy of God. James bluntly confronts Christians about the world saying, *"You adulteresses, do you not know that friendship with the world is hostility toward God? Therefore whoever wishes to be a friend of the world makes himself an enemy of God"* (James 4:4). *"Hostility toward God"* and *"an enemy of God"*–these are among the strongest, even most violent words that can be used to express the nature of the spiritual war the world wages against God and His people. John, the author of the book of Revelation, writes,

Do not love the world nor the things in the world. If anyone loves the world, the love of the Father is not in him. ¹⁶ For all that is in the world, the lust of the flesh and the lust of the eyes and the boastful pride of life, is not from the Father, but is from the world. ¹⁷ The world is passing away, and also its lusts; but the one who does the will of God lives forever" (1 John 2:15-17).

While, the Bible tells us that God loves the world (John 3:16), which means all the people who live in the world, the Bible also tells us that the system, culture, and way of life of the world is not merely indifferent to God, it hates God! Because of this, if we love God, we will not love the world.

The world and all its desires are allied and arrayed against God in this holy war. The most prominent place we see Jesus confronting this enemy is in what He says to the seventh and last church, the church at Laodicea. Jesus had nothing good to say about this church because it had been completely overcome in the spiritual war by the world. And they were totally unaware of it, which is how the world so shrewdly deceives and subtly destroys its victims! They were wealthy in the material things of this world, and their wealth seduced, sedated and deceived them. Because of their love of the things of this world, they had become lukewarm, and it made Jesus sick. Jesus said to them,

So because you are lukewarm, and neither hot nor cold, I will spit you out of My mouth. Because you say, 'I am rich, and have become wealthy, and have need of nothing,' and you do not know that you are wretched, and

miserable and poor and blind and naked'
(Revelation 3:16-17).

It is not that material wealth is wrong, for God says He will bless, provide for, and even prosper His people. But when material wealth and the things of this world become more important to us than Christ, we have become what James calls spiritual adulterers (James 4:4). When we devote more time, energy and money to the things of this world and the so-called "good life" than we do to Christ and His kingdom, the world is advancing in our lives. When we have more pleasure and enjoyment in the things and activities of the world than we do of God and His manifest presence, the world is taking ground in our lives. When we are more passionate in our pursuit of the things of the world than we are for Christ and His mission in the world, the world is overcoming in our lives.

The world continually wages holy war against Christ and His church. The Lord Jesus said,

> *If the world hates you, you know that it has hated Me before it hated you. ¹⁹ If you were of the world, the world would love its own; but because you are not of the world, but I chose you out of the world, because of this the world hates you* (John 15:18-19).

Later He said, "*In the world you have tribulation*" (John 16:33a). What is most significant about what Jesus says here is that the tense of the verb is not future, "you will have," meaning it is inevitable that at some time in the future this will happen. It is present tense. The present tense in Greek means continuous action–"you continually have." That is the nature of it–continuously present. The Greek word translated "*tribulation*" means "stress or pressure." The state of existence of the believer living in this world is continuous stress, pressure, even tribulation to make us conform to it instead of to Christ. However, as Christ goes on to say, "*but take courage, I have overcome the world*" (John 16:33b).

Jesus calls His church to overcome the world, just as He did. We will do this when our hearts are ruled and our lives are governed by true faith in Him. John wrote of this kind faith,

> For whatever is born of God overcomes the world; and this is the victory that has overcome the world–our faith. ⁵ Who is the one who overcomes the world, but he who believes that Jesus is the Son of God? (1 John 5:4-5).

The greatest battle with the world is to believe Who Jesus is–that He is the Son of God, Who became a human being, died for our sins, and rose from the dead. Intimately related to this is the battle of living for the Lord Jesus–that we keep His commandments because we truly know Him and love Him (1 John 2:3; John 14:15).

They Overcome The Flesh

While the world assaults us from the outside, the flesh wages war on the inside. In the Bible, "flesh" can designate the human body that is not evil, and also human beings. But "the flesh" Scripture identifies as our enemy is our human nature infected with the spiritual disease of sin. Sin is the evil spiritual virus that has entered the DNA of human nature to change and corrupt the totality of it–our spirit, heart, soul, mind, body, or whatever way one prefers to distinguish and label the different aspects of human nature. The power of the flesh is manifested in evil desires and deceitful thoughts that are contrary to the will of God, violate His commandments, break down and alienate relationships with God and people, and ultimately deteriorate and destroy us.

The classic description of this spiritual war is in Romans chapter 7 where Paul gives an autobiographical analysis of the power of sin waging war within him. He begins by identifying himself as "flesh" saying, *"I am of flesh, sold into bondage to sin"* (Romans 7:14). He then goes on to describe the nature of this bondage saying that in his mind he knows and agrees with the Law of God, that it is good, and that he wants to do what it says but he can't (Romans 7:15-20). Why is this? He says,

> *I find then the principle that evil is present in me, the one who wants to do good.* ²² *For I joyfully concur with the law of God in the inner man,* ²³ *but I see a different law in the members of my body, waging war against the law of my mind and making me a prisoner of the law of sin which is in my members* (Romans 7:21-23).

The law or principle of sin is the evil power that manifests and operates in fallen human nature to take over our will and make us its slave by carrying out its evil desires. Paul describes this as a spiritual war saying sin is *"waging war against the law of my mind."* Like a drug addict who agrees that his addiction is killing him, and even has the desire to be free from its power but cannot, sin holds its death grip upon human nature so that even when one wants to do God's will, he cannot. That's the nature of the flesh.

Not only Paul, but also James and Peter speak of this war. James wrote to believers, *"What is the source of quarrels and conflicts among you? Is not the source your pleasures that wage war in your members?"* (James 4:1). And Peter wrote, *"Beloved, I urge you as aliens and strangers to abstain from fleshly lusts which wage war against the soul"* (1 Peter 2:11). The way the flesh wages spiritual war in us is by evil desires that present themselves as temptations to our heart, mind and emotions, and then capture our will so that we want to do what it desires and then do it. James summarized this evil progression saying, *"Each one is tempted when he is carried away and enticed by his own lust.* [15] *Then when lust has conceived, it gives birth to sin; and when sin is accomplished, it brings forth death"* (James 1:14-15).

The Scripture characterizes the lusts of the flesh as deceitful because we are so easily deceived by evil desires (Ephesians 4:22). The only way we can detect a deadly desire is by the word of God designating it as an evil desire. Again, writing autobiographically, Paul confessed, *"I would not have come to know sin except through the Law; for I would not have known about coveting if the Law had not said, 'You shall not covet'"* (Romans 7:7). This law is the 10th Commandment, and coveting is the lust or the evil desire of sin (Exodus 20:17). There are many places Scripture exposes what is the bad fruit of an evil desire that is rooted in the flesh, but the most extensive catalogue is in Galatians chapter 5. Paul writes, *"Now the deeds of the flesh are evident, which are: immorality, impurity, sensuality,* [20] *idolatry, sorcery, enmities, strife, jealousy, outbursts of anger, disputes, dissensions, factions,* [21] *envyings, drunkenness, carousing and things like these, of which I forewarned you, that those who practice such things will not inherit the kingdom of God"* (Galatians 5:19-21).

All these actions cause a breakdown in our relationships with people and God, and on the top of the list are sexual *"immorality"* and *"idolatry."* When we survey what Jesus said to the churches in Revelation we see He addresses two of the churches about these two particular sins of the flesh that they are to overcome. The first is the church in Pergamum:

> *I have this against you because you have some there who hold to the teaching of Balaam who kept teaching Balak to put a stumbling block before the sons of Israel, to eat things sacrificed to idols and to commit acts of immorality* (Revelation 2:14).

The second church is in Thyatira to which He says,

> *I have this against you, that you tolerate the woman Jezebel who calls herself a prophetess, and she teaches and leads My bond-servants astray so that they commit acts of immorality and to eat things sacrificed to idols* (Revelation 2:20).

Christ's words to these churches are as strong as it can get: *"I have this against you."* Churches that overlook instead of overcome these sins, as well as the others, are losing the war against the flesh.

The flesh is a deadly enemy that must be overcome. Scripture reveals two critical components to conquering the flesh. The first is to die to the flesh. The word of God never says victory over the flesh comes by education or rehabilitation–it only comes by crucifixion. Paul writes in Galatians 5:23, *"Those who belong to Christ Jesus have crucified the flesh with its passions and desires."* We crucify the flesh by understanding our actual identity in Christ–that we have *"died to sin"* (Romans 6:2). Because of this, we are told *"consider yourselves to be dead to sin"* (Romans 6:11). This mindset is crucial. Scripture does not say sin is dead to us. No, like Frankenstein's monster, "Its alive!" But in Christ we are dead to sin! A dead man does not respond to sin (Romans 6:7). As a result, we are told, *"Therefore, do not let sin reign in your mortal body so that you obey its lusts"* (Romans 6:12). We are to personally actualize what we are positionally in Christ–we are dead to sin, there-fore, live as a person dead to sin! In this way, we crucify the flesh.

The second essential element to overcoming the flesh is living in the Spirit. The Holy Spirit is the power to over-come the flesh. We are to disconnect from the flesh and connect to the Holy Spirit. We do this by setting our minds on the things of the Spirit and not the flesh (Romans 8:5; Colossians 3:1-3). Writing in Galatians 5, Paul says, *"Walk by the Spirit and you will not carry out the desire of the flesh"* (Galatians 5:16). Again, we are told, *"If we live by the Spirit, let us also walk by the Spirit"* (Galatians 5:25). Having been born of the Spirit, we are to live in the Spirit. It is for this reason we are to be continuously *"filled with the Spirit"* (Ephesians 5:18), which means that we are to be ruled, governed and transformed by the Holy Spirit. Doing this, we will bear the fruit of the Spirit, which *"is love, joy, peace, patience, kindness, goodness, faithfulness, [23] gentleness, self-control"* (Galatians 5:22-23). In a word, this is being like Christ. When we live in the Spirit, we will overcome the flesh and will be the kind of church Jesus wants.

They Overcome The Devil

The third major enemy in the holy war is the devil. He is called by many names in Scripture, the two most common being *"the devil,"* which means "slanderer," and *"Satan,"* which means "the adversary." Scripture also speaks of him as *"the enemy"* (Matthew 13:39), *""the evil one"* (1 John 5:19), *"the great dragon"* (Revelation 12:9), *"the serpent"* (Revelation 12:9) and by other titles. He is commonly known by the name "Lucifer," which means "light bearer," and many believe this is his original personal name. This, however, is not what Scripture actually reveals. The name "Lucifer" is of Latin origin, not Hebrew. It was the translation of the Hebrew word "Helel" in Isaiah 14:12 by Jerome (347-420) in the Latin Vulgate and later incorporated into English by the King James Version (1609). There are actually differences of scholarly opinion of the meaning of "Helel" as seen in the New American Standard Version that translates it *"star of the morning,"* the English Standard Version as *"Day Star,"* and the New International Version as *"morning star."* Whatever name Satan is known by, he is the mastermind of all the forces of evil arrayed against God, the people of God, and all that is good and holy.

The word of God reveals that Satan was *"the anointed cherub who covers "* (Ezekiel 28:14). As revealed in the design of the tabernacle given to Moses, a cherub is an angelic or celestial being who covered the Ark of the Covenant, the place where God's manifest presence was enthroned (Exodus 25:20). Cherubs or Cherubim[4] also surrounded the most holy place, which was visually depicted in the curtains that separated that place from everything else thereby making it holy ground (Exodus 26:1). This reveals that the cherubim are the guardians of God's manifest presence, the creatures closest to God in all creation. Being *"the anointed cherub,"* the one commonly called "Lucifer" was the highest ranking of them all. But he fell into sin and in that moment became *"Satan,"* the arch adversary, opponent and enemy of God. In leading his rebellion against God, Scripture indicates he took with him one third of the angelic beings (Revelation 12:4). His destiny, along with his angels and all who follow him, is that he will be cast *"into the eternal fire"* (Matthew 24:41) *"away from the presence of the Lord and from the glory of His power"* (2 Thessalonians 1:9) in *"the lake of fire and brimstone"* (Revelation 20:10).

Through the sin of Adam, Satan took over spiritual rule of the earth and the human race to such an extent that he is called *"the god of this world"* (2 Corinthians 4:4), and the word of God speaks of his power and influence in many places. Jesus spoke of him as *"the ruler of this world"* (John 14:30; 16:11). The Scripture tells us that in tempting the Lord Jesus, the devil

> *led Him up and showed Him all the kingdoms of the world in a moment of time.* [6] *And the devil said to Him, "I will give You all this domain and its glory; for it has been handed over to me, and I give it to whomever I wish"* (Luke 4:5-6).

Jesus did not dispute this claim but resisted all the devil's temptations and for this reason He could say the devil *"has nothing in Me"* (John 14:30). Contrast this with Ephesians 2:2 which speaks of the devil as *"the prince of the power of the air, of the spirit that is now in the sons of disobedience."* Notice the word *"in"*–he is *"working in the sons of disobedience."* It is through sin that the devil is given access into the minds and hearts of people (Matthew 13:19; 2 Corinthians 4:4). We are told in 1 John 5:19, *"We know that we are of God, and that the whole world lies in the power of the evil one."*

While we often speak of this individual spiritual being as personally attacking us, he actually exercises his evil influence, control and power in people's lives through the host of fallen, evil spirits that are loyal to him and under his rule. These compose his *"kingdom"* of spiritual *"darkness"* (Matthew 12:25; Colossians 1:13). Like a military force with a hierarchy of authority and power, the Scripture tells us *"our struggle is against the rulers, against the powers, against the world forces of this darkness, against the spiritual forces of wickedness in the heavenly places* (Ephesians 6:12).

It may be surprising, but Jesus speaks about Satan and his work to four of the seven churches. To the church in Smyrna, He spoke of those who are *"a synagogue of Satan"* and that *"the devil is about to cast some of you into prison"* (Revelation 2:9,10). To the church in Pergamum, He said, *"I know where Satan's throne is"* (Revelation 2:13). To the church in Thyatira He spoke of those *"who have not known the deep things of Satan, as they call them"* (Revelation 2:24). And to the church in Philadelphia He spoke again of *"those of the synagogue of Satan"* (Revelation 3:9). The devil is hardly a minor or irrelevant figure in the world Jesus lives in, let alone a being that the modern, sophisticated world has found to no longer exist. He is relentless in his evil schemes to dominate the world and destroy churches and people's lives.

The devil, along with his evil spirits, is a real enemy we are to overcome. In his first letter, John wrote of those who are *"young men"* in the faith, in distinction to *"children"* and *"fathers,"* saying, *"I have written to you, young men, because you are strong, and the word of God abides in you, and you have overcome the evil one"* (1 John 2:14). There is a level of spiritual maturity and strength that comes from knowing and practicing the word of God. Knowing and believing the truth of the word of God is the most important thing there is to achieve victory over the devil. This is because deception and lies are his primary weapons. Jesus spoke of this saying, "*Whenever he speaks a lie, he speaks from his own nature, for he is a liar and the father of lies*" (John 8:44). And Revelation 12:9 summarizes the devil's evil work saying he "*deceives the whole world.*" It was through His knowledge of and submission to the word of God that the Lord Jesus defeated the devil and all his temptations (Matthew 4:4, 7, 10).

James wrote, "*Submit therefore to God. Resist the devil and he will flee from you*" (James 4:7). Resisting the devil is different from prayer. Prayer is addressed to God, resisting is directed toward the devil–we don't want to get these backwards! In prayer we are to humbly ask God, as Jesus taught in the Lord's Prayer, to "*deliver us from evil*" (Matthew 6:13). But we are to boldly resist the devil. We do this first by submitting to God, which means we must know His word and be obedient to it. Then, in the authority we have in Christ, we are to resist the devil to overcome him. Revelation 12:11 gives the ultimate prescription of how believers are to overcome the devil saying, "*they overcame him because of the blood of the Lamb and because of the word of their testimony, and they did not love their life even when faced with death.*" The devil is a real enemy in the holy war, and the kind of church Jesus wants overcomes him.

They Overcome False Prophets

The fourth major battlefront of the holy war is false prophets because it deals with the critical qualities of holding to the truth of God's word and exercising church discipline. While it is not often recognized, false prophets are a major concern in the book of Revelation as well as the rest of Scripture. In His classic Sermon on the Mount, Jesus warned, *"Beware of the false prophets, who come to you in sheep's clothing, but inwardly are ravenous wolves. [16] You will know them by their fruits"* (Matthew 7:15-16). He said one of the chief characteristics of this age and the end of the age is *"false prophets"* (Matthew 24:11, 24). Peter warned the church,

> *But false prophets also arose among the people, just as there will also be false teachers among you, who will secretly intro- duce destructive heresies, even denying the Master who bought them, bringing swift destruction upon themselves* (2 Peter 2:1).

And John cautioned,

> *Beloved, do not believe every spirit, but test the spirits to see whether they are from God, because many false prophets have gone out into the world. [2] By this you know the Spirit of God: every spirit that confesses that Jesus Christ has come in the flesh is from God; [3] and every spirit that does not confess Jesus is not from God; this is the spirit of the antichrist, of which you have heard that it is coming, and now it is already in the world. [4] You are from God, little children, and have overcome them; because greater is He who is in you than he who is in the world"* (1 John 4:1-4).

The concern about those who are false, and specifically false prophets is a continuous theme throughout Jesus' words to the churches in Revelation. He commended the church in Ephesus because they *"put to the test those who call themselves apostles, and they are not, and you found them to be false"* (Revelation 2:2). Testing the teaching of those who claimed to be something was not a one-time occurrence but a continuous practice of oversight and discipline in this church. To the church in Smyrna He spoke of *"the blasphemy by those who say they are Jews and are not, but are a synagogue of Satan"* (Revelation 2:9), and to the church in Philadelphia of those *"of the synagogue of Satan, who say that they are Jews and are not, but lie."* These are people with a rich religious history and the claim that they are of God because of their ethnic and cultural identity according to the flesh, but they are false. They are, as John wrote, *"false prophets"* who are of *"the spirit of the antichrist"* (1 John 4:1, 3) because they do not believe Jesus is the Christ, the Son of God. Speaking to the church in Pergamum, Christ exposed *"the teaching of Balaam"* (Revelation 2:14), who was a premier false prophet and led God's people into idolatry and sexual immorality. The same thing was happening in the church in Thyatira with *"the woman, Jezebel, who calls herself a prophetess"* (Revelation 2:20).

It is obvious that the Lord Jesus has a serious concern about the harmful and deadly effects of false prophets in the churches. They are a real enemy in the holy war who are to be overcome by teaching, testing and holding to the truth of God's word.

They Overcome Death

The fifth and final enemy to be overcome in the holy war is death. God's will for His creation is life, life in His manifest presence, but through the temptation of Satan and the sin of Adam, death came into the world. Romans 5:12 says, *"through one man sin entered into the world, and death through sin, and so death spread to all men, because all sinned."*

The Bible tells us that because Jesus overcame sin and death by His death, resurrection from the dead and ascension to heaven, He will reign at the right hand of God the Father until He has defeated every one of His enemies. The Scripture declares, *"He must reign until He has put all His enemies under His feet. The last enemy that will be abolished is death"* (1 Corinthians 15:25-26). Death is the final enemy to be defeated and Christ's resurrection and ascension guarantee this victory for all who are His.

While being born of the Spirit is the initiation of the process of resurrection (John 11:26; Ephesians 2:5), we will ultimately overcome death by our physical resurrection from the dead when *"death is swallowed up in victory"* (1 Corinthians 15:54). As followers of Christ there are a number of different ways we can face the foe of death. Certainly every believer has the possibility of fighting the enemy of death when faced with a life threatening disease or the degeneration of their body through old age. Church history and the present world crisis with the rise of fundamentalist or militant Islam has shown that one of the greatest ways believers face death is when they are being persecuted. How many believers have been put to death because they will not deny the Lord Jesus Christ but instead faithfully confess they believe He has risen from the dead and is their Lord and Savior? This is the very thing Jesus spoke about to the church in Smyrna when they were about to experience persecution and He told them *"be faithful until death and I will give you the crown of life"* (Revelation 2:10).

Because Christ has risen from the dead, we have victory over death. We do not have to fear death because *"the sting"* of death has been removed (1 Corinthians 15:55). To physically die is not the end of life as the atheist believes, but the beginning of true life in the very presence of the living Lord Jesus Christ Who is the resurrection and the life (John 11:25). As Paul wrote, *"For to me, to live is Christ and to die is gain"* (Philippians 1:21). This is because *"to be absent from the body"* is *"to be at home with the Lord"* (2 Corinthians 5:8). It will be when we arrive *"home"* in the very presence of the Lord that we will gain the final victory that He has given to us.

Christ's Call

As we see from what Jesus says to the seven churches in Revelation, the kind of church He wants is a church that overcomes. So vital is this to Him that He calls each and every church to overcome just as He overcame. Yet while He speaks to each church individually and all the churches as a whole, His specific call and challenge to overcome is not addressed to some vague group or assembly of people but personally to every one of us as individuals. He doesn't say, "If you all overcome" so that an individual might be lost in the crowd. He says, *"He who overcomes."* What this means is that we are responsible for our own spiritual lives. We are accountable to Christ for our relationship with Him—how we live, how we walk, how we obey Him. What anybody or what everybody else does is, in the end, irrelevant. On the Day of Judgment when we stand before the Lord, we will stand alone to give an account of our lives (Romans 2:16; 14:10). A spiritually mature person takes responsibility for his or her own life. That is why Jesus addresses each one of us as individuals saying, *"He who overcomes."* However, the more individuals there are in a church who are spiritually mature and overcoming, the more a church will be the kind of church Jesus wants.

Just As He Did

During World War II, numerous Christians in Nazi Germany suffered and gave their lives because of their faith in the Lord Jesus. One was the pastor, theologian and author, Deitrich Bonhoeffer. While most of the pastors and churches succumbed to the pressures of the world, the flesh and the devil, Bonhoeffer spoke out against the Nazification of the church in Germany and refused to swear allegiance to Hitler. As a pastor and leader of what was called "the Confessing Church"–because it confessed the truth of what the Bible revealed and taught about Jesus–Bonhoeffer determined that he would live his life joyfully and courageously doing the will of God even if it meant dying for Christ. As things turned out in the providence of God, he was arrested and imprisoned. Yet even while in prison, he continued to encourage his fellow prisoners to follow Christ. Under orders from Hitler, the day before the Allies set free those remaining in the prison where Bonhoeffer was held, he was executed by hanging. Sometime later, the doctor at that prison gave an account of how Bonhoeffer died. He wrote, "In the almost fifty years that I have worked as a doctor, I have hardly ever seen a man die so entirely submitted to the will of God."[5]

One of Bonhoeffer's books is entitled *The Cost of Discipleship.*[6] In it he succinctly summarizes the call of the Lord Jesus to follow Him. He wrote, "When Christ calls a man, He bids him come and die." This statement is absolutely true. Christ calls us to follow Him, to take up our own cross and die. He calls us to overcome just as He did. When we do, we will find true life–life in the Spirit, eternal life in His presence. May He give us ears to hear His call.

Study Questions
Chapter 9

1. Describe the worship that John experienced in heaven. Have you ever experienced a taste of this kind of glory on earth?

2. What is the importance of the scroll with the seven seals? Why is Jesus the only one worthy to open the scroll?

3. What is the significance of Jesus saying seven times "*to him who overcomes*"?

4. What is your Biblical understanding of the term "holy war" and what is your response to this?

5. What kind of spiritual warfare are you aware of in your own life?

6. Give some examples of waging war versus passive responses to spiritual battles we encounter in life?

7. What is the Biblical understanding of *"the world"* as one of our spiritual enemies? Where do you see this spiritual enemy threatening to influence your life?

8. How is the power of the flesh manifested, and what are the two critical components to conquering it?
(1)
(2)

9. Who is our third major enemy and what do his names reveal about him?

10. How do we achieve victory over the devil?

11. What is the fourth major battlefront, and how does Jesus expect the church to respond?

12. What is the final enemy in the holy war, and how do we as Christians face this foe?

CHAPTER 10

EACH OF THE SEVEN CHURCHES: HAS ETERNAL VALUES

Revelation 2:7b
To him who overcomes,
I will grant to eat of the tree of life which is in the
Paradise of God.

Revelation 2:10b, 11b
Be faithful until death,
and I will give the crown of life.
He who overcomes
will not be hurt by the second death.

Revelation 2:17b
To him who overcomes,
I will give some of the hidden manna,
and I will give him a white stone,
and a new name written on the stone which
no one knows but he who receives it.

Revelation 2:26-28

He who overcomes,
to him I will give authority over the nations;
27 and he shall rule them with a rod of iron, as the vessels
of the potter are broken to pieces,
as I also have received authority from My Father;
28 and I will give him the morning star.

Revelation 3:5
5 He who overcomes
will thus be clothed in white garments;
and I will not erase his name from the book of life,
and I will confess his name before My Father and before
His angels.

Revelation 3:12
He who overcomes,
I will make him a pillar in the temple of My God, and he
will not go out from it anymore;
and I will write on him the name of My God,
and the name of the city of My God, the new Jerusalem,
which comes down out of heaven from My God,
and My new name.

Revelation 3:21
He who overcomes,
I will grant to him to sit down with Me on My throne,
as I also overcame and sat down with My Father on
His throne.

He's No Fool

One of the most influential people of the last century for Christ and His kingdom was a man who died at the age of 28. His name is Jim Elliot. God only knows how many people were challenged, encouraged and motivated to commit their lives to Christ and the work of missions because of the life and death of Jim Elliot. He was a man who was zealously and wholeheartedly devoted to Christ and His glory.

As a young man, Elliot attended Wheaton College, a Christian liberal arts college in Wheaton, Illinois. He was not interested so much in the different subjects of the liberal arts courses as he was in the study of the Bible. Because of this, he chose to major in Greek, the original language of the New Testament, so he could better understand the New Testament and translate it into the language of people who did not have God's word. Elliot's passion was Christ and living by the power of the Holy Spirit according to the reality of what God's word actually taught about Christ and His demands upon those who would follow Him as His disciples. Because of this, his desire was to go into missions to take the gospel to the lost somewhere in this world.

While at Wheaton he met his wife to be, Elizabeth. After they were married, they became missionaries in Ecuador focusing their evangelism efforts on a people group called the Quechua Indians. Desiring to reach those who had never heard the gospel, Elliot and his missionary companions made contact with another tribe called the Huaorani, whom the Quechua Indians called "Acua." "Acua" means "savage," for they were a violent people who would quickly murder those outside their tribe, which proved to be true for Elliot. On January 8, 1956, while attempting to make friendly contact with them to bring the gospel to these lost souls, Elliot and four other companions encountered 10 Acua warriors who speared them to death.

In the 1950s, such a tragic occurrence happening to Christian missionaries was virtually unheard of so news of their deaths quickly spread throughout America. *Life* magazine published a full 10-page article about what happened. Details of his love and devotion to Christ were further revealed in two books, *Shadow of the Almighty* and *Through Gates of Splendor,* written by his wife Elizabeth. Through this media, the life and death of Jim Elliot became well known. As a result, countless numbers of people were challenged to give their lives to Christ and commit their lives to missions.

What motivated Jim Elliot to live and then give his life for Christ? Undoubtedly, there were many things, but foremost was that he had eternal values. What he valued most was not in this world. It is in the world to come–the eternal reward that Christ would give him. He wanted to invest what life he had in this world, which would one day pass away, into that which would never pass away. His eternal values were summarized in an entry in his journal dated October 29, 1949, in which he wrote, "He is no fool who gives what he cannot keep to gain what he cannot lose." These words express the faith of a man who understood that this world is fleeting and the world to come is forever. They are the testimony of a man who sought to invest every day of his life for Christ and His kingdom because only what is done for Christ will last. They are the confession of a man who zealously lived and died for Christ because he was motivated by the true and certain promises of Christ, that in giving what he could not keep he would gain what he could not lose–the eternal reward Christ would give to him.

The Wisest Investment You Will Ever Make

Having eternal values is valuing that which will last for eternity. This is totally different from temporary values that place the highest worth in things that will only last for a period of time, whether it is a few moments, like a drug high, a few years, like a car or clothes, or even a lifetime, like diamonds. Throughout His ministry on earth, Jesus constantly told people to have eternal values and invest their lives in that which will bring an eternal reward. He said,

> *Do not store up for yourselves treasures on earth, where moth and rust destroy, and where thieves break in and steal. 20 But store up for yourselves treasures in heaven, where neither moth nor rust destroys, and where thieves do not break in or steal* (Matthew 6:19-20).

After feeding the 5,000, He said, "*Do not work for the food which perishes, but for the food which endures to eternal life, which the Son of Man will give to you*" (John 6:27). And He said to those who suffered persecution for following Him, "*Rejoice and be glad, for your reward in heaven is great*" (Matthew 5:12). Jesus is the wisest investment advisor there will ever be.

Perhaps the greatest place in Scripture we see Jesus telling people to have eternal values is in His words to the seven churches of Revelation, and in this we see the next quality of the kind of church Jesus wants. Just as He overcame and received the eternal reward of His suffering, He encourages every one of the churches to overcome whatever challenges they face and then connects their overcoming with the promise of the eternal reward He will give them. It is clear Christ is telling these churches, and each person in all the churches, to have eternal values because there is a cost to following Him in this world. But whatever price we may pay is worth the eternal reward we will receive in the world to come, and that is why we are to have eternal values.

While Jesus gives promises of particular rewards to each church as they correspond to the specific situation each church is facing, the eternal rewards are for all who overcome. These eternal rewards will be received in the New Heaven and Earth described in the last two chapters of Revelation, chapters 21 and 22, which is the ultimate goal and destiny of every believer in Christ.

Paradise Gained

The first promise Christ gives in the letters is to the church in Ephesus, the church that was called to have a first love for Christ. He says, "*I will grant to eat of the tree of life, which is in the Paradise of God*" (Revelation 2:7).

The first tree of life was in the Garden of Eden (Genesis 2:9). The Garden was the original paradise "*in Eden*" (Genesis 2:8). It was the Garden *of* Eden–Eden being the original Garden-Temple of the manifest presence of God on the earth. The Hebrew word "*Eden*" means "pleasure, delight" and the word "paradise" is of Persian origin meaning "garden of pleasure." While there were many pleasures that Adam and Eve enjoyed, the greatest was the enjoyment of God's manifest presence as they walked with Him in the Garden. Their purpose was to glorify God and to delight in and enjoy Him forever. But instead of loving God by keeping His commandment to not eat of the tree of the knowledge of good and evil, they chose to disobey Him. As a consequence, they were condemned to the payment of sin, which is death (Genesis 2:13, Romans 6:23). Falling into sin, they were spiritually separated from God and their human nature was corrupted (Romans 5:19). In order to ensure this judgment, they were forbidden to eat of the tree of life lest they would live forever in their fallen, sinful state. This penalty was enforced by them being cast out of the Garden and holy angelic beings called cherubim with flaming swords placed at the entrance to the Garden to prevent access to the tree of life (Genesis 3:22-24).

From that time on, the only way that access to the tree of life will be granted is for a person's sins to be forgiven and cleansed. This was symbolized in the design of the Tabernacle revealed to Moses. The Golden Lampstand, which stood in the holy place near God's manifest presence enthroned on the Ark, was designed like a tree and represented the tree of life that was in the original Garden (Exodus 25:31ff.). The only way one could draw near to the manifest presence of God in the holy place of the Tabernacle was to enter through the one door of the court, come to the bronze altar where the blood was poured out to pay the penalty for forgiveness of sin, and then come to the bronze laver where one washed with water to be cleansed from the pollution of sin. All these things were prophetic types of Christ who would die on the cross–the tree of death–so that His people could be forgiven and cleansed from their sin and be able to enter Paradise, eat of the Tree of Life and receive eternal life. On the cross, Jesus spoke to the thief who came to saving faith in Him saying, *"This day you will be with me in Paradise"* (Luke 23:24).

Scripture speaks of the present third heaven, what most Christians simply call "heaven," as *"Paradise"* (2 Corinthians 12:2, 4). However, the future, eternal Paradise that Jesus promises to those who overcome will be in the New Heaven and Earth that is described as *"coming down from heaven from God"* (Revelation 21:2). This will be the ultimate and final Garden-Tabernacle/Temple of God where His people will live forever in His glorious manifest presence. Chapter 21 describes it as the ultimate Tabernacle/Temple beginning with the words, *"Behold, the tabernacle of God is among men, and He will dwell among them, and they shall be His people, and God Himself will be among them*" (Revelation 21:3). Chapter 22 describes it as the ultimate Garden of Eden and in the middle of it is *"the tree of life"* (Revelation 22:2). It will be this *"tree of life"* that gives and sustains the eternal life that Jesus promises to *"grant"* to all who are true believers in Him. This is made possible because their sins will have been forgiven and cleansed so they can live forever in the holy, manifest presence of God. This promise is repeated in Revelation 22:14, *"Blessed are those who wash their robes, so that they may have the right to the tree of life."*

The church in Ephesus was called to have first love for Christ. When we love Christ, we will keep His commandments to love God with all our hearts, minds and strength, our neighbor as ourselves, and one other as Christ loved us (Matthew 22:36-40; John 13:34; John 14:15). Adam and Eve did not keep God's command and were forbidden from eating of the tree of life in the original Paradise. Those to whom Christ will *"grant to eat of the tree of life, which is in the Paradise of God"* are those who love Him with a first love and live it by keeping His commandments.

The Winner's Wreath

The Lord Jesus gives two promises to the second church, the church in Smyrna that was called to be faithful in times of testing. They were called to be *"faithful to death,"* and to those who overcome He said, *"I will give you the crown of life"* and you *"shall not be hurt by the second death"* (Revelation 2:10b, 11). These two promises are like two sides of the same coin–the one who receives *"the crown of life" "shall not be hurt by the second death."*

The *"crown"* that Christ promises is not a "diadem," which was a royal crown (Revelation 19:12), but a "stephanos," which was a wreath awarded to victors in the games. Because the English word "wreath" does not have the connotation of being a reward to a winner in the games it is translated "crown." Nevertheless, a "stephanos" was actually a wreath–a winner's wreath awarded to a winner in the games. It would be the same as winning the gold medal in the modern Olympic games, but whereas in the Olympic games there are three medals–gold, silver and bronze–in the games of that era there was only one prize–the winner's wreath, the "stephanos."

Smyrna was famous for the games, and most everyone in the church would have understood the analogy. The esteemed value of being awarded the prize of the winner's wreath or crown was the motivation to endure all the suffering necessary to become a winner for Christ. As the saying goes, "No pain, no gain." The reason every athlete endures and works through the pain is to gain the prize they so highly value. Paul wrote to the Corinthians of this very thing saying,

> *Do you not know that those who run in a race all run, but only one receives the prize? Run in such a way that you may win. ²⁵ Everyone who competes in the games exercises self-control in all things. They then do it to receive a perishable wreath, but we an imperishable. ²⁶ Therefore I run in such a way, as not without aim; I box in such a way, as not beating the air; ²⁷ but I discipline my body and make it my slave, so that, after I have preached to others, I myself will not be disqualified* (1 Corinthians 9:24-27).

Paul contrasts the temporary values of those who run the race to receive the prize in this world of a wreath that will perish with those who have eternal values and run the race to win the wreath that will never perish. It takes great "*self-control*" and "*discipline*" in order that one may "*run in such a way that you may win*," and the reason you do this is to receive the reward of the "*wreath*" that is "*imperishable*" and eternal.

All the major writers of the New Testament speak of this winner's wreath, which is translated as "*crown.*" Knowing he was coming to the conclusion of his life on earth, Paul wrote to Timothy once again using the analogy of the games saying,

> *I have fought the good fight, I have finished the course, I have kept the faith;* [8] *in the future there is laid up for me the crown of righteousness, which the Lord, the righteous Judge, will award to me on that day; and not only to me, but also to all who have loved His appearing*" (2 Timothy 4:7-8).

Encouraging those who were enduring the trials of suffering, James wrote, "*Blessed is a man who perseveres under trial; for once he has been approved, he will receive the crown of life which the Lord has promised to those who love Him*" (James 1:12). And after giving a charge to leaders in the churches to be godly examples, Peter says, "*And when the Chief Shepherd appears, you will receive the unfading crown of glory*" (1 Peter 5:4). Whether it is called "*the crown of righteousness*," "*the unfading crown of glory*," or "*the crown of life*," it is the wreath that will be awarded to the winners who endure the pain, finish the race, and are faithful to the end. The "*crown of life*" is not an exclusive reward given to the elite group of Christians who die as martyrs for Christ. It is the reward that will be given to all true believers who are faithful to Him as their Lord. "*On that day*" they will take their place on the winner's stand to be awarded their eternal "gold medal" from "*the Lord, the righteous Judge."* Whether a person's life is a short sprint in years, like Jim Elliot or the Lord Jesus, or a marathon, like Moses or, as church tradition says, John who wrote this book, winning the eternal winner's wreath is the motivation for running the race and running it to win. And we will do it because we have eternal values.

It Cannot Happen

Corresponding to winning the winner's wreath or crown is the promise that they will not suffer the eternal destiny of those who are the real losers in life. They *"shall not be hurt by the second death."* The *"second death"* is the *"lake of fire,"* or more exactly being *"thrown into the lake that burns with fire and brimstone"* (Revelation 20:14; 21:8). Those who will suffer this eternal punishment are *"the cowardly and unbelieving and abominable and murderers and immoral persons and sorcerers and idolaters and all liars"* (Revelation 21:8).

It is most significant that while we can, so to speak, "separate the sin from the sinner," God's word does not. It is the tree that produces its fruit. The kind of fruit it produces identifies what kind of tree it is (Matthew 7:15-20). People who live their lives ruled by sin are not simply people who have sinned–they are sinners. Because of this, it is not the sin that is thrown into the lake of *"fire and brimstone"*–it is the sinner. It is not the sin of unbelief that is thrown into the lake of fire, it is the *"unbelieving."* It not the sin of murder or sexual immorality that is cast into hell, but *"murderers"* and *"immoral persons."* As John the Baptist proclaimed, *"The axe is already laid at the root of the trees; therefore every tree that does not bear good fruit is cut down and thrown into the fire"* (Matthew 3:10).

The promise to those who overcome is that they *"shall not be hurt by the second death."* The Greek word translated "*hurt*" is "adikeo." The root is "dik," and means "righteous, just." The "a" before "dik" is the negation of what is righteous or just, in other words to be treated unrighteously or to suffer injustice. The result of being wronged by this injustice is pain or hurt. This gives greater insight into the promise of Jesus, that His promise is based on the righteous judgment of God and this judgment results in two things. One is that those who are "*hurt*" in the sense of suffering the pain and agony of "*the second death*" do so because of the righteous judgment of God against them because of their sins. No one who goes to hell has suffered injustice in any way because God's judgment is righteous (Romans 1:32; 2:2-6). They have sinned and have not been forgiven the penalty of their sins. They are sinners and have not been cleansed from the pollution of their sins. They justly deserve and will receive the righteous judgment of God against them for what they have done and what they are, and they will be "*thrown into the lake that burns with fire and brimstone.*"

It may be surprising to some to realize that those who "*shall not be hurt by the second death*" also receive the righteous judgment of God. This is because their sins have been justly judged and condemned in the Lord Jesus Christ Who died in their place so that through Him they can be forgiven and cleansed from all unrighteousness (1 John 1:9). More than this, they have been declared righteous by God, being justified through faith alone in the Lord Jesus Christ as the righteousness of Christ has been credited or imputed to them (Romans 3:21-26; 4:4). They cannot be "*hurt by the second death*" because it would be utterly unrighteous for a just God to cast a righteous person into hell. They are winners in life because they have truly believed in and received the free gift of righteousness that comes through the Lord Jesus Christ.

Intimate Fellowship at His Table

The next promises are given to the church in Pergamum. This church was to hold to the truth of God's word because there were some who were teaching that believers could *"eat things sacrificed to idols and to commit acts of immorality"* (Revelation 2:14). The Lord's first promise to the one who overcomes is *"I will give some of the hidden manna"* (Revelation 2:17b).

In the Old Testament, manna was the food supernaturally supplied to the Israelites in their travels in the wilderness until they arrived in the Promised Land (Exodus 16:4, 31; Joshua 5:12). The LORD directed that a pot of this manna be put into the Ark of the Covenant to be preserved as a physical evidence and testimony to His people of His faithfulness and power to provide (Exodus 16:32-34). A Hebrew tradition held that when the temple of Solomon was destroyed, the prophet Jeremiah rescued the Ark with the manna and they believed these would be preserved until the time of the coming of the Messiah when manna would again be given as food for God's people. Another tradition, based on the manna being *"the bread of angels"* (Psalm 78:25) was that there is a treasury in heaven of manna which was believed to be *"hidden"* in a golden pot *"laid up before God"* (Exodus 16:23). Then, in the future Messianic kingdom, this manna would descend from heaven to feed those blessed of God.

Whatever the background, this food is to be contrasted to the eating of the food offered to idols that was taking place in Pergamum. Those who are faithful and hold to the truth of God's word will be given some of this manna because they will be admitted to the Messianic Banquet, the Marriage Supper of the Lamb spoken about in Revelation 19:9. There they will forever be blessed with eternal provision of *"daily bread"* (Matthew 6:11) and spiritual provision of the fullness of fellowship and communion with Christ at His table.

Along with this, the Lord promises, *"I will give him a white stone."* One of the things white symbolizes in the book of Revelation is conquering–being an overcomer. The first horse released by the first seal is white and it goes out *"conquering and to conquer"* (Revelation 6:2). The souls who overcome having been martyred for Christ are given a *"white robe"* (Revelation 6:9, 11). Jesus will return on a *"white horse"* and *"the armies which are in heaven, clothed in fine linen, white and clean, were following Him on white horses"* (Revelation 19:11, 14). In the first century when Christ gave this promise, a white stone was used as a token for admission to a banquet and public festivals. This *"white stone"* would also be a reference to admission to the Messianic Banquet in the age to come.

Then they are given *"a new name written on the stone which no one knows but he who receives it."* In Scripture, a name is not only a representation and reputation of a person but a revelation of their character. This speaks of the depth of personal knowledge, relationship and fellowship the Lord has with those who are His. He *"calls His own by name"* (John 10:3) and they share personal "secrets" with each other, for *"the secret of the Lord is for those who fear Him"* (Psalm 25:14). They will all, like John at the table of the Last Supper (John 13:23), recline on the bosom of Jesus because they have been given admission to His future table where they will share the fullness of intimate fellowship and personal relationship with Him. To be invited to dine at a table with a president, king, or emperor, would be an experience of a lifetime, and something highly valued. But it is nothing compared to being one of those who will dine at the table of the King of Kings and Lord of Lords! That will be an eternal lifetime experience and, for that reason, of eternal value.

Reigning With Him

The fourth church Jesus addressed was the church in Thyatira in which the primary concern was church discipline. Church discipline is the exercise of jurisdictional authority and the first promise Jesus gives to this church is most fitting. According to the principle *"he who is faithful in a very little thing is faithful also in much"* (Luke 16:10), the Lord's promise to those who are faithful in the exercise of authority in His church is *"I will give authority over the nations ²⁷ and he shall rule them with a rod of iron, as the vessels of the potter are broken to pieces, as I also have received authority from My Father"* (Revelation 2:26-27).

Just as He had originally been given this promise from the Father, Jesus promises to give *"authority over the nations"* to those who are faithful. This promise is recorded in Psalm 2, which is a Messianic psalm, meaning it contains prophecy about the coming Messiah. The Father's promise to His Son, who is the anointed Messiah and King, is *"Ask of Me and I will surely give You the nations as Your inheritance, the very ends of the earth as Your possession. ⁹ You shall break them with a rod of iron; You shall shatter them like earthenware"* (Psalm 2:8-9).

This promise is a major theme of God's purpose woven through the tapestry of salvation history. Authority over the earth was originally given to Adam and Eve but forfeited when they sinned and disobeyed God (Genesis 1:28). God's covenant promise to Abraham and Sarah was that *"kings will come forth from you"* (Genesis 17:6, 16) and this was repeated to Jacob whose name was changed to Israel (Genesis 35:11). The further development of this covenant promise was given to David, the king of Israel, whom God told, *"I will raise up your descendant after you, who will come forth from you, and I will establish his kingdom,"* which would be forever (2 Samuel 7:12-16). Then, as

Psalm 2 reveals, this promise was further revealed to include authority to rule over the nations of the earth. After Christ died to make atonement for sin and disarm the authority and power of Satan (Colossians 2:14-15), He rose from the dead and this authority was given to Him to be *"ruler over the kings of the earth"* (Revelation 1:5). The Lord Jesus now promises that those who are faithful and overcome will share in this authority that He received from the Father and they will *"reign upon the earth" "with Him"* (Revelation 5:10; 2 Timothy 2:12).

The power of this authority is expressed in the words, *"he shall rule them with a rod of iron,"* a phrase used in two other places in Revelation to describe the rule of the Lord (12:5; 19:15). The power of this authority will be exercised *"as the vessels of the potter are broken to pieces."* The "rod" is not a shepherd's rod, which was used to fend off predators (Psalm 23:4), but a scepter, the symbol of sovereign authority. *"Iron"* was one of the strongest metals known at the time. So great and absolute is the power of His rule that all who oppose it will be *"broken"*–shattered to pieces like an iron rod smashing a clay pot. They will not simply be cracked, they will be *"broken to pieces"*– like Humpty Dumpty, never to be put back together again! This expresses the ultimate victory of Christ and all who are His over all who reject and rebel against His God-given authority to rule. The joy of Jesus is to give us a share in His rule even as it was the Father's joy to give Him this authority.

Along with His promise of authority is the promise *"I will give him the morning star"* (Revelation 2:28). At the conclusion of the book of Revelation Christ calls Himself *"the bright morning star"* (Revelation 22:16). The morning star is the name given to the planet Venus and is the star that continues to shine as the dawn of the new day overcomes the passing darkness of the night. As a rod or scepter is a symbol of sovereignty so a star can also be a symbol of authority. Most significant in this regard is the prophecy of Balaam, about whom Jesus spoke to the previous church that taught *"the sons of Israel to eat things sacrificed to idols and to commit acts of immorality"* (Revelation 2:14). This was the same problem in the church in Pergamum that was called to be faithful to exercise jurisdictional authority in church discipline. Balaam prophesied,

> *I see him, but not now; I behold him, but not near; a star shall come forth from Jacob, a scepter shall rise from Israel, and shall crush through the forehead of Moab, and tear down all the sons of Sheth* (Numbers 24:17).

In this word, the *"star"* and the *"scepter"* are equated as symbols of authority. Just as the first prophecy of Christ was that He would *"crush the head"* of the serpent (Genesis 3:15), it is the *"star"* who has authority who will *"crush the forehead"* of the enemies of God. Jesus is that star, *"the bright morning star,"* who brings the dawn of the day of God to defeat the powers of darkness. Jesus promises those who are faithful in the right exercise of church authority that they will be given *"the morning star."* They will be given authority with Him as the *"lords"* and *"kings"* He has made to be His *"kingdom"* (Revelation 1:6; 17:14; 19:16). They will reign with Him in the dawn of the new day that will come when the dark power of the enemies of God are completely defeated.

Priests in God's Holy, Manifest Presence

To the church in Sardis that was called to be real, Jesus gives three promises that are three aspects of one glorious future reality–being priests in the holy, manifest presence of God. As Christ has made those who overcome to be a *"kingdom,"* He has also *"made them to be "priests"* (Revelation 1:6; 5:10). This will fulfill the eternal purpose of God for His people that they will be to Him *"a kingdom of priests"* (Exodus 19:6). While under the Law of Moses only those of the physical lineage of Aaron could be priests, under the New Covenant inaugurated by Christ all who are His are made to be *"a holy priesthood"* (1 Peter 2:5) with the foremost privilege, honor and blessing being granted access to the holy, manifest presence of God.

God revealed to His people in the Old Covenant period that a priest had to be clothed in holy, clean garments in order to approach and be accepted before His manifest presence enthroned above the Ark in the holy place (Exodus 28:1-5, 38, 41, 43; Zechariah 3:1-5). Christ says those who overcome will be *"clothed in white garments"* (Revelation 3:5). Along with conquering, white is the symbol of the spiritual cleanliness and purity that is essential to be in the holy, manifest presence of God. *"White garments"* or *"robes"* are spoken of seven times in Revelation (3:4, 18; 4:4; 6:11; 7:9, 13; 19:14) and all are in the manifest presence of God. The twenty-four elders who are around the throne of God are *"clothed in white garments"* (Revelation 4:4). The martyrs whose souls are *"underneath the altar"* are given *"a white robe"* (Revelation 6:9, 11). All the saved before the throne are *"clothed in white robes"* (Revelation 7:9, 11). Christ promises those who overcome that they will be given *"white garments"* not only making them justified, having been saved from the penalty of sin, but completely sanctified, having been saved from the pollution of sin. Because of this, they will be able to approach, be completely accepted and able to live forever in the glorious and holy manifest presence of God.

Christ then promises, "*I will not erase his name from the book of life*" (Revelation 3:5). In a number of places, the Bible reveals that God has a book in which are written the names of those who will inherit eternal life (Exodus 32:32-33; Psalm 69:28; Daniel 12:1; Luke 10:20; Philippians 4:3; Hebrews 12:23) and for this reason it is called "*the book of life.*" The ominous words of Revelation 20:15 make known, "*if anyone's name was not found written in the book of life, he was thrown into the lake of fire.*" These will be cast "*away from the presence of the Lord*" (2 Thessalonians 2:9). Those whose names are in "*the book of life*" will live forever in His manifest presence.

Because the Lord's promise is that one's name will not be erased from the book of life, some have inferred that there is a real possibility of a person losing their salvation and their name being "*erased from the book of life.*" This inference should not be made for a number of reasons, among them being as follows:

(a) There are many instances in Scripture where an explicit statement is made and from this a false inference can be made–and that is the point, it is a false inference. The foremost example of this is the book of Romans where the major arguments proceed in response to false inferences (Romans 2:3; 3:1, 3, 5, 7; 6:1, 15; 7:7; 8:12; 9:6, 14, 19; 10:16; 11:1). Great caution should be used in making an inference, especially as in this promise of Christ when the inference actually contradicts His express promise that one's name will not be erased from the book of life.

(b) The nature of Christ's word is not a threat but a promise of assurance. To infer a threat from this would be to make "*the book of life*" a "book of probation" and one's salvation ultimately dependent on their works in this world. To the contrary, Revelation 13:8 speaks of those "*whose name has been written from the foundation of the world in the book of life*"–"*the foundation of the world*" being the creation of the world before which God by His grace chose those who would forever be in His holy, manifest presence (Ephesians 1:4).

(c) This is an explicit declaration of assurance just as much as are Christ's declarations "*I am with You always*" (Matthew 28:20), "*the one who comes to Me I will certainly not cast out,*" (John 6:37) and "*I will never desert you, nor will I ever forsake you*" (Hebrews 13:5). No one should infer from these promises that the possibility exists for Christ to do the exact opposite of what He says He will do, that He will not be with His own, that He would cast one out or that He would abandon and forsake us. Christ gives the promise that one's name will not be erased because it cannot be erased. It is a promise of blessed assurance to the one who overcomes.

Having our name written in the book of life is required to receive eternal life, as it is also essential to serve as a priest forever in God's presence. Upon the return from the exile under the leadership of Ezra, the temple was to be rebuilt and the priesthood restored. However, there were certain people of whom it was said, "*These searched among their ancestral registration, but they could not be located; therefore they were considered unclean and excluded from the priesthood*" (Ezra 2:62). The names of the priests had to be recorded in the book of "*ancestral registration*" to be accepted as clean in order to serve as a priest in the temple. Because one's name is in the "*registration*" of "*the book of life,*" they will be able to serve God as priests in His future Temple of the New Heaven and Earth.

The third promise confirms what has already been promised: "*I will confess his name before My Father and before His angels*" (Revelation 3:5). This is a restatement of what Christ declared during His earthly ministry (Matthew 10:32; Luke 12:8). Christ is revealing that He is "*the Advocate with the Father*" for all who are His because He is the One Who made propitiation for their sins (1 John 2:1-2). While

His confession before the Father pleads for the legal pro-nouncement that one be declared righteous before God, the Biblical background includes that of the High Priest Joshua who stood before God with filthy garments being *"accused by Satan"* and *"the angel of the LORD"* interceding on his behalf. Joshua is then clothed with clean garments to be able to perform the service of the LORD, being given free access and charge of the courts of the LORD (Zechariah 3:1-7). The *"angel of the LORD"* at that time was the preincar-nate Son of God. His promise for the future is that He will be the Advocate *"before the Father"* who will *"confess"* the names of those who overcome. Their names will be in the *"registration"* of *"the book of life,"* and they will be clothed in *"white garments"* thereby making them acceptable to serve as holy priests in the manifest presence of God in the ulti-mate temple that God Himself will build.

The Dwelling Place of God's Glory

The sixth church is in Philadelphia to which Christ revealed Himself as having *"the key of David."* They were to go through the *"open door"* to fulfill their assignment (Revelation 3:7-8). *"The key of David"* is the symbol of authority for governing the royal household of David. To this church Christ promised,

> *He who overcomes, I will make him a pillar in the temple of My God, and he will not go out from it anymore; and I will write on him the name of My God, and the name of the city of My God, the new Jerusalem, which comes down out of heaven from My God, and My new name* (Revelation 3:12).

While at first sight the promises concerning *"the temple"* and those concerning a *"name"* may seem unrelated, they are actually intimately connected. In Deuteronomy chapter 12, God commanded His people to *"seek the LORD at the place which the LORD your God will choose from all your tribes, to establish His name there for His dwelling, and there you shall come"* (Deuteronomy 12:5). This would be *"the place in which the LORD will choose for His name to dwell"* (Deuteronomy 12:11). As these verses reveal, the *"name"* of God was not only the identification of God but the very manifest presence of God which would dwell in the place He would choose–His name and His manifest presence being essentially related. That place became the temple in Jerusalem, the city of David, the city of God (1 Kings 3:1; 8:1; 11:32; Psalm 46:4; 48:1, 8). The temple of God is the house of God because God's manifest presence lives and dwells in it. As the glory of God's manifest presence filled the tabernacle (Exodus 40:30) so it also filled the temple in Jerusalem (1 Kings 8:11). With the transition to the New Covenant, the temple of God became the people of God (1 Corinthians 3:16; 2 Corinthians 6:16). Ephesians 2:19-22 states,

> You are God's household, [20] having been built on the foundation of the apostles and prophets, Christ Jesus Himself being the corner stone, [21] in whom the whole building, being fitted together, is growing into a holy temple in the Lord, [22] in whom you also are being built together into a dwelling of God in the Spirit.

The words *"growing into a holy temple"* are revealing–it is an organic temple! This is the Scriptural combination of the Garden Tabernacle/Temple of God, and this *"dwelling of God in the Spirit"* is *"the household of God,"* which is the people of God.

The progressive restoration and revelation of God's Garden Tabernacle/Temple will culminate in the New Heaven and Earth foretold in chapters 21 and 22 of Revelation. Chapter 21 describes the Tabernacle/Temple and chapter 22 the Garden of Eden. Christ's promise to the one who overcomes is *"I will make him a pillar in the temple of My God, and he will not go out from it anymore."* Revelation 21:22 says, *"I saw no temple,"* which means there will not be a physical temple made by human hands. The temple Christ speaks of is the living dwelling place of God in His people. This promise reveals not only that those who overcome will be priests who can dwell in the manifest presence of God but that the glory of God's manifest presence will dwell in them. This will be the fulfillment of what Paul spoke of as *"the riches of the glory"* of God *"which is Christ in you"*–no longer *"the hope of glory"* but the full realization of it (Colossians 1:27)!

When Solomon built the temple in Jerusalem, Scripture says there were two pillars that he gave the names *"Jachin,"* which means "Yahweh establishes," and *"Boaz,"* which means "strength" (1 Kings 7:21). Jesus promises those who are made pillars in the future temple of God, *"I will write on him the name of My God, and the name of the city of My God, the new Jerusalem, which comes down out of heaven from My God, and My new name."* A name gives a person their identity. Further insight into understanding what this means comes from two passages in the book of Revelation. Revelation 7:4 says, *"And I heard the number of those who were sealed, one hundred and forty-four thousand sealed from every tribe of the sons of Israel."* These are *"sealed"* to mark them as belonging to God and members of the people of God. Then in Revelation 14:1, John writes *"Then I looked, and behold, the Lamb was standing on Mount Zion, and with Him one hundred and forty-four thousand, having His name and the name of His Father written on their foreheads."* The seal with which the 144,000 are marked is the name of God–the names of the Lamb and the Father. The promises Jesus gives to those made pillars give them their true identity and seal them as belonging to and being in covenant relationship with God, as citizens of *"the new Jerusalem"* where God dwells, and as belonging to Jesus Christ, *"the corner stone"* of God's dwelling place. This will be the ultimate fulfillment of Christ's words in the Upper Room, *"In that day you will know that I am in My Father, and you in Me, and I in you"* (John 14:20).

The Greatest Reward There Could Ever Be

It was to the seventh church, the church in Laodicea that Christ gives the culminating promise. He said, *"I will grant to him to sit down with Me on My throne, as I also overcame and sat down with My Father on His throne"* (Revelation 3:21). During the Lord's earthly ministry, His disciples James and John thought that He was about to bring the kingdom of God to earth and they wanted to share in the glory. So they came to Him with the request, *"Grant that we may sit, one on Your right and one on Your left, in Your glory"* (Mark 10:37). They wanted to be seated next to Jesus because they wanted to be as close as possible to the glory. Jesus' response was, *"You do not know what you are asking. Are you able to drink the cup that I drink, or to be baptized with the baptism with which I am baptized?"* (Mark 10:38). Jesus was telling them the cost of following Him as well as the devotion required to pay the price in order to be given such a reward. Their response was, *"We are able,"* thereby confessing their commitment to follow Him (Mark 10:39). They valued what they would gain greater than the loss they would suffer for following Christ. Jesus then went on to say,

> *The cup that I drink you shall drink; and you
> shall be baptized with the baptism with which
> I am baptized. [40] But to sit on My right or on
> My left, this is not Mine to give; but it is for
> those for whom it has been prepared* (Mark
> 10:39-40).

In complete contrast to the devotion of James and John, the church in Laodicea was lukewarm in its devotion to Christ. He called it to *"be zealous and repent"* so it could receive the eternal reward He promised (Revelation 3:19). He drank *"the cup"* and had been *"baptized with the baptism"* of His passion and had overcome. He had been raised from the dead and ascended to heaven to be enthroned at the right hand of God the Father. Now He promises those who overcome, those who are zealous for Him, those who are burning with holy desire and love for Him and pay the price of following Him that they will be enthroned with Him. Like James and John they will do it because of what they value most–the eternal reward they will receive from Christ. But far greater than the request of James and John that they be seated next to Christ's throne in glory, the Lord promises those who overcome will sit on His throne!

To sit down with Christ on His throne is the greatest reward there could ever be because it means that we will be closer to God the Father and the glory of His manifest presence than any other creatures in the whole universe. There are millions, perhaps billions of angels who worship God in heaven around His throne (Revelation 5:11), but they are not as close to the throne of God the Father as the twenty-four elders (Revelation 4:10). And the twenty-four elders who are seated on their thrones are not as close to the throne of the Father as the Living Creatures (Revelation 4:6). And the Living Creatures are not as close to the Father as the Lamb Who is seated on His throne at the right hand of His Father–as close as one can possibly be. The riches of His grace, goodness and glory are so exceedingly great that He not only gave up all to become a human being, to suffer and be *"slain to purchase for God with His blood men from every tribe and tongue and people and nation"* (Revelation 5:9), then rise from the dead and ascend to heaven to be enthroned at the Father's right hand, but He grants that all who overcome, all who love Him with burning zeal, all who live for Him with wholehearted devotion and pay the price, whatever it may be, to follow Him will share in His glory and be enthroned with Him next to the Father for ever and ever! What greater reward could there ever be! What could ever be of greater value!

The Wisest Investment You Will Ever Make

The book of Hebrews says God *"is a rewarder of those who diligently seek Him"* (Hebrews 11: 6). Those who have eternal values will not merely seek the reward of the things Christ has promised, they will seek Him. He is the greatest reward we will ever receive. Because we value Him as of the greatest worth, He will give us the greatest reward. We will be seated with Him on His throne at the right hand of God the Father. To be as close as possible to behold the most the most beautiful, magnificent and majestic Being there is, to be next to Him in Whose presence there is *"fullness of joy"* and *"pleasures forever"* (Psalm 16:11), to bask in the glory of the most glorious Being there is in the universe is the greatest reward there could ever be! Truly the one who "gives what he cannot keep to gain what he cannot lose" is no fool. He will be among those who will have made the wisest investment you can ever make. Are you listening with ears that hear?

Study Questions
Chapter 10

1. What is the next quality of the kind of church Jesus wants? In what way does your life reflect this call of Christ for believers to live this way?

2. What is the first promise of eternal reward that Christ gives to the church?

3. Describe the ultimate Garden of Eden?

4. What does it mean to you to fight the good fight to receive *"the crown* or *winner's wreath of life"*?

5. Discuss the phrase "separating the sin from the sinner."

6. What is the promise Jesus gives to those who overcome concerning *"the second death"*?

7. How does manna fit into the promises of God?

8. Who will be given authority over the nations and how is this theme seen throughout the Scriptures?

9. What is the greatest privilege of a priest of God and how is the priesthood made possible?

10. How do you understand Jesus' promise that one's name will not be erased from the Book of Life and do you have confidence that your name is in this book?

11. How are the name of God and His manifest presence essentially related?

12. What is the greatest reward that you could ever be given and what does it require?

CHAPTER 11

ALL OF THE SEVEN CHURCHES: LISTENS TO WHAT THE SPIRIT SAYS

Revelation 2:7
He who has an ear, let him hear what the Spirit says to the churches.

Revelation 2:11
He who has an ear, let him hear what the Spirit says to the churches.

Revelation 2:17
He who has an ear, let him hear what the Spirit says to the churches.

Revelation 2:29
He who has an ear, let him hear what the Spirit says to the churches.

Revelation 3:6
He who has an ear, let him hear what the Spirit says to the churches.

Revelation 3:13
He who has an ear, let him hear what the Spirit says to the churches.

Revelation 3:22
He who has an ear, let him hear what the Spirit says to the churches.

What Were They Thinking?

He said it the last night He would spend with His disciples before He died. After washing their feet, Jesus was reclining at the table with them as they celebrated the Passover in the Upper Room in the city of Jerusalem. Over the past three years that they had been with Him, they had seen Him do works that no one had ever done before, care for people most did not care for, and say things no one had ever said before. He had personally called them to follow Him, and devoting their lives to Him as His disciples, they left everything to be with Him (Mark 3:14; 10:28). Pouring His life into them, He gave them power and authority to preach the gospel, heal the sick, and cast out demons, and He sent them out to bring the kingdom of God into people's lives just as He had brought it into their lives (Matthew 10:7-8; Luke 9:1). He taught and trained them, admonished and rebuked them, but most of all, lived before and loved them. Through it all they grew to know Him, depend upon Him, and love Him as their Lord and Leader (John 13:34). They had come to believe He was the Messiah, the Son of God, who would bring God's kingdom to their nation once again and they were going to be right there with Him (Matthew 16:16; 20:21; Acts 1:6). All their hopes and dreams for their futures were placed on Him. But then, seemingly out of nowhere, He told them something they could hardly believe, something they did not want to believe–He was leaving! What looks did they give each other? What thoughts raced through their minds? What emotions filled their hearts?

Through the course of the evening, Jesus continued to tell them a number of times that He was going away, but they didn't understand what He was saying (John 13:33; 14:2, 3, 4, 12, 28; 16:5). Like a fog creeping in at night, their hearts filled with confusion, sadness and grief until Jesus finally acknowledged what they were feeling and said, *"Because I have said these things to you, sorrow has filled your heart"* (John 16:6). We can only imagine how they might have responded. Perhaps some were speechless. Perhaps some were stunned. Perhaps some thought, "Well, yeah! All that we have done with you and for you! All that we have given up to follow you! And all that we hope will happen because of you! Now you keep telling us you're leaving! What else should we feel?" *"But,"* He went on to say, *"I tell you the truth, it is to your advantage that I go away"* (John 16:7a).

Once again, we can only imagine what they were thinking. "What! What are you saying? Advantage...what kind of advantage?" The Greek word translated *"advantage"* means "better, benefit, or profit." Jesus was saying, "You will be better off, it will be of greater benefit for you, and your life will have a far richer profit if I go away." What now would have been going through their minds when they heard this? "How could that be? What could be better than having you right here with us, talking with us, teaching us, and loving us just as you have done for the last three years?"

Why He Had to Go Away

Jesus immediately shifts from empathy to explain why He must leave. He says, *"for if I do not go away, the Helper*

will not come to you; but if I go, I will send Him to you" (John
16:7b). "*The Helper*"–literally in the Greek "*the one called
along side*"–the One Who can be called "the Comforter,
the Encourager, the Intercessor, the Advocate." Jesus had
already spoken three times about this One He called "*the
Helper.*" First, He said,

> I will ask the Father, and He will give you
> another Helper, that He may be with you
> forever; ¹⁷ that is the Spirit of truth, whom
> the world cannot receive, because it does
> not see Him or know Him, but you know Him
> because He abides with you and will be in
> you. ¹⁸ I will not leave you as orphans; I will
> come to you (John 14:16-18).

Next He said,

> These things I have spoken to you while
> abiding with you. ²⁶But the Helper, the Holy
> Spirit, whom the Father will send in My
> name, He will teach you all things, and bring
> to your remembrance all that I said to you
> (John 14:25-26).

Then the third time, He said, "*When the Helper comes,
whom I will send to you from the Father, that is the Spirit
of truth who proceeds from the Father, He will testify about
Me*" (John 15:26). It would have been very clear to them
Who "*the Helper*" is–He is the Holy Spirit.

After saying He must "*go away*" so that He can send
the Holy Spirit, Jesus goes on to speak at length about the
Spirit, saying,

> *And He, when He comes, will convict the world concerning sin and righteousness and judgment; ⁹ concerning sin, because they do not believe in Me; ¹⁰ and concerning righteousness, because I go to the Father and you no longer see Me; ¹¹ and concerning judgment, because the ruler of this world has been judged. ¹² I have many more things to say to you, but you cannot bear them now. ¹³ But when He, the Spirit of truth, comes, He will guide you into all the truth; for He will not speak on His own initiative, but whatever He hears, He will speak; and He will disclose to you what is to come. ¹⁴ He will glorify Me, for He will take of Mine and will disclose it to you. ¹⁵ All things that the Father has are Mine; therefore I said that He takes of Mine and will disclose it to you* (John 16:8-15).

These words reveal a great deal about the Holy Spirit. Far from being an impersonal force or power, He is a Person, having all the attributes of a personal being. He is Someone like Jesus for He is "*another Helper.*" He is Someone they "*know;*" Someone Who will "*be with them;*" even Someone Who "*will be in*" them. Jesus only speaks of Him as a Person, never saying, "It," but always using the personal pronouns ""*He*" or "*Him*"—"*that He may be with you forever,*" "*the world does not see Him or know Him, but you know Him because He abides with you,*" "*He will teach you all things,*" "*He will testify about Me,*" "*He, when He comes,*" "*when He, the Spirit of truth, comes, He will guide you into all the truth; for He will not speak on His own initiative, but whatever He hears, He will speak; and He will disclose to you what is to come,*" and "*He will glorify Me.*" Certainly these are Trinitarian declarations for Jesus speaks of the Father, Himself and Holy Spirit as different Persons, yet, His oneness with the Holy Spirit is made known when He says He Himself will come to them through the manifest presence of the Holy Spirit (John 14:18).

Jesus told them He *had* to leave so the Holy Spirit could come. He *must* go away to the Father. He *must* ascend to the right hand of God the Father in heaven so that there, carrying out His ministry as High Priest for His people, He will *"ask the Father"* to send the Holy Spirit. Then *"the Father will send"* the Holy Spirit in the name of Jesus because He *"proceeds from the Father."* And the Holy Spirit will come from the Lord Jesus as well, for He says, *"I will send Him to you."* The Holy Spirit Who anointed Jesus with the fullness of power for ministry to be the Messiah, the Holy Spirit Who empowered Him to do the works He did, the Holy Spirit Who inspired Him to speak the words He spoke, the same Spirit was going to come to them. Unless Jesus died, rose from the dead, and ascended to the Father in heaven, He could not send Him. *"But,"* Jesus said, when He comes it would be to their *"advantage."*

What Are We Thinking?

These words of the Lord Jesus need to be seen in the greater context of the ministry of these men. Some time before Jesus said this, He had given them *"power and authority over all the demons and to heal diseases. ² And He sent them out to proclaim the kingdom of God and to perform healing"* (Luke 9:1-2). This means they had already received and experienced something of the power and authority of God. Yet now Jesus tells them He will send them the Holy Spirit. Just as Jesus had to be filled with the manifest presence of the Holy Spirit to receive power for His ministry (Luke 4:1, 14, 18-19), so they had to receive a greater manifestation of the empowering presence of the Holy Spirit for their lives and ministries. And the astonishing words of Jesus put in stark contrast and make it absolutely clear that being filled with and empowered by the Holy Spirit is better than having Christ right there with them!

Christ's words were true not only for those men, they are true for all who are His. For many, perhaps most Christians, it is hard to understand, let alone believe how it could be better for us to have the Holy Spirit than to have Jesus right here with us–talking with us, teaching us, training us and, most of all, loving us. So the question has to be asked: what are we thinking? Jesus is the One Who said this! Jesus is the One Who said the presence and power of the Holy Spirit in our lives is of greater advantage, fuller benefit and richer blessing than for He Himself to be right here with us in the flesh–even in His resurrected glory! Perhaps so many find this hard to understand and believe because they have never encountered and experienced the manifest presence and power of the Holy Spirit in the way Jesus spoke about it.

He Kept Telling Them

Receiving the empowering presence of the Holy Spirit was so important to Jesus that He not only spoke of it many times during His last evening with these men, He continued to tell them about the Spirit's coming on numerous occasions during the forty days after He rose from the dead until He ascended to heaven. On the very day He rose from the dead He told them, *"I am sending forth the promise of My Father upon you, but you are to stay in the city until you are clothed with power from on high"* (Luke 24:49). Then, right before He ascended to heaven, He gathered them together with the express purpose of telling them that they were *"to wait for what the Father had promised"* because *"You will receive power when the Holy Spirit comes upon you"* (Acts 1:4, 8). Undoubtedly these men felt great sorrow that Jesus was going away. Yet what joy and anticipation filled their hearts as, not only they, but 120 men and women gathered together in the Upper Room to wait and pray for the promise of the Father that Jesus continuously told them He would send them? What thoughts filled their hearts then? What thoughts fill our hearts now?

He Will Speak to Them

When Jesus spoke to His disciples about the Holy Spirit during that Passover meal, He revealed many aspects of the Spirit's ministry. He told them that, as He had been with them, the Holy Spirit will *"be with you forever,"* that *"He will teach you all things,"* that *"He will convict the world,"* and, most of all, *"He will glorify Me"* (John 14:16; 15:26; 16:8, 14). Truly, Christ was telling them that the living, dynamic, Personal presence of the Holy Spirit would be working in their lives and ministries. Then, in His closing and culminating words about the Holy Spirit, He summarized that which is the key to the Spirit's ministry in their lives and how He would glorify Jesus–He will speak to them. Jesus said,

> He will not speak on His own initiative, but whatever He hears, He will speak; and He will disclose to you what is to come. *14* He will glorify Me, for He will take of Mine and will disclose it to you. *15* All things that the Father has are Mine; therefore I said that He takes of Mine and will disclose it to you (John 16:13-15).

Christ said the Holy Spirit would Personally speak to them and in this way disclose the things of Christ–the things Christ wanted them to know–and in this way the Spirit would glorify Christ. Because the role of the Spirit would be to speak to them, their responsibility was to listen to what He says.

The Final Word

Just as the Lord's closing word to His disciples that night about the Holy Spirit was to listen to what the Spirit will say, so His culminating word to each one of the seven churches in the book Revelation is that they are to listen to what the Spirit says. His final word to the seven churches shows that what He said to His disciples was not exclusive to those few men who would become the foundation of the New Covenant church–it was for all the churches and for each individual in every one of the churches. Like a recurring refrain in a gospel song, Jesus repeats Himself seven times saying, *"He who has an ear, let him hear what the Spirit says to the churches"* (Revelation 2:7, 11, 17, 29: 3:6, 13, 22). While He had a specific word for each church, what He said about the Holy Spirit was *"to the churches"*–to all the churches. Just as the number seven is the number that symbolizes completion, Christ's closing word to all seven churches shows that for a church to be complete it must *"hear what the Spirit says."* Still, more to the point, while His word was for all the churches, He spoke directly to each individual in a church saying, *"He who has an ear, let him hear."*

Listening to what the Spirit says is one of the two things Christ says to all of the seven churches–the other being that they *"overcome."* But not only is it one of the two, it is the last thing He says to them. With these words He completed His address to the seven churches thereby emphasizing that it was the one thing He wanted them to be left with, the last taste in their mouth from the meal He gave them, the final take away. Making this His final word to the churches, Jesus nailed down the culminating characteristic of the kind of church He wants–it listens to what the Spirit says.

The Holy Spirit is Essential

The New Testament makes it clear that a church can never be the kind of church Jesus wants apart from the empowering presence of the Holy Spirit. It can be said that the Christian life is life in the Spirit because the Holy Spirit is essential for every area of our lives in Christ (Romans 8:1ff.). Our walk is to be in the Spirit (Romans 8:4; Galatians 5:16, 25). Our worship is to be in the Spirit (John 4:23-24). Our witness is to be in the Spirit (Acts 1:8). Our work is to be in the Spirit (1 Corinthians 12:11). And our warfare is to be in the Spirit (Matthew 12:28).

The key to living in the Spirit is to perceive, discern and recognize *"the things of the Spirit,"* in other words, to listen to what the Spirit says (Romans 8:5; 1 Corinthians 2:14-16). This is why Jesus said to each person in all of the churches, *"He who has an ear, let him hear what the Spirit says to the churches."* The ministry of the Holy Spirit is of vital concern to the Lord Jesus because it is through the Holy Spirit that He speaks, communicates and makes known His will to His church, to particular churches, and to individuals.

Christ Speaks through the Holy Spirit

Throughout the course of salvation history, God spoke to His people, as the very first verse of the book of Hebrews says, *"in many different ways"* (Hebrew 1:1).

He would communicate in the way that pleased Him, whether through an audible voice, visions one saw, words that one heard, burdens that one received, dreams or any other way that He chose (Exodus 20:1; Numbers 12:6-8). These various ways of communicating are spoken of as *"the word of the LORD"* coming to someone and the foremost way this communication was summarized was of God *"speaking"* (Genesis 15:1; 1 Samuel 3:7; 15:10; 2 Samuel 7:4; Luke 3:2).

When God spoke, He would give different commands to obey and this was described as listening to God's voice (Genesis 22:18; Exodus 15:26; 19:5; Deuteronomy 13:4; 30:20; Psalm 95:7; Hebrew 3:7ff.). The manifestation of sin and rebellion against God is described as people not listening to His voice (Genesis 3:17; Numbers 14:22; Judges 2:20). While God can and does communicate through angels, and did speak directly through "the Angel of the LORD" Who was the preincarnate Son of God (Genesis 16:7ff.; 21:11ff.; Exodus 3:2ff.; Zechariah 3:1ff.), His primary means of communication was through the Holy Spirit (Numbers 11:17, 25-26; 2 Samuel 23:2; Nehemiah 9:20; Psalm 106:33; Isaiah 48:16; Micah 3:8; Matthew 22:43; 1 Peter 1:21). This is how Christ said He would communicate to His church. That night in the Upper Room He said He would speak to His disciples through the Holy Spirit, saying, *"But when He, the Spirit of truth, comes, He will guide you into all the truth; for He will not speak on His own initiative, but whatever He hears, He will speak"* (John 16:13). These words were not exclusively for the Apostles as is obvious from the fact that decades later, after most if not all but John had died, Jesus says to the seven churches *"He who has an ear, let him hear what the Spirit says to the churches."* Christ explicitly says He is speaking to each church and every person in every church through the Holy Spirit.

The Holy Spirit Makes Known Christ's Will

The critical importance of this is understood by asking this most practical question: If the resurrected Lord Jesus Christ is living at this moment in time-space history in His glorified human body seated at the right hand of God the Father in heaven, how will He communicate His will to His church and individuals in His church? He does not communicate with His physical voice in His glorified body for it is limited by the laws of the created order. He could send an angel, as we read in the New Testament He did on certain occasions (Acts 5:19-20; 8:26; 10:3; 12:7-8; 27:23; Revelation 1:1; 22:6). Some Christians suppose the Bible is enough for this purpose. However, while the Scriptures are enough to make known essential theological truths necessary to believe for salvation as well as guidelines necessary to know the *general* will of God, the Bible does not give revelation or illumination to anyone as to the *specific* will of God for their lives. Jesus said, "*My sheep hear My voice*" (John 10:27). How have His sheep, not only in the days of His earthly ministry, but through the centuries in increasing numbers through out the earth heard His voice? Further, while the Bible says Christ calls people to ministries, it does not reveal to anyone what that ministry is or where and to whom they are to go to fulfill that ministry (Ephesians 4:7-11). What is the primary way He communicate His will?

One of the major principles Christians use to discern God's will is evaluating the circumstances of their life. We can seek to discern Christ's will from providential events, the opening and closing of doors, and the appearance of outward circumstances to indicate that something may be His will. But that is the point–they are *outward* circumstances, and sometimes outward circumstances are not actually His will.

The New Testament reveals that the primary way we hear Christ speaking and discern His will is through the working of the Holy Spirit. For example, one of the most precious things we can have is the assurance of our salvation–the knowledge that when we die we will go to heaven. The New Testament reveals that it is not merely knowledge of the truth of written word of God that gives us actual assurance for, as is so often the case, many true believers know the Bible but don't know if they are saved. Actual assurance of salvation comes from the witness of the Holy Spirit in our hearts, as Romans 8:16 says, *"The Spirit Himself testifies with our spirit that we are children of God."* It is by the witness, the testimony, the communication of the Holy Spirit to our inner person in our hearts that Christ speaks to us and gives us assurance that we are His. Then, concerning Christ's will for us in serving Him, we are told in the book of Acts how He did this in the church in Antioch. It says, *"While they were ministering to the Lord and fasting, the Holy Spirit said, 'Set apart for Me Barnabas and Saul for the work to which I have called them'"* (Acts 13:2).

The primary way Christ communicates His will is through the Holy Spirit. As He said of the Spirit, *"He will not speak on His own initiative but whatever He hears, He will speak."* What He will speak is what the Lord Jesus tells Him to speak, and there are many ways He can and will *"speak."* Because of this, it is absolutely critical for churches and each and every person who is a believer in Christ to discern what the Spirit says for when they listen to the Spirit they will be listening to Christ.

We Hear with Our Hearts

How do we listen to what the Spirit is saying? The Bible tells us the primary organ for hearing what the Spirit says is our heart. Just as God created the physical senses of eyes to see and ears to hear in the physical world, so He created the human heart to be the instrument by which we perceive the things of the Spirit.

Jesus spoke of this on a number of occasions, perhaps the most significant being when He was teaching with parables. In answer to the question, *"Why do You speak to them in parables?"* (Matthew 13:10), He answered,

> *I speak to them in parables; because while seeing they do not see, and while hearing they do not hear, nor do they understand.* ¹⁴ *In their case the prophecy of Isaiah is being fulfilled, which says, 'You will keep on hearing, but will not understand; You will keep on seeing, but will not perceive;* ¹⁵ *For the heart of this people has become dull, with their ears they scarcely hear, and they have closed their eyes, otherwise they would see with their eyes, hear with their ears, and understand with their heart and return, and I would heal them.'* ¹⁶ *But blessed are your eyes, because they see; and your ears, because they hear* (Matthew 13:13-16).

It is with the eyes and ears of the heart that we *"understand"* and *"perceive."* The heart can *"become dull"* so that we have ears that *"scarcely hear"* and eyes that are *"closed"* so that we do not *"see."* Or we can be *"blessed"* because we have eyes that see and ears that hear.

The Cell Phone of the Heart

In certain ways, our hearts are similar to cell phones. A cell phone is a physical instrument that picks up invisible information and data transmitted on radio frequencies. In order for the cell phone to function properly, it must be turned on by the power source and connected to the carrier to receive the message or data that is being sent. It can receive downloads with which it can be upgraded. It is also possible for a cell phone to be damaged in some way or have a "glitch" so that it cannot or does not properly receive the information being sent.

Like a cell phone, our hearts are the spiritual instruments by which we pick up the invisible information and data transmitted in the invisible spiritual realm. In order to be able to receive communication from God, our hearts must be "turned on"–they must be made alive by the power of the Holy Spirit connecting our spirits to God. If a person's heart is not "turned on," they will not "*understand*" or "*perceive*" what the Spirit is saying. It doesn't matter how much information God sends, a person will not receive it. They will have eyes but not be able to see and ears but not be able to hear. The original connection with God takes place when one is born of God by the Spirit. When a person is born of the Spirit, they are given the capacity to see and hear so that they can "*understand*" and "*perceive*" the things of the Spirit.

The existential difference between a person who is able to receive the things of the Spirit and one who cannot is starkly contrasted by Paul in 1 Corinthians. He wrote,

> *But a natural man does not accept the things of the Spirit of God, for they are foolishness to him; and he cannot understand them, because they are spiritually appraised.* [15] *But he who is spiritual appraises all things, yet he himself is appraised by no one.* [16] *For who has known the mind of the Lord, that he will*

instruct Him? But we have the mind of Christ
(1 Corinthians 2:14-16).

Paul is not identifying different levels of spirituality but distinct categories of humanity–two completely different kinds of people. The Greek word translated *"natural"* is *"psychikos"* and literally means "soulish"–"a soulish man." It means a person whose animating source of power is their soul. They function, think, reason, perceive, understand only by the limited capacity of the instrument of their soul which is not connected to the Holy Spirit. Their heart is like a cell phone that has not been turned on to God by being born of the Spirit. To be precise, they have a functioning "cell phone" of their soul but it has never been connected to the Holy Spirit. They can and will receive spiritual information from *"the prince of the power of the air, of the spirit that is now working in the sons of disobedience* (Ephesians 2:2), but they will not *"accept the things of the Spirit of God."* The *"soulish"* person *"cannot understand"* *"the things of the Spirit of God, for they are foolishness to him."* They simply don't get it.

Categorically different is the *"spiritual"* person who *"has the mind of Christ"* which is *"the Spirit of God."* Because we are born of the Spirit, the "cell phones" of our hearts have been connected to God and we can receive and *"accept the things of the Spirit."* Being born of the Spirit, we are to grow in maturity in Christ, continually receiving "downloads" from the Holy Spirit so that we can have an "upgrade" in our walk with Christ as we are transformed to become more like Him.

In Need of an Upgrade

While a person can be born of the Spirit and given the capability to hear what the Spirit is saying, they can still live according to their soul and not according to the Spirit. They remain spiritually immature, living no different than non-Christians. This is what Paul went on to say to the Corinthians, writing,

> And I, brethren, could not speak to you as to spiritual men, but as to men of flesh, as to infants in Christ. ² I gave you milk to drink, not solid food; for you were not yet able to receive it. Indeed, even now you are not yet able, ³ for you are still fleshly. For since there is jealousy and strife among you, are you not fleshly, and are you not walking like mere men? (1 Corinthians 3:1-3).

This, sadly, is the way too many Christians and too many churches live–"*like mere men*," like ordinary men, like everyone else. This is why the world sees them and the church as not being any different, except that they are religious. They need the "receivers of their hearts" healed. They need the "glitches" in their broken and wounded hearts reprogrammed. While they are "*walking like mere men*," they are crawling in Christ, remaining "*infants in Christ.*" Even when the Spirit is speaking, they do not "*accept the things of the Spirit.*" They are functioning, reasoning, thinking, perceiving and understanding at best according to their soul, at worse according to their flesh. As a result, the fruit of their lives is the works of the flesh–"*jealousy, strife*," sexual sin, pride, anger–and "*the things of the Spirit*" are "*foolishness*" to them." They simply do not get it. Instead, they "*grieve*" and "*quench*" or put out the fire of the Spirit (Ephesians 4:30: 1 Thessalonians 5:19). Churches predominantly filled with such people are like those in the book of Revelation with whom the Lord Jesus was not pleased. They need a spiritual upgrade.

Grow in Maturity

Once we have been born of the Spirit, it is God's will for us to grow spiritually "*until we all attain to the unity of the faith, and of the knowledge of the Son of God, to a mature man, to the measure of the stature which belongs to the fullness of Christ*" (Ephesians 4:13). One of the distinguishing realities of an infant is that while they can hear what their father and mother may say, they don't understand it. They must grow and mature in discernment to accurately perceive and understand what they are saying. The same is true for us spiritually–we must grow spiritually to hear and discern what the Spirit is saying. We must "*be transformed by the renewing of our minds so that will be able to prove–to test to discern–the will of God.*"–in other words, what the Spirit is saying and how He is leading us (Romans 12:2).

Just as there are things that are essential to make it possible for a baby to grow and mature, so there are things that are vital for us to grow and mature in Christ and hear His voice. The book of Hebrews identifies three of these in chapter 5. It says,

> For though by this time you ought to be teachers, you have need again for someone to teach you the elementary principles of the oracles of God, and you have come to need milk and not solid food. [13] For everyone who partakes only of milk is not accustomed to the word of righteousness, for he is an infant. [14] But solid food is for the mature, who because of practice have their senses trained to discern good and evil" (Hebrews 5:12-14)

Tuned

The first and most important thing that is essential to become spiritually mature and hear Christ's voice is an accurate understanding of the word of God. It should go without saying that whatever the Holy Spirit says will always be according to the written word of Scripture that He inspired (2 Timothy 3:16). The word of God is like the perfect "tuning fork" that resonates with the pure frequency of God when the Holy Spirit makes known what it actually means. As we grow in the knowledge of the word of God, our minds and hearts will be transformed and we will be "tuned" to what the Spirit is saying. We will grow from being a spiritual *"infant"* who has only learned *"the elementary principles"* of the *"milk"* of the word of God to become spiritually *"mature."*

Paul's words to the church in Corinth and these from the book of Hebrews make it clear that the primary reason Christians remain spiritual *"infants"* is that they are *"not yet able to receive" "solid food."* A baby can't handle meat. They don't want it because they aren't able to receive it. That is the way it is with many Christians–they are not *"accustomed to the word of righteousness."* And as Hebrews states, such people may have been Christians for a long time, a time during which *"they ought to have become teachers."* How many churches are filled with Christians who simply want short sermons with simple "practical how-to principles" to "make it through the week"? They are living in the power of their souls or according to the flesh and are not any different than people of the world. While Christ is in their hearts, they are on the throne of their hearts. Because of this, they do not listen to what the Spirit says because their hearts have not been "tuned" by the word of God.

A spiritually mature person has a holy hunger for the *"solid food"* of Scripture. They have a holy craving for the meat of the word because they have a first love for Christ, hold to the truth of God's word, and are zealous for Him. Christ is reigning in their hearts and lives by the empowering presence of the Holy Spirit and, because of this, they want to hear what the Spirit is saying. In order to grow in spiritual maturity, they will faithfully read the Scriptures on their own, study the word in groups, and listen to the word of God in churches that teach and preach "the whole counsel of God." Because of this, they will grow to have *"ears to hear what the Spirit says."*

Trained

It's one thing to sit in a crowd and watch athletes on a field playing to win. It's another to get in the game. Those who want to get in the game will train themselves to win. That's what Hebrews says mature Christians do so that they can grow in Christ and be able to discern what the Holy Spirit is saying. We are told *"the mature"* are those *"who because of practice have their senses trained to discern good and evil."* This is the second thing that is essential to listening to what the Spirit says–to be trained.

The Greek word translated *"trained"* is *"gymnadzo"* from which we get our English word "gymnasium." A gym is a place where people exercise and practice. People who faithfully go to a gym or an exercise facility want to get in shape and stay in shape. They want to be healthy, and they know that to be healthy they need to work out. Athletes who want to win will have a passion to practice so they can be trained to respond instantly to what is happening in the game. The same is true spiritually. To become spiritually mature, we must *"have our senses"*–the eyes and ears of our hearts–*"trained to discern good and evil"*–to know what the Spirit is saying and what is not of the Holy Spirit.

Every four years, the Olympic games are celebrated in which the greatest athletes in the world compete to "win the gold" in their respective sports. All of them have been given great athletic gifts or they wouldn't be there. But it is not only their amazing athletic gifts that separate them from those who are sitting in the stands cheering them on. When you listen to the testimonies of the medal winners, they all say that it was their dedication to training that made them the athlete they became. Every true Christian has been given the awesome gift of the Holy Spirit. What separates the spiritually *"mature"* from spiritual *"infants"* is their passion to *"practice,"* their holy desire to never stop working out to train the eyes and ears of their hearts to *"discern"* what the Spirit is saying.

Taught

The third thing that is vital to grow spiritually is to be in a church that has a healthy level of spiritual maturity. It is not about the quantity of people in the church, as if the more who attend the better the church. It is about the quality of spiritual life in the culture of the church. Jesus said, *"A disciple is not above his teacher"* (Matthew 10:24). The healthier the level of spiritual maturity, the greater the potential for a person to grow into spiritual maturity and the church to become more fully like Christ.

Hebrews speaks of Christians who are spiritual *"infants"* who should have grown to become *"teachers."* They were not in a church in which they were being taught and trained to grow in *"the things of the Spirit."* Because of this, they remained *"infants"* in the crib, or merely crawling. To become spiritually mature, we must be in a church where hearts are burning with first-love and zeal for Christ, where lives are being transformed through times of testing as they hold to the truth of God's word and others accountable to live it, and where people are real followers of Christ and fulfilling His will and assignments for their lives. It will be a church in which the leaders and teachers have a holy passion to press on to be like Christ because they are pursuing the manifest presence of Christ. They will be teachers who know how to train people to tune their hearts to what the Holy Spirit is saying.

People who want to learn how to sing or play a musical instrument can take it up themselves, and they will become capable to one level or another. If they want to become more proficient, they will take lessons from a teacher who knows more than they do. However, if they want to become accomplished and play with excellence, they will seek to be taught by the best they can find. Because they have excellent teachers, they will be trained to sing with their voice and play their instrument with a beauty, harmony and oneness that resonates to the depths of human hearts.

The same is true of life in the Spirit. Christians who are mentored, trained and discipled by mature believers will not merely reproduce notes from the page of music of the Bible, they will transcend to the heights of the spirit of the music because their hearts will be tuned to hear what the Spirit is saying. They will have ears to hear.

The Symphony of the Lord

The Lord Jesus wants to sing and play His magnificent music through the symphony orchestra of His church. Reigning now from heaven at the Father's right hand, He is conducting His masterpiece through the Holy Spirit. As we have ears to hear what He says by listening to the Spirit, we will play on key, we will play in harmony, and we will play for His glory. As we listen to His voice, we will walk in the Spirit, work in the Spirit, witness in the Spirit, war in the Spirit and above all worship in the Spirit, and the music of heaven will be heard on earth.

And as His church grows in spiritual maturity by listening to what the Spirit says, the beauty, splendor and glory of God will come to earth because the reality of the Living Lord Jesus Christ will be seen and heard. It will be the kind of church Jesus wants because it will be like Him, listening to Him and ultimately reigning with Him. When this takes place, His holy desire and purpose for His church from before creation will be fulfilled because the glory of His manifest presence will fill the earth as the waters cover the sea! May He give us ears to hear!

Study Questions
Chapter 11

1. Briefly share one personal highlight from the chapter.

2. What is one thing that was a surprise to you from this chapter?

3. How do you think you would have felt if you had been there with the disciples and heard Jesus say He was leaving?

4. Where was Jesus going and why was it necessary for Him to go away? Why did Jesus say it was better that He leave?

5. What is your response to Jesus saying that being filled with the empowering presence of the Holy Spirit is better than having Jesus right there with you?

6. What is the key to the Spirit's ministry in our lives and the church?

7. How would you describe the Person of the Holy Spirit and has your understanding of Who He is grown?

8. What is the last thing Jesus says to each of the seven churches that reveals the culminating characteristic of the kind of church He wants?

9. Why is the Holy Spirit so essential to individual lives and the church at large?

10. How do we listen to the Holy Spirit and what must we do to hear what He is saying?

11. Paul describes two distinct categories of humanity. What are they and where do you see yourself?
(1)
(2)

12. What three essentials to spiritual growth and listening to the Spirit are found in Hebrews 5:12-14. In which of these do you see your need for growth?
(1)
(2)
(3)

END NOTES

1. C. S. Lewis, *The Lion, the Witch and the Wardrobe*, New York: HarperCollins, 1994.

2. Roger Nicole, "New Testament Use of the Old Testament," *Revelation and the Bible*, ed. Carl. F.H. Henry (Grand Rapids: Baker, 1958), pp. 137.

3. The essential doctrines of fundamental Islam and historic Christianity demonstrate that Allah of Islam is not the God of Christians.

(1) Concerning God: Muslims are absolute monotheists, utterly rejecting the Trinity. The greatest sin in Islam is Shirk, which is to attribute to Allah "partners" or "associates," in other words, to believe in the Trinity.

(2) Concerning the Person of Christ: While believing Jesus, who is called "*Isa*," to be a prophet, had a miraculous birth, and did miracles, Muslim doctrine teaches that the Lord Jesus Christ is not the only begotten Son of God, did not die on the cross (Qur'an, 4:157), and did not rise from the dead.

(3) Concerning salvation: Muslims believe a person will be rewarded paradise on the basis of their works. Christians believe a person is saved by grace through faith

alone in the finished work of the Lord Jesus Christ who died on the cross for their sins and rose from the dead.

The rejection of the essential Christian doctrine that the Lord Jesus Christ is the only begotten Son of God is declared by Muslims five times a day in their prayers. Besides not praying in the Name of the Lord Jesus Christ, they declare in Arabic the following that is translated into English, "Say, He is Allah, the One. Allah is All Independent. Neither He begot anyone nor He was begotten. And none is equal to Him in any way" (translation Bilal Zuberi–http://bilalzuberi.com/2006/10/02/what-do-muslims-say-in-their-prayers-5-times-a-day/)

The following are verses from the Qur'an that are inscribed in the Dome of the Rock in Jerusalem stating these doctrines of Islam concerning the Lord Jesus. They state:

"In the name of God, the Merciful the Compassionate. There is no god but God. He is One. He has no associate. Unto Him belongeth sovereignty and unto Him belongeth praise. He quickeneth and He giveth death; and He has Power over all things. Muhammad is the servant of God and His Messenger. [conflation of Qur'an 64:1 and 57:2]

"O People of the Book! Do not exaggerate in your religion nor utter aught concerning God save the truth. The Messiah, Jesus son of Mary, was only a Messenger of God, and His Word which He conveyed unto Mary, and a spirit from Him. So believe in God and His messengers, and say not 'Three' – Cease! (it is) better for you! – God is only One God. Far be it removed from His transcendent majesty that He should have a son." [Qur'an 4:171]

"Oh God, bless Your Messenger and Your servant Jesus son of Mary. Peace be on him the day he was born, and the day he dies, and the day he shall be raised alive! Such was Jesus, son of Mary, (this is) a statement of the truth concerning which they doubt. It befitteth not (the Majesty of) God that He should take unto Himself a son. Glory be to Him! [Qur'an 19:34-36] (www.islamicawareness.org/History/Islam/Inscriptions/DoTR.html]

4. The word "cherubim" is a transliteration of the Hebrew meaning "cherubs," the root being "cherub" and the "im" the Hebrew plural. In the rabbinic tradition, it was believed the basic meaning of "cherub" was "childlike" and this led to the popular idea of cherubs being like plumb little babies. In actuality, a cherub is an awesome angelic being, and among their assignments was *"to guard the way to the tree of life"* with *"the flaming sword"* (Genesis 3:24).

5. *The Cost of Discipleship,* New York: MacMillian, 1959.

6. Eric Metaxas, *Bonhoeffer,* Nashville: Thomas Nelson, 2010, p. 532.

ABOUT THE AUTHOR

B ill Hyer was born and raised in Southern California, lived in Hawaii, and came to Christ at the age of 18 in the Jesus Movement. He graduated with a Bachelor of Arts *Summa Cum Laude* in Biblical Studies from Wheaton College, Wheaton, Illinois, and a Master of Divinity *Magna Cum Laude* from Gordon-Conwell Seminary, South Hamilton, Massachusetts. He and his wife, Michelle, are blessed with two sons, their wives and five grandchildren. Bill has served churches in California, Florida Massachusetts, South Carolina and Mississippi. He is the Academic Dean and on the Leadership Team of *The College of Prayer, International*, a worldwide movement whose purpose is "mentoring, training and equipping Christian pastors and leaders to reach a lost world through a revived church" For more information regarding *The College of Prayer, International*, go to www.collegeofprayer.org.

CPSIA information can be obtained
at www.ICGtesting.com
Printed in the USA
LVOW01s0044280416
485648LV00002B/2/P